SHARIA, MUSLIM STATES AND INTERNATIONAL HUMAN RIGHTS TREATY OBLIGATIONS: A COMPARATIVE STUDY

SHARIA, MUSLIM STATES AND INTERNATIONAL HUMAN RIGHTS TREATY OBLIGATIONS: A COMPARATIVE STUDY

Nisrine Abiad

British Institute of
International and
Comparative Law

Published and Distributed by
British Institute of International and Comparative Law
Charles Clore House, 17 Russell Square, London WC1B 5JP

British Library Cataloguing in Publication Data
A Catalogue record of this book is available from the British Library

ISBN 978–1–905221–41–7

This publication has been produced by the British Institute of International and Comparative Law (BIICL) with the assistance of the European Union. The views expressed in it are those of the author(s) and can in no way be taken to reflect the views of either the European Union or BIICL. BIICL is a registered charity and an independent research institute committed to supporting high standards of scholarship in all aspects of international and comparative law.

Typeset by Cambrian Typesetters
Camberley, Surrey
Printed in Great Britain by Biddles Ltd,
King's Lynn

Contents

Acknowledgments

I would like to thank all those who provided support and invaluable assistance during the various stages of this work. First and foremost among them are the European Commission for giving us the opportunity to undertake research on this contemporary and most interesting of subjects.

Enormous thanks must be given to Professor Robert McCorquodale for his essential support and advice, particularly during the most critical and determinant final phase of the work, especially for having read the entire work and thoroughly commenting on it.

Special thanks also goes to Professor Gillian Triggs and Aphrodite Smagadi for their supervision and encouragement during the early stages of the work, and to Aphrodite in particular for having read the entire work and providing precious comments on it. My thanks to Victor Kattan for also reading and commenting on some parts of the work, as well as kindly providing the picture for the cover, and to Orla Fee for her efficient role in the production process of this publication.

Particular thanks to Ayla Karmali and Sakina Rizvi for their precious input, without their assistance this work would simply not have been accomplished the way it is

I would also like to thank all those who assisted me during the various stages of the work, specifically Emena Efeotor for compiling the materials and editing, as well as Armin Seif Amir-Hosseini, Michelle Chan, Suzan Davis, P Nawas Deen, Kate Jones, and Sushil Kumar.

Particular thanks to Nurhalida Mohammad Khalil for having undertaken the research on Malaysia

Special thanks to those who commented on my paper which was based on the findings of the research and which was presented at a colloquium on 'Islam, the application of Sharia and Human Rights' held in London on the 5th June, namely Professor Shaheen Ali, Professor Javaid Rehman, and Dr. Reza Eslami.

Dr Nisrine Abiad

Foreword

The European Union and the Islamic Republic of Iran initiated a *Comprehensive Dialogue*[1] in 1998 as the basis for collaboration in numerous areas, ranging from energy, trade and investment, refugees and drugs control, to the Middle East peace process, non-proliferation of weapons of mass destruction, the fight against terrorism and human rights. The *Human Rights Dialogue*[2] was officially launched in the context of this bilateral cooperation in 2002 as the necessary platform for legal experts to exchange views on human rights issues of mutual interest to both parties through a series of roundtable discussions. This enhanced collaboration was intended to enable all parties to acquaint themselves with the perception and legal protection of human rights at the international level and in Iran.

To this end, the British Institute of International and Comparative Law undertook a project on 'Human Rights in International Law and Iran'. The primary objective of the project is to foster the dialogue between international and Iranian legal scholars, practitioners and intellectuals on international and Islamic human rights standards, in order to achieve consensus on the character of human rights values and, ultimately, to contribute to the adoption and the effective implementation of major international human rights instruments in Iran.

One of the outputs of this project is the publication of a compilation of human rights legal materials designed as a practical guide and reference book for lawyers and others involved in human rights issues, consisting of two parts, one on International Law (*Sourcebook of International Human Rights Materials*) and one on Iranian Law (*Introduction to the Iranian Legal System and the Protection of Human Rights in Iran)*.

The second output of this research project is the present comparative study, which examines the ratification and implementation of the core international human rights treaties among Muslim States. This was an ambitious project that sought to identify patterns followed by Muslim States in their engagement with international human rights treaties and the extent of their implementation at the national level. The purpose of this analysis was to appreciate what motivated a positive engagement by these States with international human rights law and what effect, if any, Sharia (both as religious

[1] For a brief history of the relations between the European Union and Iran, see http://ec.europa.eu/external_relations/iran/relations_en.htm (last accessed 12 June 2008).

[2] The Human Rights Dialogue was set up in 2002 on the basis of the principles enshrined in the Universal Declaration of Human Rights and the International Covenant on Civil and Political Rights ratified by Iran in 1975. Four rounds were held between 2002 and 2004 before the suspension of the Dialogue in 2005. More information available at: http://ec.europa.eu/external_relations/iran/humanrights_en.htm (last accessed 12 June 2008).

doctrine and practice) had on the ratification of international human rights treaties and their implementation at the national level. Indeed, the study is unique because it provides a comprehensive analysis of Muslim State practice at key stages, beginning with government ratification at the international level, to legislative implementation, and to judicial practice among both secular and Sharia courts within the State.

The challenges presented by such a study were considerable, due to such factors as: the many states concerned; the vast amount of information about the state, Sharia and the translation of international human rights law into national practice through legislation, court judgments, and government policy; the difficulty in identifying and locating key materials, which often were found in Arabic or Farsi and thus required translating; and the many ways of approaching the issues concerned and thus determining the best methodology. Research was undertaken in London, Paris and Beirut, and with interviews conducted with judges of Sharia courts. The research was enhanced by a selection of key examples across a spectrum of States and so it aims to provide a very useful tool for comparative research in the area.

The impact of the research project was demonstrated by its positive reception at the colloquium held at BIICL in June 2008. At this colloquium, experts from Iran and from other Muslim states discussed the findings of the comparative study and contributed their knowledge, experiences and research in this area. The experts strongly recommended that the work be translated into Arabic and widely disseminated, due to its important contribution to debate and discussion on these issues.

The Institute is indebted to the European Commission for initiating and funding the project, and for being supportive and flexible throughout it. Finally, I express my sincere thanks to Nisrine Abiad for her very hard work in authoring this research and for her effective and inspired management of this project.

Professor Robert McCorquodale
Institute Director
British Institute of International and Comparative Law

Introduction

An analysis of the relationships between Islamic law and international human rights law needs to be undertaken since many Muslim States have made various reservations to international human rights conventions which place limits upon their ratification and implementation. Significantly, many of the limitations are grounded in Sharia. Yet, at the same time, Muslim States provide examples of domestic legislative amendments which not only apply human rights law but which also remain within the very framework of the Sharia.

This study uses a comparative approach when analysing Muslim State practices, with a view to identifying any patterns followed by Muslim States in making declarations and reservations to the main international human rights instruments. Particular focus is placed on the role of Sharia in influencing the ratification of international human rights treaties and their domestic implementation through legislative amendments and court jurisprudence. By undertaking such analysis, the study hopes to determine to what extent Sharia is used by Muslim States to justify their limitations to the scope of international human rights treaties. This study will analyse the various roles of Sharia in order to expose any contradicting practices or inconsistencies which hinder the advancement of human rights and which use Sharia as an excuse to limit the State's engagement with international human rights law. Additionally, the study hopes to analyse the extent to which Sharia has actually been used to improve and implement human rights standards in the Muslim world.

CULTURAL PRACTICE AND POLITICAL CLIMATE

It is important to clarify that although this study is focused on the impact of Sharia on the human rights attitudes and practices of Muslim States, we do not assume that Sharia is the only influencing factor. Rather, the study seeks to examine whether Sharia is merely one factor among many which influences human rights practices and if its effect on human rights practices, whether positive or negative, largely depends on how it is used and by whom. Indeed, it may even be argued that the impact of Sharia appears minimal when put in the broader context of human rights practices in Muslim States. This is because, generally speaking, it is the governments of Muslim States that are largely responsible for human rights abuses. Moreover, when it comes to the implementation of many human rights, specifically those concerning the rights of women and children, pervading patriarchal cultures and norms play a significant part in limiting the advancement of human rights in Muslim societies.

A stark example of the impact of local culture is illustrated by the continuing practice of female genital mutilation (FGM) in Muslim societies despite efforts by governments to outlaw the practice and by authoritative Muslim scholars such as the Grand Sheikh of Al-Azhar to denounce the practice as forbidden in Islam. The practice is known to have been pre-Islamic and is unknown in certain parts of the Muslim world such as Iran and Saudi Arabia.[1] Nevertheless, attempts by the Egyptian Government to limit and later ban (with medical exceptions) the practice in 1997 had no effect on the prevalence of FGM practice, as evidenced by the 2005 Egypt Demographic and Health Survey (EDHS) which found that among girls between the ages of 15 and 17, 77 per cent had been subjected to the practice.[2] In 2007, FGM was completely outlawed in Egypt following the death of a young girl.[3] Not only does the continuing practice demonstrate the strong influence of culture on the observance of human rights, it also demonstrates that governments may also be held accountable for abuses when they fail to take an assertive role in inculcating these norms into domestic practice by means other than law.

Aside from the existing patriarchal culture that suppresses equality and maintains the status quo of male dominance within Muslim societies,[4] the major contributing factor to human rights violations in Muslim States has been their political structure and institutions which allow for their abuse.[5] The heavily interdependent relationship between State infrastructure and religion, as seen in many Muslim States from Iran and Pakistan to Saudi Arabia, also contributes to a situation whereby governments and their agencies are able to neglect human rights standards or positively inflict human rights abuses on their citizens whilst invoking Islamic considerations as a justification for these acts and omissions. Yet, as one commentator remarked, 'neither Islam nor its culture is the major obstacle to political

[1] Simon Ingram, UNICEF Deputy Executive Director Rima Salah visits Egypt, 14 April 2005 (http://www.unicef.org/infobycountry/egypt_26107.html).

[2] UNICEF, Media Backgrounder: Female Genital Mutilation/Cutting (FGM/C) in Egypt (http://www.unicef.org/egypt/media_4115.html).

[3] Magdi Abdelhadi, BBC Arab Affairs, Egypt forbids female circumcision, 28 June 2007 (http://news.bbc.co.uk/1/hi/world/middle_east/6251426.stm).

[4] See generally: Valentine M Moghadam, 'Women, Citizenship, and Civil Society in the Arab World', in *Human Rights in the Arab World: Independent Voices* (Anthony Chase and Amr Hamzawy (eds), University of Pennsylvania Press, 2006) 89; Julika Erfurt, 'Committee on the Elimination of Discrimination against Women,' 30th Session 12–30 January 2004 (Women's International League for Peace and Freedom) (http://www.wilpf.int.ch/publications/CEDAW_Report_Jan_2004.html).

[5] Anthony Chase, 'The Tail and the Dog: Constructing Islam and Human Rights in Political Context,' in *Human Rights in the Arab World: Independent Voices* (Anthony Chase and Amr Hamzawy (eds), University of Pennsylvania Press, 2006) 27.

modernity, even if undemocratic rulers sometimes use Islam as their excuse.'[6] This abuse of State power is most stark in relation to violations of some of the most fundamental civil and political freedoms which are essential to a free and democratic society and guaranteed by the International Covenant of Civil and Political Rights, a treaty most of the States in this study have ratified.

An examination of a cross-section of Muslim States reveals that the same types of violations occur across the spectrum, despite the differences in their treatment of Sharia within the hierarchy of norms.[7] This indicates that Sharia is not the chief contributor to many of the human rights abuses that are perpetrated in these States. Moreover, a recent study by Price on the correlation between a commitment to Islamic law and the practice of torture found that the relationship was 'insignificant'.[8]

That study also revealed that the worst human rights records were generally found in States with either a pervasively authoritarian and Islamic political structure (such as Saudi Arabia, Pakistan and Iran where Sharia is intricately woven into the fabric of the constitution and legal system); or in States with a secular political structure (as in the case of Syria and Tunisia where Sharia has little to do with the governing elite). This strongly suggests that, although the implementation of Sharia may be a common denominator among the States, it does not necessarily determine whether a State will comply with international law. Indeed, in a comparative study of the human rights scores of Muslim-majority States with those of a control group consisting of non-Muslim developing States, Price found that Islamic considerations were insignificant with respect to human rights practices.

FRAMEWORK AND METHODOLOGY

International Standards

The main international human rights instruments examined in this study consist of those related to the human rights law enshrined in the 1948 Universal Declaration of Human Rights and the main global international human rights treaties. These are: the International Covenant on Civil and Political Rights (ICCPR);[9] the International Covenant on Economic, Social and Cultural Rights (ICESCR);[10] the Convention on the Elimination of All

[6] Robin Wright, 'Islam and Liberal Democracy: Two Visions of Reformation', at www.mtholyoke.edu/acad/intrel/rwright.htm (last accessed on 15 January 2008).

[7] Daniel Price, 'Islam and Human Rights : A case of deceptive first Appearances', 41 *J Sci Study Religion* 213 (2002).

[8] ibid.

[9] Adopted 1966 and entered into force in 1976.

[10] Adopted in 1966 and entered into force in 1976.

Forms of Racial Discrimination (CERD);[11] the Convention on the Elimination on All Forms of Discrimination Against Women (CEDAW);[12] the Convention Against Torture and Other Cruel, Inhuman or Degrading Treatment or Punishment (CAT);[13] and the Convention on the Rights of the Child (CRC).[14]

Sharia at a glance

It is important to clarify what is meant by 'Sharia', and what defines a 'Muslim State'. Sharia comprises 'the totality of divine categorisations of human acts',[15] the aim of which is to foster obedience to God and serve and protect religion, life, lineage, property and intellect.[16] The substance of Sharia can take the form of positive law or prescriptive norms and moral exhortations. These rules and norms of Sharia are derived from a methodological interpretation of the Quran and the prophetic Sunnah, a process termed *'ijtihad'*. [17] Further sources of Sharia are generally thought to include *ijma* (consensus) and *qiyas* (reasoning by analogy), while *istihsan* (juristic preference) and *maslaha* (public interest) are also the basis of some rules.[18] The rules and norms 'derived from the Quran and the Sunna' and 'developed by means of human juristic efforts'[19] have been categorised by scholars as 'obligatory' *(wajb)* and 'prohibited' *(haram),* which are generally unequivocal and legally enforceable; or, 'recommended/praiseworthy' *(mandub)* and 'disapproved/reprehensible' (*makruh*) which are mainly issues of norms and morality rather than divine law.[20] The rules relating to matters that are *wajb* or *haram* are limited in number; however, they are more difficult to review due to the precision of their expression in the Quran and Sunnah.

Sharia takes the form of a 'comprehensive and detailed corpus of law', which has been 'continuously adjusted to changing circumstances'.[21] This

11 Adopted in 1966 and entered into force in 1969.

12 Adopted in 1981 and entered into force in 1981.

13 Adopted in 1984 and entered into force in 1987.

14 Adopted in 1989 and entered into force in 1990.

15 Weiss, Bernard, *The Spirit of Islamic Law* (University of Georgia Press, 1998) 18.

16 Abou El Fadl, Khaled, *Rebellion and Violence in Islamic Law*, 27.

17 Weiss, Bernard: *'The Theory of Ijtihad'* (1976) 26 American Journal of Comparative Law.

18 Hallaq, *The Origins and Evolution of Islamic Law* (Cambridge, 2005) 144–146.

19 Muhammad Khalid Masud, Brinkley Messick, David S Powers, 'Muftis, Fatwas, and Islamic legal Interpretation', in *Islamic Legal interpretations, Muftis and their Fatwas* (Muhammad Khalid Masud, Brinkley Messick, David S Powers (eds) (Harvard University Press, 1996) 3, 4.

20 Rahman, Fazlur, *Islam* (2nd edn, Chicago University Press, 1979) 32.

21 Muhammad Khalid Masud, Brinkley Messick, David S. Powers, 'Muftis, Fatwas, and Islamic legal Interpretation' in *Islamic Legal interpretations, Muftis and their fatwas*

flexibility is important as Islamic jurisprudence recognises that different contexts and situations result in different interpretations, approaches and rulings. Thus, a key feature of Sharia is the principle of *ikhtilaf* (accepted diversity of opinion) where multiple rulings and opinions regarding a single issue are as valid as each other.[22] The concept is based on the Prophetic hadith which states: '[D]ifferences of opinion within my community are a sign of the bounty of Allah.'[23]

Historically, juristic opinions were mainly developed according to the methodologies and principles of each *madhhab* (school of thought). Within Sunni Islam there are four main schools of thought—*Hanafi, Maliki, Hanbali and Shafi'I*. These schools are still of considerable influence today. Within Shia Islam there are a number of different sects; however, most Shia Muslims are 'Twelvers' and follow the *Jaafari* legal school of thought. The *Jaafari* legal school recognises the Quran and various Sunnah as sources of law but add to it the practices of the 12 imams.

Shia identity emerged within the first century of Islam where, following the death of the Prophet of Islam, disagreements emerged as to who should lead the Muslims.[24] The Shia Muslims believed that leadership should go to the family of the Prophet and refused to recognise the three *caliphs* that ruled following the death of the Prophet. Although this appears to be a largely political difference, other significant differences in relation to theology, philosophy and legal jurisprudence soon emerged between Sunni and Shia Islam. That said, the above exposition of Sharia is generally common to both Sunni and Shia Islam and, furthermore, many of the legal opinions developed by jurists since the 7th century are still in use among Muslim States today. Therefore, where Sharia or Islamic law are referred to in this study, it refers to either classical/traditional legal norms or those enshrined in the personal status and family laws of Muslim States.

Muslim States selected for this study

The term 'Muslim States' may be defined as those States where the majority of the population are Muslim and where the State is a member of the Organisation of the Islamic Conference (OIC).[25] The OIC defines itself as

(Muhammad Khalid Masud, Brinkley Messick, David S. Powers (eds) (Harvard University Press, 1996) 3, 4.

22 Coulson, *Conflicts and Tensions in Islamic Jurisprudence* (University of Chicago Press, 1969).

23 Cited in NJ Coulson, *Conflicts and Tensions in Islamic Jurisprudence* (University of Chicago Press, 1969).

24 Dakake, Maria Massi, *The Charismatic Community: Shi'ite Identity in Early Islam* (State University of New York Press, 2008) 1–2.

25 The Organization of the Islamic Conference (OIC) is the second largest inter-governmental organization after the United Nations which has membership of 57 States spread over four continents.

an inter-governmental organisation of 57 States which represents the collective voice of the Muslim world.[26] As it is beyond the capacity of this study to analyse all 57 States, only a cross-section of 10 Muslim States have been chosen, namely: Bahrain, Egypt, Iran, Lebanon, Malaysia, Morocco, Pakistan, Saudi Arabia, Turkey and Tunisia.

These States have been selected to represent the diversity of schools of thoughts in Islam, and the different degrees of the application of Sharia in Muslim States. Within the study, particular attention has been paid to Bahrain and Lebanon because they have a significant Jaafari–Shia population, thus making the study both more comprehensive, and more relevant to the broader research project on 'human rights in international law and Iran'.[27]

Some of the defining features of the States selected for this study are as follows:

a) Bahrain's status as a constitutional monarchy in which Islam has a strong constitutional and legislative impact, in addition to an interesting dynamic between a Shia Jaafari majority and Sunni Maliki and Shafi'i minorities;
b) Egypt's place as both the largest Arab State, and the centre of Sunni Hanafi Islamic jurisprudence by virtue of Al Azhar University. The acknowledgment of Islam in the Egyptian legal system is found in the constitutional strengthening of the status of Islam in 1982, the jurisprudence of the Supreme Constitutional Court and the interpretation of the constitutional amendments by the judiciary, which have allowed for flexibility in the interpretation of Sharia;
c) Iran's status as the beneficiary State of the comprehensive project within whose framework this study is carried out. Iran is also representative of a Shia Islamic State in which the religious leader has the ultimate authority;
d) Lebanon has a *sui generis* position as a multi-confessional State where 18 officially recognised religious sects have a share in the overall political and constitutional structure of the Lebanese State. It is particularly interesting to study the impact of the delegation of sovereignty to the religious groups in the field of family law and its impact on the engagement of Lebanon with international human rights instruments.[28] The Muslim

[26] See http://www.oic-oci.org/oicnew/page_detail.asp?p_id=52.

[27] The primary objective of the project was to foster the dialogue between international and Iranian legal scholars, practitioners and intellectuals on international and Islamic human rights standards, in order to achieve agreement on the character of human rights values and ultimately contribute to the adoption and the effective implementation of major international human rights instruments in Iran.

[28] See below at 88–89.

population of Lebanon represents a majority and is divided mainly between Sunni and Shia;[29]

e) Malaysia's 13 States and 3 federal territories uniquely illustrates differing approaches to the application of Sharia within the same State;
f) Morocco's status as a Muslim monarchy that mainly follows Maliki doctrine; it has an interesting combination of Islamic and secular features in the legal system;
g) Pakistan's position as an avowedly Islamic State which mainly follows the Sunni Hanafi school of thought;
h) Saudi Arabia's standing as a Sunni Islamic State over which a monarchy presides and where the Quran is the Constitution. Saudi Arabia follows a specific trend within the classical Hanbali School known as Wahhabi;
i) Turkey's status as a secular State since the early 1920s despite 99 per cent of the population of Turkey being Muslim.
j) Tunisia's reforms which have significantly advanced the rights of women and children compared to other Muslim States. Tunisia follows the Maliki school of thought.

Methodology

This study aims to analyse the impact of Sharia on the ratification and implementation of international human rights treaties. It is extremely large in scope, and it could not be undertaken in the course of 18 months or contained in one volume. Instead, the study acts as a first step in elucidating the subject through its comparative approach, addressing some illustrative aspects of the relationship between Islam, Muslim State practices, and international human rights law. Research for this work has been conducted in the UK, France and Lebanon. Before conducting this study, charters summarizing the status of ratification of the human rights treaties of 56[30] Muslim States were prepared: the dates of accession and ratification, the reservations lodged for each, and the objections made against them. An interview at Dar el Fatwa, Lebanon, on the role of Sharia tribunals, was carried out by the author in March 2007. Documents in Arabic have been thoroughly consulted (court decisions, legislation, and academic literature); however, the lack of available documentation was a permanent concern in the course of this research. For this reason, each of the selected States has not necessarily been analysed in every section, and, sometimes, examples from Muslim States outside the defined selection are mentioned when relevant and where available.

29 A minority of Druze exists in Lebanon.

30 Palestine is a Member State to the OIC but is not included in the charters we have prepared.

Purpose and Contents of this Study

Two different phases will be analysed by this study: (1) the role of Sharia on the ratification of international human rights treaties; and (2) the impact of Sharia on the translation of the international human rights law into domestic practice in terms of both legislation and jurisprudence.

Chapter 1 of this study will provide in Section 1, a background of Sharia in terms of both substance and form, analysing the relationship between human rights and Sharia. Section 2 will clarify the relationship between Islam and the Constitutions of the selected Muslim States and the role of Sharia within the national legal system.

Chapter 2 shall first analyse, in Section 1, the impact of Sharia on the ratification of international human rights treaties and its influence on State abstentions from voting on human rights treaties and state limitations to the scope of the international human rights treaties. Section 2 will specifically analyse the role of Sharia on the ratification process of international human rights treaties.

Finally, Chapter 3 of the study will analyse the impact of Sharia on the implementation of international human rights law into domestic practice by looking at both legislation and jurisprudence. Section 1 documents the incorporation of international human rights treaties into the domestic law of Muslim States. Section 2 then undertakes a brief survey of the compatibility of legislation with human rights law. Section 3 will demonstrate the implementation of legislative amendments undertaken within the framework of Sharia and, lastly, Section 4 will discuss the role of the judiciary in the application of human rights law in the Muslim States selected for this study.

By analysing the role of Sharia in shaping the attitudes and policies adopted by Muslim States with regard to international human rights law, this study hopes to add to and serve as a resource for those currently engaged in the popular debates over the relationship between Islam and international law.

CHAPTER ONE

The Interrelationship between Islamic Law and Human Rights

The interrelationship between Islamic law and the concept of human rights relies predominantly upon two interwoven factors. The first relates to the substance of Sharia itself, and the second to the status of Sharia within the domestic legal system of each Muslim State—its place in what is commonly referred to as the 'hierarchy of norms'. The combination of these two factors determines the impact that Islamic doctrine has on the status and effectiveness of human rights norms in each State. More specifically, it appears to strongly influence the implementation and degree of adherence to the multiple international human rights treaties that the States concerned have ratified.

Section One The Substance of Sharia and its Relation to the Concept of Human Rights

In dealing with the relationship between Sharia and human rights, an exploration and understanding of pre-Islamic Arabia,[1] its culture, laws and traditions, is necessary. This inquiry serves not only to provide an historical context within which to view the changes brought by Sharia to the region, it also facilitates an appreciation of those customary laws and traditions that were later incorporated into Islam and have contributed to the doctrinal landscape of the religion as it stands today.[2] After comparing customs in pre-Islamic Arabia to the reforms brought by Sharia, this introductory section of the study examines the dual nature of the relationship between Sharia and human rights by further examining the normative confrontation between the two from a material perspective.

[1] Pre-Islamic society was composed of numerous tribes which lived in the desert and in towns under varying economic circumstances.

[2] See A Rahim, *The Principles of Islamic Jurisprudence: According to the Hanafi, Maliki, Shafi'I and Hanbali Schools* (Kitab Bhavan, New Delhi, 1994) 1.

1. THE HISTORICAL PERSPECTIVE OF ISLAM: A POSITIVE IMPACT

Before the advent of Islam, Arabia was composed primarily of tribal societies.[3] Tribal populations settled in large urban centres such as Medina and Mecca, which contained large and powerful populations and consisted of several clans linked together by kinship and interest.[4] In addition to these, nomadic tribes known as the Bedouin were prevalent throughout the Arabian Desert; the only difference between the Bedouin and the other tribes being that the latter enjoyed a more settled lifestyle.[5] The majority of Arabs at this time were idolaters, a relatively smaller number were Christians, and even fewer were Magians.[6] Medina and parts of southern Arabia also contained a large and influential community of Jewish Arabs.[7]

The following section aims to highlight the positive impact that the advent of Islam brought to the Arabian Peninsula. For instance, even seasoned critics of Islam have conceded that the religion bestowed rights on women as early as the 7th century that women in the West were unable to obtain until only relatively recently—such as the right to vote.[8] Indeed, the progressive nature of Sharia at this time enabled a significant improvement in the socio-legal life of the people in this region, even in terms of what would now be described in modern discourse as 'human rights'. These changes occurred most notably in the following areas: (a) criminal law and procedure; (b) economic rights; and (c) women's rights.

(a) Criminal law and procedure

Arabian society was traditionally based upon two sets of laws: the sedentary-supporting transactional laws; and the tribal laws that were dependent on the customary laws of the Bedouin.[9] Both groups followed the same set of customary laws in criminal matters, and although there was no settled form of constitutional governance, each tribe was led by an

[3] See generally MGS Hodgson, *The Venture of Islam: Conscience and History in a World Civilization, Vol 1: The Classical Age of Islam* (University of Chicago Press, Chicago, 1974) 103–45 (describing the pre-Islamic society from agrarian cultures to the Roman empire). See also M Watt, *Islam and the Integration of Society* (Routledge & Keagan Paul Ltd, London, 1961) 4–43 for a discussion on the place of economic and social factors in the historical background of the development of Islam.

[4] A Rahim (n 2) 2–3.

[5] ibid.

[6] ibid 3.

[7] ibid 2–3.

[8] AE Mayer, *Islam and Human Rights: Tradition and Politics* (Westview Press, Boulder, CO, 1995) 94.

[9] See W Hallaq, *The Origins and Evolution of Islamic Law* (CUP, Cambridge, 2005) 17–18.

elected chief.[10] The chief was generally a male who garnered a reputation of nobility and wisdom amongst his tribe. He was charged with the task of representing his tribe in its relations with other tribes.[11] If an offence was committed by one member of the tribe against another, the culprit would be surrendered to the chief for punishment. Tribal opinion and assent enforced the chief's decision.[12] However, if the culprit's family refused to surrender him and were powerful enough, the family would break away and join another tribe, becoming their *ahlaf* ('sworn allies'). If the culprit himself ran away to take refuge within a rival tribe, he would bear the label of *dakhil* ('one who has entered') within the new tribe.

Dispute resolution was based on the complainant adducing proof in support of his claim. If there were no witnesses and the defendant denied the charges, an oath to that effect would be taken by the defendant and he would be absolved from all liabilities.[13] Upon the agreement of both parties, soothsayers made judgments. If the suspect was a slave, torture was sometimes used to coerce a confession.[14]

Punishments for crimes against the person generally took the form of retaliation and were commutable by a payment of blood-money or compensation for the injury.[15] If an injury resulted in the person's death, the tribe or family had the right to demand satisfaction from the culprit—this form of retaliation was modified according to the position and status of the parties' families or of the tribes concerned. If a member of an inferior tribe killed an individual who was of a nobler tribe, the monetary compensation would be doubled; alternatively, the blood of two men could be called upon for one slain member, of a male instead of a female, and of a freeman instead of a slave.[16] No distinction was made with regards to whether the killing was intentional or otherwise.[17] If the tribes were at peace with one another and the accused denied the charge, as long as a number of men belonging to his tribe pledged their oaths to his innocence, the matter would be dropped entirely.[18]

Other forms of punishment that were prevalent during this time included cutting off the right hand of a thief. In other communities in

10 See generally W Montgomery Watt, *Muhammad at Mecca* (Clarendon Press, Oxford, 1953) 16–23 (discussing the importance of tribal solidarity and its politics); M Lippman, S McConville and M Yerushalmi, *Islamic Criminal Law and Procedure: An Introduction* (Praeger, New York, 1988) 77.

11 See Montgomery Watt (n 10) 22.

12 See Rahim (n 2) 3; Lippman, McConville and Yerushalmi (n 10) 77–78.

13 See Rahim (n 2) 5.

14 ibid.

15 See Rahim (n 2) 6; Lippman, McConville and Yerushalmi (n 10) 78.

16 See Rahim (n 2) 6 (citing *Tafsir-i-Ahmadi*, 57).

17 ibid 4.

18 ibid.

Medina adulterers were punished by having their faces blackened and by being flogged. If the adulterer was poor, he would also be stoned to death.[19]

The rise of Islam signalled a shift in the basis of the social foundation, expanding the basic social unit from simply the extended family to one which was placed within a community of believers (*ummah*).[20] The religion emphasized the importance and strength of the family and recognized rights of both men and women. Reforms in criminal law were also brought about by Islam.

First, the Quran prescribed a specific system for criminal procedure.[21] Islamic law requires the proper appointment of a judge (*qadi)* to decide on the claims (*dawa*) of disputants.[22] It also establishes a requisite number of witnesses for particular crimes. The oath taken by the accused or the alleged victim still had considerable sanctity, but was no longer a *conclusive* test as to the nature or veracity of a claim but viewed rather as a guarantee of truth. The primary principle underlying the Islamic law relating to evidence is that the decree or order of the court should be based on certainty and not conjecture.[23] The new system contained elaborate rules to determine the credibility of witnesses and guard against the court being misled.[24] The use of coercion or torture as a method of ascertaining the truth was also prohibited.[25] Furthermore, Islam entrenched the assumption of innocence as a fundamental principle within the legal system. It was therefore necessary for a court to be utterly convinced of the guilt of the accused before prescribing punishment.[26]

[19] ibid 6.

[20] JL Esposito with NJ DeLong-Bas, *Women in Muslim Family Law* (2nd edn, Syracuse University Press, New York, 2001) 14; see also W Coggins, 'Succession in Traditional Islamic Law' (2004) 60 Journal of the Missouri Bar 180, 181.

[21] For details on procedural and evidentiary rules in Islamic law: see Rahim (n 2) 346–63; R Peters, *Crime and Punishment in Islamic Law: Theory and Practices form the Sixteenth to the Twenty-first Century* (CUP, Cambridge, 2005) 6–68. See also AO Sherif, 'Generalities on Criminal Procedure under Islamic Sharia' in MA Haleem, AO Sherif, and K Daniels (eds), *Criminal Justice in Islam: Judicial Procedure in the Sharia* (IB Tauris, London, 2003) 3–16; S Ibrahim and N Mehemeed, 'Basic Principles of Criminal Procedure under Islamic Sharia' in Haleem, Sherif and Daniels, ibid 17–34.

[22] See Peters, ibid 8–11 (elaborating principles regarding law enforcement agencies and procedure).

[23] MS al-'Awaa, 'The Basis of Islamic Penal Legislation' in MC Bassiouni (ed), *The Islamic Criminal Justice System* (Oceana Publications, Inc, New York, 1982) 141.

[24] For specific conditions relating to the capacity and competency of witnesses: See Rahim (n 2) 358–59.

[25] KA El Fadl, *Islam and the Challenge of Democracy* (Princeton University Press, Princeton, 2004) 23.

[26] See MS El-Awa, 'Confession and Other Methods of Evidence in Islamic Procedural Jurisprudence' in Haleem, Sherif and Daniels (n 21) 111–30; MM Salama, 'General Principles of Criminal Evidence in Islamic Jurisprudence Confession and Other Methods of Evidence in Islamic Procedural Jurisprudence' in Bassiouni (n 23) 109–22.

The penal system was also reformed to establish two distinct categories of crime and punishment: 'determined crimes' or *hadd* crimes, those crimes expressly identified in the Quran or the Sunnah and having prescribed punishments; and 'discretionary crimes' *(taa'zir)*, those acts that neither the Quran nor the Sunnah cite as being criminal.[27] Determined crimes are divided into two further categories: crimes of *Hudud* (offences attracting prescribed *hadd* punishments); and crimes of retribution (*qisas*) and compensation (*diyya*), committed in retaliation to a prior offence. *Hudud* crimes, defined as violations of the claims of God, are penalized in order to protect public interests within Muslim society, such as public property and security, the family structure, conjugal and familial relationships and personal reputation.[28] The six *hudud* offences under traditional Islamic law and their prescribed punishments are:[29] (1) theft, requiring the amputation of a hand (*sariqah*);[30] (2) rebellion or highway/armed robbery, requiring death, crucifixion, cross-amputation of the hand and foot or banishment (*hirabah*);[31] (3) adultery and fornication, requiring 100 lashes respectively (*zina*);[32] (4) false accusations of unchastity, requiring 80 lashes (*qadhf*);[33] (5) apostasy, punishable by death; and (6) intoxication, punishable with 40 or 80 lashes (*sharb al-khamr*).[34]

Crimes of retribution (*qisas*) and compensation (*diyya*) include intentional homicide, bodily injury or other types of physical harm committed against the person. These are labelled separately because the punishments imposed are either retributive and equivalent to the injury sustained, or they allow a monetary compensation to be furnished as recompense for the victim's injuries. The pecuniary compensation is imposed only if the victim (or his legal guardians) waives his right to demand retribution or if the crime committed is not executable.[35]

Crimes of *taa'zir* are discretionary offences and carry corrective punishments. The penal laws created under this framework were designed to protect society's political, social and economic systems.[36] The heads of State are granted discretionary powers over the regulation of these offences.[37]

The establishment of these substantive and procedural penal laws heralded in by the advent of Islam marked an improvement to the existing pre-Islamic systems. The Islamic criminal system introduced a *qadi*, whose selection was based on knowledge and fairness, to resolve issues where previously a tribal chief, chosen partially for his claims to nobility, would

[27] al-'Awaa (n 23) 127.
[28] ibid.
[29] See M Baderin, *International Human Rights and Islamic Law* (OUP, Oxford, 2005) 79.
[30] Qu'ran 5:38.
[31] Qu'ran 5:33.
[32] Qu'ran 24:2.
[33] Qu'ran 24:4.
[34] See Baderin (n 29) 79; Rahim (n 2) 344.
[35] al-'Awaa (n 23) 127.
[36] ibid 128.
[37] See Rahim (n 2) 345.

have presided over disputes. Procedurally, disputes and claims used witnesses and established rules to prove or disprove charges. The accused was no longer simply handed over to the tribal chief but held to be innocent until formally convicted. Furthermore, judgments by soothsayers were no longer permitted. Under Islam, torture and coercion became an unacceptable means of ascertaining the truth[38] and witnesses were evaluated in an attempt to determine the appropriate value that should be attributed to their testimony. The principle of equality was implemented through various parts of the penal law, including the establishment of a uniform compensatory amount for crimes of retribution irrespective of nobility or birth. These were called *qisas*, crimes where punishment was strictly determined by Sharia. Punishments were enforced without regard to the kinship ties (*nasab*) of either the victim or the accused.[39]

(b) Economic rights

In addition to the changes observed within the criminal law and procedure, Islam modified certain financial dealings as well. Financial transactions in pre-Islamic Arabia were subject to interest and this kind of usury was rampant at the time.[40] Arabs, generally living at subsistence level and under pressing need, would borrow money from merchants and money-lenders only to be faced later with excessive increases to the original sum of the loan. These increases were based on charges of interest that accrued when the borrower could not meet the repayment deadline. The borrower could gain an extension for repayment, but at an exorbitant rate.[41] Islam prohibited these practices which constituted *riba*—'illicit gain' or 'usury', which involves 'enrichment without justification which upsets the balance of benefits'.[42] There were more changes, some of which were quite revolutionary and ahead of their time.

(c) Women's rights

Another area of revolutionary reform brought about by Islam's arrival centres on women in early Arabia. The treatment of women in pre-Islamic Arabia is generally seen to be poor by comparison, although this contention

38 For details on treatment of confession in Islam see MS El-Awa, 'Confession and Other Methods of Evidence in Islamic Procedural Jurisprudence' in Haleem, Sherif and Daniels (n 21) 111–130.

39 See Rahim (n 2) 345.

40 ibid 14.

41 See B Seniawski, 'Riba Today: Social Equity, the Economy, and Doing Business Under Islamic Law' (2001) 39 Columbia J Transnational L 701, 707–8.

42 N Comair-Obeid, *The Law of Business Contract in the Arab Middle East* (Kluwer Law International, The Hague, 1996) 43.

has generated some debate.[43] Some scholars point to women like Khadijah Bint Khuwailed (later to become Muhammad's first wife) as an example of pre-Islamic female social and economic independence.[44] However, during this early period, female participation in business ventures was typically contingent on male permission and support and it is unclear exactly how widespread this practice was.[45] Other scholars laud Islam for elevating the relatively low position of women in pre-Islamic Arabia.[46] However, historical evidence available points towards a blend of both notions, where women who were relatively independent were 'living side by side with hopelessly enslaved ones'.[47]

The influence of Islam in improving conditions for women can be seen most prominently in the following legal institutions and concepts: (i) marriage; (ii) dissolution of marriage; and (iii) property ownership and inheritance.

(i) Marriage

Despite indications of several types of marriage—patrilineal and patrilocal; patriarchal; matrilineal and matrilocal; uxorilocal; polyandrous; and polygamous—being evident in pre-Islamic poetry[48] and other sources, women were generally placed under the control of a husband and lived with him and his tribe following a patrilineal/patrilocal pattern.[49]

[43] cf L Ahmed, 'Women and the Advent of Islam' (1986) 11 Signs 665 (declaring the matriarchal elevated status of women within matriarchal Arabia) with A al-Hibri, 'A Study of Islamic Herstory: Or How Did We Ever Get into this Mess?' in A al-Hibri (ed), *Women and Islam* (Pergamon Press, Oxford, 1982) (arguing that despite the existence of some goddesses, Islam raised the status of women in Arabia); see also G Nashat, and J Tucker, *Women in the Middle East and North Africa: Restoring Women to History* (Indiana University Press, Indianapolis, 1999).

[44] See N El Saadawi, 'Women and Islam' in A al-Hibri (ed), *Women and Islam* (Peragamon Press, Oxford, 1982) 196. See also Ahmed (n 43) 665–91; JI Smith, 'Women in Islam: Equity, Equality, and the Search for the Natural Order' (1979) 47 Journal of the American Academy of Religion 517–37.

[45] JL Esposito and NJ DeLong-Bas, *Women in Muslim Family Law* (2nd edn, Syracuse University Press, New York, 2001) 13.

[46] MC Ali, *The Proposed Political, Legal, and Social Reforms in the Ottoman Empire and Other Mohammadan States: Reforms Under Moslem Rule* (Education Society Press, Bombay, 1883) 111–13.

[47] al-Hibri (n 43) 210.

[48] Some strong women did receive tribute in poetry; however, women in general are not prominent in pre-Islamic literature. Esposito and DeLong-Bas (n 45). See also I Lichtenstadter, *Women in the Aiyam Al-'Arab: A Study of Female Life During Warfare in Pre-Islamic Arabia* (Royal Asiatic Society, London, 1935) (stating that women are seldom mentioned in *Aiyam al 'Arab*—that branch of Arab literature that deals with Bedouin warfare during the *Jahiliyah*—and that women rarely take part in raids and warfare); but see Ahmed (n 43) 665–91.

[49] Esposito and DeLong-Bas (n 45) 12–13.

Four types of marriage that were practised in pre-Islamic Arabia are generally outlined. The first, *nikah-e-am*, was a form sanctioned by Islam, where a man asks another for the hand of the latter's daughter or ward and then marries her by giving her a dower.[50] The second, *nikah-e-istebza*, was a custom through which a husband asked his wife to go to a famous person he had selected for sexual intercourse, and to reside with the latter until she had conceived by him. Once her pregnancy had become apparent, the woman would return to her husband. This form of sexual activity is said to have been based on the desire to secure a noble seed for the glorification of the husband's clan. The third form, *nikah-ul-jama*, involved up to ten men engaging in sexual relations with one woman. If she conceived and delivered a child, she could assemble the men and ascribe the child to whichever one she chose. The man would be unable to deny paternity. Finally, *nikah-e-baghaya* was a form of marriage through which an unlimited number of men would visit a woman who would not refuse any visitors. These women were classed as prostitutes and labelled themselves as such by fixing a flag to the doors of their tents. In this form of marriage, if a woman gave birth, the men that frequented her house would be assembled and a physiognomist would decide to whom the child belonged.

Various other forms of sexual union were prevalent among the pre-Islamic Arabs.[51] Marriage by capture and purchase were also highly prevalent practices. Marriage by purchase involved the payment of a sum of money to the bride's guardian and another sum of *sadaqa* (charity) to the bride herself. The amount of the purchase price would vary and could be quite large if the woman was regarded as a prospective mother of warriors.[52] Marriage by capture occurred when a man parted a woman's hair with his spear and lifted her such as to carry her away by force.[53] A woman was not considered a free agent and her consent for marriage was of no importance. Any of a woman's male relatives: her father, brother, cousin or any other male guardian, had the right to give her away in marriage to whomsoever they chose. *Sighar*, another form of marriage, developed out of the custom of one man telling another that he would

[50] Rahim (n 2). It is important to note that in pre-Islamic Arabia the dower was presented to the bride's father and with Islam, the *mahr* was changed to be a gift for the bride herself.

[51] *Nikah-ul-khadan* was a form of a concealed marriage, entered into on the belief that there was nothing wrong in the concealment of marriage. However, open marriages were considered inauspicious. *Nikah-ul-badal* was the exchange of wives between two men who would seal the arrangement with the promise: 'leave your wife for me and I will leave my wife for you'. *Nikah-bil-um* was the custom through which a son would acquire his father's wife aside from his own mother, as she was regarded as inheritable property. Two sisters were taken into marriage by a single man through *nikah-bainal-ukhtain*.

[52] KN Ephroz, *Women and Law: Muslim Personal Law Perspective* (Rawat Publications, Jaipur, 2003) 29.

[53] ibid; See also R Levy, *An Introduction to the Sociology of Islam, Volume I* (Williams and Norgate Limited, London, 1957) (discussing how capture reduced women to mere chattels).

marry his daughter or sister to the other, in exchange for the other's daughter or sister becoming his wife. This form of marriage enabled each of the two girls to be the dower for the other girl.[54] Guardians of orphan children had the same unbridled power and often married girls off and misappropriated their property.

While men in pre-Islamic Arabia indisputably enjoyed far greater liberties than women in respect of marriage, certain restrictions were placed on them with regards to whom they could marry. An Arab male was prohibited from marrying his mother, grandmother, sister, daughter or granddaughter, although those that followed the Magian were permitted to marry their daughters and sisters.[55] Arabs were, however, allowed to marry stepmothers, cousins, or wives' sisters; they could also marry two sisters at the same time, or a woman and her niece.

Islam resulted in the overall improvement of the status of women in the 7th century with new customs and laws that signalled radical departures from customary law in ancient Arabia.[56] Through Islam, significant reforms were implemented with respect to women's rights, including the prohibition of female infanticide.[57] The institution of marriage ('*nikkah*') was reformed and appreciated as a highly religious and sacred covenant in the form of a legal contract authorizing intercourse and encouraging procreation.[58] Group marriages, 'flag' marriages, marriage exchange and prostitution were all forbidden by Islam.[59] Dower rights were granted to women in order to safeguard their economic position after marriage.

After the arrival of Islam, marriages in Muslim societies began to be classified according to their degree of validity, which in turn affected the rights that were granted to the partners. In order to secure all of the important rights that were available within marriage, the *nikkah* had to be completely lawful ('*sahih*') and valid. '*Batil*' (void and foundationally bad marriages) and '*fasid*' (unlawful but foundationally good marriages), either limited or completely denied the spouses their legal rights.[60] A *batil* marriage was an unlawful union that accorded neither mutual rights nor any obligations to the spouses. Marriages that were prohibited on the grounds of shared kinship or consanguinity, affinity, or fosterage were all considered *batil*.[61]

54 Ephroz (n 52) 30.

55 See Rahim (n 2) 9.

56 Esposito and DeLong-Bas (n 45) 12–14.

57 Smith (n 44) 520. Female infanticide also became characterized as a crime against God (not just man). al-hibri (n 43) 212. See also Rahim (n 2).

58 cf Esposito and DeLong-Bas (n 45) 15 and Ephroz (n 52).

59 Ephroz (n 52) 37.

60 Esposito and DeLong-Bas (n 45) 17–18.

61 See JJ Nasir, *The Status of Women Under Islamic Law and Under Modern Islamic Legislation, Second Edition* (2nd edn, Graham & Trotman, London, 1994) 20 (elaborating categories with respect to *batil* marriages). See generally Esposito and DeLong-Bas (n 45) discussing 'consanguinity'.

The factors used to determine whether a union would be prohibited on the grounds of shared kinship are laid out in the Quran.[62] Relations that were prohibited included those with the man's ancestors and descendants, the descendants of his first ascendants, and the first descendants of every ancestor, however far back in the lineage.[63]

In addition, the marriage of a Muslim woman to more than one husband at the same time is considered *batil*. Under this kind of marriage (or lack thereof), upon the death of one partner, the other will not be entitled to any inheritance. Children resulting from a *batil* marriage are considered illegitimate and as such are not entitled to inherit either.[64] Because this marriage is considered null and void, there is no formal requirement to dissolve the relationship.

A '*fasid*' marriage is considered unlawful either because it lacks legal formality or there is a particular impediment that is either temporary or may be removed. Those issues regarding the formality of the marriage that may be rectified refer generally to practices such as marriages contracted with less than the requisite number of witnesses or marriages that were conducted in secret.[65] Temporary impediments are based on pre-existing marriages, irrevocable divorce and religion. Once the *qadi* (judge) has been made aware of such an irregular marriage he must either legalize the relationship or terminate it.[66] A *fasid* marriage may theoretically become *sahih* ('lawful') once the impediment has been removed,[67] but has no legal effect until consummation. Furthermore, even after consummation, only partial rights will attach to the partners. The wife will possess dower rights but will have none in respect of maintenance due (*nafaqa*). Although there is no mutual right of inheritance between the spouses, the children, now considered legitimate, will be entitled to inherit.

A *sahih* marriage avoids the prohibitions imposed on *batil* and *fasid* marriages, conforming to the legal requirements of marriage and conferring on the partners all legal rights and obligations. The contractual nature of

[62] Quran, 4:23: 'Prohibited to you (For marriage) are:—Your mothers, daughters, sisters; father's sisters, Mother's sisters; brother's daughters, sister's daughters; foster-mothers (Who gave you suck), foster-sisters; your wives' mothers; your step-daughters under your guardianship, born of your wives to whom ye have gone in,—no prohibition if ye have not gone in;—(Those who have been) wives of your sons proceeding from your loins; and two sisters in wedlock at one and the same time, except for what is past; for Allah is Oft-forgiving, Most Merciful'.

[63] Nasir (n 61) 20.

[64] See Esposito and DeLong-Bas (n 45) 19.

[65] See Esposito and DeLong-Bas (n 45) 18. The general consensus of jurists finds that for a marriage to be considered lawful there must be two male witnesses, or a man and two women who are each adult, sane and free. The witnesses must hear and understand both the offer and acceptance of the *nikkah*. See also Nasir (n 61) 13.

[66] Esposito and DeLong-Bas (n 45) 18.

[67] Nasir (n 61) 23.

the marriage, a novel concept under Islam, transformed the status of the woman from a mere object for sale to a genuine party to the agreement, the conclusion of which requires her consent. Muslim men may contract their own marriages; however, a Muslim woman must typically have a male guardian (called a '*wali*') to contract the marriage on her behalf.[68] Although some scholars cite the Quran as conferring the right of independence to a Muslim woman to enter into the *nikkah* without the involvement of a *wali*,[69] the general consensus among the schools of thought is that the woman is unable to conduct her own *nikkah* without a guardian.

Thus, most pre-Islamic unions would be seen as *batil* within the framework of Islamic law. As outlined earlier, *nikah-e-istebza* (whereby a husband sent his wife to a famous man in order to conceive a child with him), *nikah-ul-jama* (whereby a woman would have sexual relations with a group of men and then conceive a child) and *nikah-e-baghaya* (sex with prostitutes) were outlawed. These pre-Islamic exchanges that enabled men to treat women as movable property were forbidden. Similarly, *nikah-bil-um*, the practice of inheriting a deceased father's wife as property, and marriage by purchase and capture of a Muslim woman were also prohibited. It is also interesting to note that within these reforms, Islam did retain some elements of the *nikah-e-am* type of marriage.

The Islamic law derivative of the *sahih nikah* reformed marriage to include a woman's consent. It also changed the practice where the bride's price was given to the bride's father, instead treating it as a dower (*mahr*) and giving it to the bride directly, thereby changing the woman's status from mutable property to a partner in an agreement. With regard to the consent of the woman and the guardianship duties of the *wali*, according to some schools of thought[70] the *wali* was perceived to have also been granted the power (*jabr*) to arrange marriages in respect of minors which could not be annulled at puberty.[71] This view was supported on the assumption that the *wali* would not have sinister motives in arranging the marriage.[72] This is despite the change in the legal age of marriage, which also came with the advent of Islam and was established for both Muslim men and women of sound mind to the age of puberty. It is important to note that there is no

68 The Hanafi school of law theoretically allows women of legal majority to contract their own marriage. Esposito and DeLong-Bas (n 45) 15.

69 See MA Syed, *The Position of Women in Islam: A Progressive View* (SUNY Press, Albany, NY, 2004) 38; see also Qu'ran.

70 Both *Maliki* and *Shafii* believe the consent of the *wali* is essential; the *Shi'i* do not. The Hanafi school of thought is cited by al-Marghinani in Syed (n 69) 38: 'the marriage contract of a free woman who has reached the age of majority and is possessed of understanding, is complete with her own consent, whether she is a virgin or has never been married before, though it may not have been confirmed by her guardian'.

71 Esposito and DeLong-Bas (n 45).

72 ibid 12–13.

Quranic injunction against child marriages, although this custom already existed in pre-Islamic Arabia.

Child marriages, multiple and loose forms of unions between men and women, promiscuity and 'temporary marriages' (*'muta'a'*) were also quite common in pre-Islamic Arabia.[73] Under pre-Islamic Arab custom, men could possess an indeterminate number of wives (*kasrat-e-izdewai*).[74] Furthermore, a man was unrestricted as to the number of slave girls he might possess[75]—the only limit imposed being that of the man's means, opportunity and inclination.[76]

Islamic law modified these customs and limited polygamy. As discussed above, marriages involving one woman and more than one man were considered *batil*. However, a Muslim man may legitimately have up to four wives.[77]

There is considerable debate surrounding this issue. Jurists cite the Quranic text within *Sura Nisa* as supporting polygamy (or up to four wives). Verse 4:3 provides

> [I]f you fear you cannot deal justly with the orphans, then marry such of the women that appeal to you, two, three or four; but if you fear that you cannot be equitable, then only one'.[78]

Other jurists argue that this Quranic injunction must be viewed within the social context of the period, which saw vast numbers of widows and orphans of men who had died in battle, in need of protection and support.[79] The contention is that as the social context has altered, the general reform of polygamy created by the Quran's express limitation should be extended to allow only for monogamous relationships in our modern times. On this topic, Mohammed Ghari Fatemi stated that:

> It seems plausible to suggest that traditional *fiqhi* norms should be considered the first steps, but not the last, made by early Muslims to improve women's rights. That is to say, the ultimate goal of Islam has been the achievement of a just society with just relationships. It is obvi-

[73] Ephroz (n 52) 26.

[74] Esposito and DeLong-Bas (n 45) 28.

[75] Rahim (n 2) 9.

[76] ibid 9.

[77] Esposito and DeLong-Bas (n 45); J Rehman, 'The Sharia, Islamic Family Laws and International Human Rights Law: Examing the Theory and Practice of Polygamy and Talaq' (2007) 21 Intl J of L Policy and the Family 108.

[78] Qu'ran 4:3.

[79] Esposito (n 52) 625, specifically states that the context of the Battle of *Uhud* is especially instructive in the reading of the Qu'ranic verse conceding to polygamy, as the battle had caused the death of a substantial portion of the male Muslim population. Esposito and DeLong-Bas (n 52) 19.

ous that in a society like pre-Islamic Arabia the elimination of all culturally rooted inequalities was not feasible. Quranic teachings, however, set forth justice as the ultimate goal of all divine religions.[80]

Some scholars also argue that rather than sanction polygamy, the Quran may in fact be interpreted as implicitly permitting only monogamy. This is done by reading verse 4:3 in conjunction with a later verse,[81] which provides: 'Ye are never able to be fair and just among women, even if you tried hard…' (4:129),[82] thus countering the equity caveat stated in verse 4:3. This issue continues to be debated amongst scholars although, in general, Muslim jurists continue to uphold the male's right to marry up to four wives. In any event, Islam's reduction of the number of wives in a polygamous marriage to four, and even then, *only* in instances where the man is able to provide equally for all four, when compared to the previous situation in pre-Islamic Arabia in which unlimited polygamy was tolerated, is generally seen as a positive reform.[83]

Lawful sexual relations between Muslim men and women are generally confined to these general terms. An exception is a form of marriage called '*mutaa*', which is accepted as a valid form within minority interpretations of Islam. *Mutaa* marriages are temporary and a pre-defined term for the marriage—for example, one month, one year—is established from the outset of the union. It confers rights and responsibilities upon both spouses, also imposes obligations towards and rights for any resulting children. *Mutaa* was allowed in the 10th year of Hijra but in most schools of thought it has since been forbidden. *Shia* Islam still allows for *muta'aa* [spelling???] to take place but tradition refers to it as *Sighe*.

(ii) Dissolution of marriage

In addition to the reforms outlined above with regard to the manner in which marriage was entered into and the rights and obligations conferred by it, Islam also reformed the mechanisms surrounding the end of a marriage. With respect to divorce, a man in pre-Islamic Arabia was just as free to release himself from the union as he was to enter into it. This spontaneous and arbitrary form of divorce was customarily referred to as '*talaq*'. There was neither a particular procedure to be observed nor the necessity of a reason to be given for initiating the divorce. The man held all

[80] S Mohammad Ghari and S Fatemi, 'Autonomy and Equal Right to Divorce with Specific Reference to *Shi'I Fiqh* and the Iranian Legal System' (2006) 17 Islam and Christian–Muslim Relations 281, 286.

[81] Azizah Alhibrih 216.

[82] Que'ran 4:129.

[83] See generally Esposito and DeLong-Bas (n 45); Rehman (n 77); Ephroz (n 52).

the power in the relationship and was free to exercise it at whim. It was also within his discretion as to whether he would dissolve the marriage absolutely so as to set the woman free to remarry or not. The man could even revoke the divorce and then resume the marital union at a later point, customs revealing that men often divorced women by repeating the word '*talaq*' many times, and then took them back, and then divorced them for a further time.[84] Men in pre-Islamic Arabia were also able to suspend a marriage by making a declaration: the man would renounce and she would then cease to live with him; however, the wife was not free to remarry.

Ila was another form of divorce whereby the husband renounced his wife by swearing that he would have nothing to do with her again. This was perceived by some to be a type of 'suspended marriage' and by others as an instant separation. '*Zihar*' was an irrevocable divorce that was successfully executed when the husband told his wife that she was 'like the back of his mother'. The wife did not have a corresponding right to divorce. Her family could arrange a separation by returning the dower, or by rejecting it if it had not already been paid. This form of dissolution was called a '*khula*'. Once a woman was absolutely separated from her husband, she did have the option to remarry—but was unable to do so until after a waiting period (known as '*iddat*') had elapsed.[85] This period, imposed so that it could be ascertained whether the woman was pregnant, was also enforced upon the death of the husband for a term of one year.[86]

Islam restructured the dissolution of marriage. First, with respect to the termination of marriage upon the death of the husband, the wife no longer had to mourn for one year as the *idaat* period was shortened to approximately three months, although some traditions still implement the full year for the sake of culture.[87] Furthermore, marriages are terminated with immediate effect if either spouse commits apostasy.[88]

As noted earlier, Islam promoted family and kinship relationships as central to society. As such, marriage became the basic building block of society. It was, and continues to be, traditionally viewed as a permanent institution[89] and divorce was accordingly seen as abhorrent.[90] Many Quranic injunctions sought to limit the earlier frequency and facility of divorce in Arabia.[91] Although divorce is permitted in Islam, it is regarded as a last resort in cases where spouses can no longer live together in

[84] Abdul Rahman citing tale of 10 *talaq* pronouncements.
[85] Rahim (n 2) 910.
[86] ibid.
[87] al-Hibri (n 43).
[88] Nasir (n 61) 103.
[89] With the exception of *mutaa* in the *shia* school of thought.
[90] The Prophet is reported to have said: 'of all things permitted, divorce is the most abominable with God'. See also Rahim (n 2) 319 (citing Fathu'l-Qadir, vol iii, p 326).
[91] Esposito and DeLong-Bas (n 45) 27.

harmony, thereby defeating the very purpose of marriage by remaining together. *Talaq* is the general term used to indicate divorce. It literally means 'a repudiation' and signifies one spouse's release of the other spouse from the marriage bond, whether through repudiation or legal process. There are several forms of divorce that may be discussed in five categories: (1) *talaq* (proper); (2) *talaq al-tafwid*; (3) *khul and mubaraah*; (4) *lian and faskh*; and (5) apostasy.

Talaq (proper) constitutes the husband's right to divorce his wife and is initiated when he makes a particular pronouncement, stating that the marriage is dissolved. Although the Quranic verses indicate the undesirability of divorce, there are no specific restrictions on the husband's right to divorce that incorporate a legal guard against abuses of the practice. Hanafi law also permits conditional, contingent, or qualified pronouncements that may be enacted at the occurrence of a future event or at a future time.[92] Hanafi law also considers the following spoken words: 'You are divorced', 'I have divorced you', or 'I divorce my wife', to be of immense gravity and that action alone is seen as having effect. This also means that these words, whether spoken in jest, under duress or under the influence of alcohol are still considered to be valid and effective. Under Hanafi law, the husband's right to divorce is unencumbered and the woman does not even have to be present nor must she be informed of the proceeding.[93]

Divorce can either be revocable ('*raji*') or irrevocable ('*bain*').[94] The revocable form is traditionally viewed as the approved form—breaking the classification of *talaq* down further to allow for *talaq al-sunnahh* (divorce that is initiated in keeping with prophet Mohammed's teachings) and *talaq al-bidah* (divorce that does not follow the prophet's teachings).[95] *Talaq al-ahsan* and *talaq al-hasan* are further classifications of *talaq al-sunnahh*.[96] *Talaq al-ahsan* is the more proper and orthodox form of divorce and takes place during the period of *tuhr* (or 'purity'—the period when the woman is not menstruating).[97] Under this type of divorce, the husband pronounces a single invocation of divorce and abstains from sexual intercourse with his wife during the period of *iddah*. *Iddah* is the period of waiting a woman must observe before she can remarry following the divorce or death of her husband.[98] During the entire *iddah* period, the pronouncement is revocable, providing time and space for the husband to reconsider or enter into

[92] ibid 29.
[93] ibid 29–30.
[94] Nasir (n 61).
[95] Esposito and DeLong-Bas (n 45).
[96] ibid.
[97] Rahim (n 2).
[98] A Rahman, *Shariah: The Islamic Law* (Ta-Ha Publishers, London, 2008) 307–12. (The period of *Iddah* is three menstruation cycles for a woman who menstruates and three months for a woman who does not.) The Qur'an (65:4) states: 'Such of your women as have passed the age of monthly courses, for them the prescribed period, if [you] have any doubts, is three months, and for those who have no courses (it is the same): for those who are pregnant, their period is until they deliver their burdens ...'.

family arbitration. However, the divorce becomes irrevocable once the *iddah* period is complete.[99]

The *ahsan* divorce is the form that is least disapproved of because of the kind treatment shown to the wife under it. The marriage's period of suspension is not long, and there is no prohibition against the wife remarrying her husband as there has only been one pronouncement of *talaq*. Furthermore, the wife may still retain her inheritance rights if her husband dies during her *iddah*, and vice versa.

The second classification of *talaq al-sunnahh*, the *hasan* form, retains the structure but not the spirit of the Quranic injunctions.[100] This divorce is enacted by uttering the three *talaq* pronouncements during successive periods of *tuhr*, with no sexual intercourse taking place within those times. This third pronouncement renders the divorce irrevocable and remarriage is only possible after the wife marries another man, consummates that marriage and is then lawfully divorced. The period of the *idaah* must also be fulfilled after the third pronouncement.

The irrevocability of the divorce after the third pronouncement was implemented to stop the pre-Islamic practice of divorcing a wife and taking her back several times. It also stops a Muslim man from divorcing his wife, and taking her back several times to push her to divorce him and relinquish her dower, or make some other financial sacrifice.[101]

Talaq al-biddah, the disapproved form of divorce, does not allow for any period of reconsideration. It is immediately irrevocable. The first form of *talaq al-biddah* consists of three successive proclamations of divorce within the same period of *tuhr*. Generally, this form is invoked with the utterance of *talaq* in three sentences repeated consecutively, or just one sentence: 'I divorce you thrice'.[102] Another form of *talaq al-bidah* is comprised of one single irrevocable oral or written proclamation of divorce. It may be made during a period of *tuhr* or at any other time and causes the marriage to dissolve immediately.

On occasion, although the words of *talaq* are not spoken, the conduct of the husband may have the effect of repudiation. In such a case, the husband must swear that he will have nothing to do with his wife and, after having made this oath, must abstain from sexual relations with her for a period of

[99] Esposito and DeLong-Bas (n 45).

[100] ibid.

[101] ibid 31. See Quran, 2:228: 'Divorced women shall wait concerning themselves for three monthly periods. Nor is it lawful for them to hide what Allah Hath created in their wombs, if they have faith in Allah and the Last Day. And their husbands have the better right to take them back in that period, if they wish for reconciliation. And women shall have rights similar to the rights against them, according to what is equitable; but men have a degree (of advantage) over them. And Allah is Exalted in Power, Wise.'

[102] See Ephroz (n 52) 278–85 (detailing the difference of opinion among jurists about the validity of the triple pronouncement *talaq)*.

four months. This type of divorce is called '*ila*'.[103] According to the Hanafi view, it is an irrevocable divorce, whereas the Malikis, Shafiis, Hanbalis and *shia* Muslims make the separation subject to a pronouncement of divorce by the husband or to a suit by the wife.[104]

The second category of divorce, '*talaq al-tawfid*' is a right to divorce which a husband may delegate to his wife.[105] A woman's right to divorce in Islam is relatively limited and this type of divorce commits control over the relationship into the woman's hands. The husband may assign his wife this right in three different ways: the first, '*al'ikhtiar*', entails a husband permitting his wife to 'choose herself' or 'divorce herself'; the second method, '*al'am'ru bil yade*', involves a husband saying to his wife: 'your business is in your hands'; and the third, '*al'mashi'at*', entails the husband stating: 'if you wish it, divorce yourself'.[106]

The third category of divorce entails an element of mutuality, where both parties to the marriage agree to a divorce. A '*khul*' divorce is initiated by the woman and then accepted by both parties. The *khul* generally includes the wife giving some compensation to her husband—typically a part or all of her '*mahar*'. However, some scholars note that based on verse 4:19 of the Quran, the *khul* may take place without the furnishing of consideration.

When both the husband and the wife want to separate, the divorce may take the form of '*mubaraah*'. The correct procedure for this divorce under Hanafi law involves the arrangement of a meeting in which the husband will propose a dissolution of the marriage and the wife will formally accept it.[107] Where this occurs, the divorce is irrevocable.

The final category of divorce, of which there are two types, accommodates judicial intervention in the proceedings. In '*lian*', the first of the two in this category, the husband accuses his wife of having committed adultery, although without adducing any legal evidence in corroboration of the charge.[108] The wife may, in effect, bring a counter-suit, requiring her husband to either swear an oath to support his claim, or to issue a retraction. The wife must also be prepared to swear a similar oath professing her innocence (if she denies the charge). Both man and wife will declare their oaths with the knowledge that verses 24:6–9 of the Quran promise the wrath of God upon the perjurer. Once the suit is filed, they may no longer engage in sexual intercourse and as long as this condition has been fulfilled, the husband will be permitted to divorce his wife once the oaths have been made. If for some reason he declines to do so, the court may intervene and

[103] Rahim (n 2) 321.
[104] Nasir (n 61) 75.
[105] Esposito and DeLong-Bas (n 45).
[106] Rahim (n 2) 321–22.
[107] Esposito and DeLong-Bas (n 45) 32.
[108] ibid.

dissolve the marriage, should the parties not agree to forgive each other. The ensuing divorce will be irrevocable. The second type of divorce in the 'judicial' category is that of '*faskh*', a process of annulment afforded through the judge (or the '*qadi*'). This judicial rescission of the marriage contract is generally initiated upon the court receiving a petition from a wife.

The major schools of law differ with respect to the number and kinds of divorce that are legitimately available to women. The Hanafi school provides the narrowest remit of divorce that may be successfully instigated by a woman. Judicial dissolution may only occur under Hanafi law if the following six factors are present in the relationship: (1) the marriage is 'irregular'; (2) a person who has the option to dissolve the marriage does so; (3) the parties are connected through fosterage; (4) the marriage was contracted by non-Muslims who subsequently adopted Islam or vice versa; (5) the husband is unable to consummate the marriage; or (6) the husband is missing. If the husband is missing, the marriage may be terminated by the court after a certain period of time on the presumption that the husband is dead and the wife is a widow.[109]

The Maliki construction of this concept is perceived to preserve the most rights for women in its interpretation of divorce. It allows a woman to divorce her husband on the grounds of his cruelty, refusal or inability to maintain her, his desertion or the contraction of a serious disease or aliment that would render the marriage harmful for the wife.

These mechanisms for dissolving and repudiating marriages illustrate significant changes to the social structure in pre-Islamic Arabia and the rights that women were afforded. The institution of divorce, although still affording men more rights than women in marriage, was structured in such a way as to provide some measure of support to women. The pre-Islamic constructs allowed husbands an indeterminate number of revocable divorces, which threatened women with the intolerable position of being bound in a perpetual cycle of divorce and marriage to the same man. Husbands were effectively able to hold their wives hostage as they were not free to remarry without their express permission. *Ila* and *zihar* are two forms of divorce that survived the arrival of Islam and have continued within its tradition. However, as noted earlier, these were not without significant modifications to those doctrines being made and, in any event, most jurists view these two latter forms of marriage, along with *lian*, as having little practical relevance today. [110]

[109] Esposito and DeLong-Bas (n 45) 32.
[110] ibid 74–75.

(iii) Property ownership and inheritance

Pre-Islamic Arabian custom recognized the right of every free man and woman to own property. Slaves were an exception as they were considered property themselves.[111] Therefore, a free woman was able to own property in pre-Islamic times; however, her property was not secure unless she was under the protection of her parents, husband or another male relative. But this in itself was not an adequate solace as, if her protectors were dishonest in dealing with her property, she would be afforded no real remedy.[112] Furthermore, women were barred from inheriting under pre-Islamic custom—property owned by a woman must have been acquired by trade, commerce or be a gift from her parents and relatives.[113]

In contrast, an Arab man could dispose of his property at will, which could include giving it away in its entirety to anyone he wanted, leaving his family in want. He could also choose an heir to his property to the exclusion of others. If a man died intestate, suitable beneficiaries were identified and determined by consanguinity, adoption or compact[???]. It appears in these situations that the tribal chief would divide the estate amongst the male relatives—the female relatives (wives, sisters and mothers) were excluded from inheritance deliberations. However, the estate was considered liable for the widow's *mahr* (the dower she received upon marriage.) Some tribes also held the estate responsible for her maintenance.[114]

The advent of Islam reconstructed most of these norms and property rights as women were introduced to the Arab world for the first time. A woman was now allowed to own, manage and inherit property, and she would also be able to retain it after marriage.[115] Neither spouse automatically acquired an interest in the property of the other purely because of marriage.[116] Inheritance under Islam became a formal system, where rules regarding beneficiaries were based on the principle that the property of the deceased should devolve proportionately to those with consanguinity or affinity claims.[117] The pre-Islamic custom of entrusting property to a mature male relative (who could physically fight) on behalf of the tribe, to the exclusion of members of the family, was discontinued to ensure that the family was provided for.[118] Under Islamic inheritance laws, the direct family of the deceased—a son, father, husband, daughter, mother, or wife,

111 Rahim (n 2) 12.
112 ibid 14.
113 al-Hibri (n 43).
114 Rahim (n 2) 15.
115 Qu'ran 4:7.
116 Esposito and DeLong-Bas (n 45) 23.
117 Rahim (n 2) 329.
118 Esposito and DeLong-Bas (n 45) 37.

can never be totally excluded from inheriting.[119] Furthermore, widows were no longer seen as part of the inheritance to be handed from man to man and were mandated an inheritance from their deceased husbands' estates.[120] However, because slaves were still viewed as property within Islam, they were unable to inherit. Although Islam reformed financial laws and prohibited *riba* so as to end indentured servitude, the legal system still recognized slavery as an institution.[121]

In addition to the disparities evident in the treatment of men and women as far as marriage and divorce were concerned, Arabian society also practised female infanticide. The *Hamasa* (an anthology that contains pre-Islamic narrative) includes a saying to the effect that the grave is the best bridegroom and that the burial of daughters is demanded by honour.[122] The act of female infanticide was prompted by the view that the birth of a daughter was a calamity.[123] Alternatively, some views suggest that female infanticide was driven by poverty and a sense of shame[124] and was already in decline by the dawn of Islam. However, this decline is attributed to the realization that selling or marrying off their daughters for a large dowry was far more profitable than burying them.[125]

Islam also brought various other reforms pertaining to women. These include prohibiting males from expelling menstruating women from their homes and refusing to eat from the same pot as them.[126] Education and learning became an equal duty of both men and women. Men were also prohibited from taking Muslim women as prisoners of war.

119 Rahim (n 2) 332–33.

120 Rahim, ibid.

121 See Qu'ranic Surah. Slavery, practised in Arabia (and most parts of the world) before Islam, was a big source of labour and profit. Slaves were treated inhumanely and Islamic reforms in the area were targeted to ameliorate those conditions. Nothing within the Qu'ran sanctioned or advocated slavery. Its passages continually recommended the compassionate treatment for slaves and prescribed the freeing of slaves as recompense for certain sins. Jurists acknowledge that Islam tolerated the practice, but simultaneously advanced its gradual eradication. Today, no Muslim State will formally admit the practice and most have ratified international instruments abolishing slavery or related practices.

122 See R Levy, *An Introduction to the Sociology of Islam: Vol I* (Williams & Norgate, London, 1957) 132.

123 Rahim (n 2).

124 See Levy (n 122), discussing rational explanations given for female infanticide and the potential origin of the action in the idea of sacrifice. al-hibri (n 43) 209 (citing Mahmasani on the practice of female infanticide by Northern Arabs of Jahiliyah).

125 This also shows a heightened economic pragmatism. See W Montgomery Watt (n 10) 1–4, discussing the importance of tribal solidarity and its politics.

126 al-Hibri (n 43).

2. FROM THE MATERIAL PERSPECTIVE: SHARIA LAW AND HUMAN RIGHTS—A NORMATIVE CONFRONTATION?

The above section demonstrated Islam's contribution to the reformation of the socio-legal and economic context of early pre-Islamic Arabia. This section will continue with an analysis of how this same Islam is currently engaged in a normative confrontation with modern international human rights norms. Indeed, despite the advent of Islam bringing some improvements to human rights conditions as demonstrated, the substance of Islamic norms still remain problematic from the perspective of human rights.

A significant proportion of substantive Islamic law is either in harmony with human rights (for instance, in regard to certain rules relating to economic, social and cultural rights), or has no obvious bearing on human rights at all (such as the rules governing private religious rituals).[127] However, there are components of Islamic law that present challenges when viewed through the lens of international human rights law. As asserted by Abdullahi Ahmed An-Naim, 'some principles of Sharia are in direct and irreconcilable conflict with some major human rights norms' and therefore 'the implementation and enforcement of those Sharia principles will necessarily violate the corresponding human rights norms'.[128] These controversies may be found specifically within the Islamic provisions relating to: (a) the criminal and penal justice system, and the laws, procedures and punishments relating to select crimes; (b) the legal rules governing religious freedom and religious minorities; and (c) women's legal status.[129]

In relation to the Islamic norms that raise human rights concerns, some Muslim countries have legislated to include various changes in their domestic legal codes in order to temper the full effect that those provisions would otherwise have, while other countries implement the provisions with an even sharper traditional interpretation. Further still, some countries have never abided by them. This section, however, focuses on some controversial aspects of Islamic law as derived from the different Islamic school of jurisprudence,[130] with the view of highlighting its conflict with international human rights standards.

127 NK Modirzadeh, 'Taking Islamic Law Seriously: Ingos and the Battle for Muslim Hearts and Minds' (2006) 19 Harvard Human Rights Journal 191, 201.

128 AA An-Na'im, 'The Application of Sharia (Islamic Law) and Human Rights Violations in the Sudan' in T Lindholm and K Vogt (eds), *Islamic Law Reform and Human Rights Challenges and Rejoinders* (Nordic Human Rights Publications, Oslo, 1993) 135.

129 See Modirzadeh (n 127) 201.

130 See above at x–xi.

(a) Islamic criminal law and procedure

Within Islamic criminal law the main issues arise under crimes that prescribe pre-determined punishments, namely, crimes of *Hudud* and crimes of *qisas* and *diyya*.[131] The issue of *qisas* and its retributive punishment for intentional homicide highlights the controversy between the acceptability of the death penalty within Islam and the prohibition against it within international law.[132] Furthermore, as discussed earlier, the *hudud* crimes have fixed mandatory punishments (*'uqubat muqaddara'*) that are based on the Quran or Sunnahh. These fixed punishments cannot usually be amended, altered, commuted, substituted, changed or waived except in exceptional circumstances. This is often evidenced by the famous case of Caliph Umar, where he cancelled the *hadd* punishment for theft due to famine and the resulting hunger. This may demonstrate that various *hudud* are dependent on context, an argument further supported by the principle of 'over-riding social necessity/essential interests (of Islamic law)' (*al-masalih al-daruriyah*). Another example where a *hadd* penalty was lifted during the reign of Caliph Umar concerned a man who had committed *zina*—illicit sexual relations. The Caliph found that the man accused was ignorant of the law and stated, 'there is no *hadd* except regarding what one has knowledge of'.[133] Indeed, there are even disagreements among scholars as to the necessary extent of intention, such as where one mistakenly commits a prohibited action.[134] Offences detailed in the Quran and intentional homicide and wounding are often categorized together to form *hudud* crimes. However, Hanafi and Shia scholars hold that in order to constitute a *hudud* crime, the conduct concerned must entirely or at least predominantly have included a violation of a claim of God, or in other words, a violation of public interest.[135] This classification of crimes excludes homicides and wounding because those are based on claims of men. Following the Shia and Hanafi classification, the six *hudud* offenses are: theft (*sariqah*); rebellion (*al-baghiye*) or highway or armed robbery (*hirabah*);[136] unlawful sexual intercourse (*zina*); false accusation of unlawful

[131] See earlier discussion for a comparison between pre-Islamic and Islamic norms.

[132] See Second Optional Protocol to the ICCPR enacted to abolish the death penalty: <http://www.unhchr.ch/html/menu3/b/a_opt2.htm>. See also JH Wyman 'Vengence is Whose? The Death Penalty and Cultural Relativism in International Law' (1997) 6 Journal of Transnational Law and Policy 543.

[133] PR Powers, *Intent in Islamic Law: Motive and Meaning in Medieval Sunni Fiqh* (Brill, Leiden, 2005) 193.

[134] Powers, ibid 190–93. Powers cites as his example the different opinions between Abu Hanifa, Imam Shafii i, Ibn Qudama and the Hanbali school related to a man having sex with a woman whom he mistakes as being his wife. However, such defences of mistake do not apply in the case of unlawful killing according to Ibn Qudama.

[135] Peters (n 21) 52.

[136] It is worth noting that some schools differ on the six—some allow seven and some pick either rebellion or highway robbery and some merge them as one.

sexual intercourse (*qadhf*); apostasy; and the consumption of alcohol (*sharb al-khamr*).[137] Fixed penalties are carried out in public as the principle purpose of *hadd* punishments is to act as deterrents to others, and as they are imposed for 'violations of claims of God', their terms may not be waived. The carrying out of *hadd* punishments may only be delayed or suspended in cases of doubt as to the guilt of the accused, or they may be postponed if there is a risk of severe harm being caused to the perpetrator, for instance, a death sentence imposed on a pregnant woman would be postponed until she has had her child and weaned it.

The fixed penalty for theft is the amputation of the right hand.[138] In the Shia school, only the four fingers are amputated, because the palm and thumb are required for the proper completion of prayers (or '*namaz*').[139] The crime of theft ('*sariqa*') is strictly defined.[140] The act must include the following five elements: (1) the surreptitious taking away; (2) of movable property with a certain minimum value ('*nisab*'); (3) which is not partially owned by the perpetrator; (4) nor entrusted to him; (5) from a place which is locked or under guard ('*hirz*'). As the first requisite element of theft necessitates that the perpetrator must take 'surreptitiously', some scholars have maintained that the stealing of goods from a market stall in broad daylight is not surreptitious and hence the fixed penalty of amputation is not appropriate in this case.[141] According to the Mailiki and Shia schools, the value (*nisab*) of the stolen goods must be at least 8.91 grams of silver or 1.06 grams of gold, or 29.7 grams of silver according to the Hanafi school. The goods must have legal value and be capable of being owned (so the crime of theft excludes the kidnapping of free persons as they cannot be owned). In addition, the goods cannot have been either under the accused's protection or have been owned, even partially, by him. Therefore, a person stealing from the State, a store assistant stealing from the shop he tends, and an embezzler will not be punished with the fixed penalty of amputation. Finally, the owner is responsible for the security of his belongings and therefore the fixed penalty cannot be applied if the owner did not guard or store his goods in an adequately secure place. In addition to these restrictions, Hanafi law prohibits the fixed penalty for the theft of perishable food.

137 See Peters (n 21) 53; see also M Baderin, *International Human Rights and Islamic Law* (OUP, Oxford, 2005) 79. See also Rahim (n 2) 344.

138 This is based on Qu'ran 5:38: 'as for the thief, both male and female, cut off their hands. It is the reward of their own deeds, an exemplary punishment from God. In case of second offense, the left foot is removed'.

139 Moulana Naqvi, Death penalty event, WCL 2006.

140 *Sariqa* is distinguished from *ghasb* or unlawfully taking away property, which is described as a tort with civil remedies involving the return of the stolen objects or damages and a discretionary punishment. Peters (n 21) 56.

141 Peters, ibid 56; Lippman, McConville and Yerushalmi (n 10) 45.

Hirabah is a complex doctrine involving highway or armed robbery. The crime of rebellion is sometimes also incorporated into this offence based on the words of the Quran which condemn the 'spreading corruption on earth'.[142]

Extramarital sex, more commonly called '*zina*' is considered to be one of the greatest sins in Islam. Islamic law only permits sexual intercourse within a marriage or between a slave woman and her master.[143] The fixed penalty for '*zina*' is either 100 lashes for a free person or 50 lashes for slaves, followed by a period of banishment lasting one year.[144] The Hanafi school of thought does not include banishment in the punishment, and the Maliki do not banish women.[145] The Shia school also requires men who have committed *zina* to shave off their beards. A punishment of death by stoning is imposed on a specific category of people (known as '*muhsan*'). In Sunni jurisprudence, '*muhsan*' are categorized as free, Muslim[146] adults who have previously engaged in legitimate sexual relations in marriage (even if the marriage is no longer continuing). The Shia school of thought defines *muhsan* as a free Muslim in a position to have legal sexual intercourse with an available partner and not absent on a long journey or imprisoned. The fixed penalty of lashes is found within verse 24:2 of the Quran and the sentence of death by stoning is found in the *hadith*.[147]

The essential element for the *hadd* crime is the actual penetration by the man into the vagina.[148] The act of penetration must be corroborated by four witnesses or the confession must be made four times in court. Shia law also permits the testimonies of two men and four women or one man and six women. The Hanabali and Shia schools also include anal intercourse in the definition and consider sexual acts without penetration as *hadd* offences as well. Other Sunni schools instead allow the *qadi* (the judge) discretion in the sentencing of such crimes. Most schools equate homosexual intercourse to unlawful heterosexual intercourse but assign different punishments. The Maliki school inflicts death by stoning, and some Shafi'i and Hanbali scholars insist on death by the sword. Shia jurists leave to the discretion of the judge the method by which death will be implemented: by using a sword,

142 Quran, 5:33: 'The punishment of those who wage war against Allah and His Messenger, and strive with might and main for mischief through the land is: execution, or crucifixion, or the cutting off of hands and feet from opposite sides, or exile from the land: that is their disgrace in this world, and a heavy punishment is theirs in the Hereafter'.

143 On the abolition of slavery in Muslim States, see below at 21.

144 Lippman, McConville and Yerushalmi (n 10) 56; YY Bambale, *Crimes and Punishments under Islamic Law* (Malthouse Press, Nigeria, 2003).

145 The other schools that do banish women require that she be accompanied by a close male relative to watch over her.

146 Shafii school allows *dhimmi* (person of book). Peters (n 21) 61.

147 See Peters (n 21) 60.

148 Peters, ibid 59–62; Bambale (n 144).

stoning, throwing the perpetrator from a high wall or burning him to death. The Hanafi school of thought does not equate homosexual intercourse to the *hudud* crime of unlawful intercourse and leaves the exact nature of the punishment to the entire discretion of the *qadi*.

Another *hadd* offence is that of '*qadhf*', the allegation that an individual has engaged in unlawful sexual intercourse; the crime may also be alleged in cases where an individual, whose mother must be a Muslim and a free person, denies his legitimate descent.[149] The penalty, derived from verse 24:4–5 of the Quran, is 80 lashes and discreditation as a future witness in legal disputes.

The consumption of wine ('*sharb al-khamr*') is also explicitly forbidden in the Quran.[150] Chapter 5, verse 90 forbids the practice and the punishment is found within a *hadith*, which narrates the Prophet Mohammed punishing a man who had consumed wine with 40 lashes, a punishment that was later repeated by Abu Bakr.[151] However, when Caliph Umar came to power, he consulted people and decreed that the lightest fixed punishment in respect of this crime should be 80 lashes. The Shafi'i school follows the Prophet Mohammed's precedent and penalizes the consumption of alcohol with 40 lashes. Other schools maintain that the punishment is 80 lashes, as exemplified by Umar. Drinking is not considered a *hudud* crime for non-Muslims. For alcoholic beverages other than wine, there is some disagreement as to the corresponding penalties and the correct classification of legality. The majority of theoretical schools in Islam analogize all alcohols to wine and thereby extend the punishment, although Hanafi'i scholars only impose penalties to the individual who actually gets intoxicated as a result of his consumption of wine.

The act of apostasy, (or '*ridda*'), is a public renunciation of Islam by words or conduct.[152] Considered a *hadd* offence in most schools of thought, the punishment for apostasy is death based on a *hadith* of the Prophet Mohammed stating: 'If someone changes his religion, then kill him.'[153] Most schools also offer the apostate a period of three days in which to repent and remove any uncertainty. The Hanafi and Shia schools do not consider apostasy a *hadd* offence. Considering apostates to be potential traitors or enemies of the State, they hold that only males should be executed and that women should be imprisoned until they repent. The

149 Peters (n 21); AA Mansour 'Hudud Crimes' in C Bassiouni (ed), *The Islamic Criminal Justice System* (Oceana Publications, Inc, New York, 1982) 195–201.

150 See also Lippman, McConville and Yerushalmi (n 10) 53–54.

151 Peters (n 21).

152 Peters (n 21); Mansour (n 149) 195–201; E Boyle-Lewicki, 'Need World's Collide: The *Hudad* Crimes of Islamic Law and International Human Rights' (2000) 13 New York Intl L Rev 43; see also D Forte, 'Apostasy and Blasphemy in Pakistan' (1994) 3 Connecticut J Int L 27.

153 Peters (n 21) 65 (citing *Asqalani, bulugh* no 1019).

women are also to be beaten every third day within Hanafi law or at the hours of ritual prayer according to Shia scholars. Hanafi law does not necessitate the grace period to allow for repentance, although it does recommend it. Shia jurists allow only converted Muslims to have the grace period but those born as Muslims may not revoke their apostasy and must be put to death.

An important aspect of *hudud* crimes is that, in practice, the nature of the doctrine makes convictions very difficult to obtain.[154] Strict evidentiary rules are put in place and the accused may take advantage of extensive opportunities to use the notion of uncertainty ('*shubha*') as his or her defence. With regards to theft, uncertainty is presumed if a person steals from his son, wife or debtor. Duress is also a defence in respect of *hadd* crimes.[155] Rape for the victim is not a *hudud* crime because although unlawful sexual intercourse occurs, the coercion and duress elements invalidate the application of the penalty. A special exception is also available through repentance, as noted above in the case of apostates.[156] Moreover, illustrated above, each crime is narrowly defined and any similar act that falls outside of the precise definition may not be punished with the fixed punishment, but only at the *qadi's* discretion.

In addition to strict evidentiary and prosecutorial requirements, the punishments themselves have exacting standards.[157] With respect to flogging, the executioner of the lashes may not raise his arm above his head to the extent that the armpit is visible. The force of the lashes inflicted varies with the nature of the crime committed. The Shia and Hanbali scholars only allow for flogging by palm leaves, twined clothes or shoes. Other schools also recognize that the least painful method of flogging should be used when punishing the culprit for intoxication. The blows must be equally distributed over the body, except for sensitive areas including the head and genitals. The lashing should not be fatal.

With respect of capital punishment, the normal method employed is beheading by sword. Different approaches are permitted (as highlighted above) although none may be used against a pregnant woman until after she has delivered the child and weaned it. Furthermore, when death by stoning is prescribed, care must be taken with the size of the stones so that they are not too small to prolong the time for the killing of the condemned, nor too large to kill him too soon. Within the Hanafi'i school, the witnesses

[154] However in contemporary state practices many are punished for *hudud* crimes: see eg Shabnum Rahmati Interview: Judiciary Spokesman on Stoning of Jafar Kiani (July 11 2007). See also R Peters, 'The Islamisation of Criminal Law: A Comparative Analysis' (1994) 34 Die Welt des Islams 246–74.

[155] Peters (n 21) 23.

[156] ibid 27.

[157] Peters (n 21); See also Lippman, McConville and Yerushalmi (n 10) 77–91 (detailing the concept of punishment in Islamic criminal law).

upon whose testimony the culprit was convicted must throw the first stone so as to ensure that the testimonies were not withdrawn.

Irrespective of the difficulties in obtaining convictions for *hudud* crimes and the elaborated methods for applying the penalties, it must be noted that the punishments do pose a normative conflict with certain international human rights norms.[158] These punishments are simply irreconcilable with contemporary norms of human rights.[159] The Universal Declaration of Human Rights (UDHR) contains an absolute prohibition on torture and cruel, inhuman or degrading treatment. It also includes 'the right to freedom of thought, conscience and religion' and the right to equal protection of the law. The International Covenant on Cultural and Political Rights (ICCPR) provides similar protections and prohibits torture and cruel punishment even during times of national emergency and protects the guarantee of freedom of thought, conscience and religion. Other core instruments that protect against cruel and torturous treatments include the Convention Against Torture and Other Cruel, Inhuman or Degrading Treatment or Punishment (CAT);[160] the UN Second Optional Protocol to the International Covenant on Civil and Political Rights, aiming at the abolition of the death penalty, and the UN Convention on the Rights of the Child (CRC).

The penalties of flogging, capital punishment, death by stoning, and amputation are contrary to international law principles as each of these can be identified as cruel, degrading or torturous.[161] With respect to the death penalty, though the Optional Protocol is aimed at abolishing capital punishment, the ICCPR does allow for a 'sentence of death' to be imposed 'for the most serious crimes'.[162] Nevertheless, it is unlikely that unlawful sexual relationships would be considered sufficiently serious to warrant the death penalty.

(b) Freedom of religion

The criminalization of apostasy directly counters freedom of thought,

158 See generally Boyle-Lewicki (n 152) 43.

159 See generally MS El-Awa, *Punishment in Islamic Law* (American Trust, Indianapolis, 1982).

160 Convention Against Torture and Other Cruel, Inhuman or Degrading Treatment or Punishment, UN GAOR, Supp No 51, 197, UN Doc. A/39/51 (1984) ('imposing a duty to prevent acts of torture in any territory under its jurisdiction.'); see also Declaration on the Protection of All Persons from Being Subjected to Torture and Other Cruel, Inhuman or Degrading Treatment or Punishment, UN GAOR, Supp No 34, 91, UN Doc A/1034 (1975).

161 E Boyle-Lewicki (n 152) 70–76; See also E Peiffer, 'The Death Penalty in Traditional Islamic Law and as Interpreted in Saudi Arabia and Nigeria' (2005) 11 William and Mary Journal of Women and the Law 507; R Postawko, 'Towards and Islamic Critique of Capital Punishment' (2002) 1 UCLA Journal of Islamic and Near Eastern Law 269.

162 ICCPR, Article 6(2).

conscience, religion or belief, as embodied by international instruments.[163] As human rights instruments protect freedom of religion, it is improbable that apostasy would be viewed as a serious crime.[164] In addition to the instruments detailed above, religious coercion is also prohibited through the ICCPR, which provides that '[n]o one shall be subject to coercion which would impair his freedom to have or to adopt a religion or belief of choice'.[165] Therefore, neither offensive words nor conduct renouncing a particular faith or adopting another merits punishment under human rights norms.

(c) Women's legal status

In addition to conflicts between human rights instruments and *hudud* penalties within Islamic criminal law, many conflicts also occur with respect to women's legal status. Within Islamic criminal procedure, discrimination against women may be found within the dual witness rule—mandating the testimony of two women instead of one in lieu of one male witness. This is derived from the Quranic injunction in 2:282, which states:

> And get two witnesses out of your own men, and if there are not two men, then a man and two women, such as you choose for witnesses so that if one of them errs, the other can remind her.

However, it is commonly argued that this is not a general rule but merely particular to financial transactions based on the context of the verse. This is because the Quran, in 24: 6–9, explicitly equates the testimonies of man and woman as equal.[166]

---

163 See eg Article 26 ICCPR; Muslim history demonstrates both religious persecution and tolerance: recent examples of State-sponsored persecution include the targeting of Ahmedi's in Pakistan: See law review.

164 Universal Declaration of Human Rights, Art 18 (stating 'everyone has the right to freedom of thought, conscience and religion; this right includes freedom to change his religion or belief, and freedom, either alone or in community with others and in public or private, to manifest his religion or belief in teaching, practice, worship and observance').

165 ICCPR art 18.

166 Quran, 24: 6–9: And for those who launch a charge against their spouses, and have (in support) no evidence but their own, their solitary evidence (can be received) if they bear witness four times (with an oath) by Allah that they are solemnly telling the truth;

And the fifth (oath) (should be) that they solemnly invoke the curse of Allah on themselves if they tell a lie.

But it would avert the punishment from the wife, if she bears witness four times (with an oath) By Allah, that (her husband) is telling a lie;

And the fifth (oath) should be that she solemnly invokes the wrath of Allah on herself if (her accuser) is telling the truth.

Other provisions that discriminate against women are found within Islamic personal status law. Although there is some debate over the acceptance of polygamy in marriage, there are still provisions that allow for it.[167] Moreover, as detailed earlier, divorce rights are not equally shared by both men and women. Men enjoy the right of unilateral divorce through *talaq*, whereas women are limited to divorce either under specific circumstances, such as the man's impotence, or with the consent of the husband and the relinquishing of a monetary amount (*khul*).

Child custody (*hadanah*)[168] is also predisposed to paternal preference. Elaborate rules regarding *hiazanat* have been made by jurists based on the references in five Quranic verses regarding childcare.[169] In Hanafi law, the divorced mother has the right to the custody of her male child until he is aged seven and of the female child until puberty, set at the age of nine.[170] According to Shafi'i and Hanbali schools, the mother has the right of custody of the child (male or female) up to the age of seven, after which time the child has the right to decide which of the two parents he or she wishes to reside with.[171] Shia Ithna-Ashari rules hold that the mother has the custody of the son until the age of two and the daughter until the age of seven.[172] Upon the remarriage of the woman, the children will be automatically assigned to the custody of the father as long as he is an able and proper guardian.[173]

Finally, although a woman may inherit under Islam, which is admittedly a positive reform from pre-Islamic times, she does not inherit at the same level as her male counterparts. The Islamic inheritance laws (*'ilm-ul-fara'id*) incorporate one of the most comprehensive and detailed succession schemes.[174] There exist several tiers and hierarchies in the distribution of

167 J Rehman, 'The Sharia, Islamic Family Laws and International Human Rights Law: Examining the Theory and Practice of Polygamy and *Talaq*', 21 *International Journal of Law, Policy and the Family* 108.

168 For a discussion on the three types of guardianship of the child (guardianship of the infant, guardianship of education, and guardianship of property) see JJ Nasir, *The Status of Women Under Islamic Law and Under Modern Islamic Legislation, Second Edition* (Graham & Trotman London 1994) 130.

169 MA Syed, *The Position of Women in Islam: A Progressive View* (State University of New York Press New York 2004) 77; see also David Powers *Studies in Qu'ran and Hadith: The Formation of the Islamic Law of Inheritance* (University of California Press Berkeley 1986).

170 JL Esposito with NJ DeLong-Bas, *Women in Muslim Family Law, Second Edition* New York: Syracuse University, 2001, 35.

171 MA Syed, *The Position of Women in Islam: A Progressive View* (State University of New York Press, New York, 2004), 79.

172 ibid,163, 165–166.

173 JL Esposito with NJ DeLong-Bas, *Women in Muslim Family Law, Second Edition* (New York: Syracuse University, 2001) 36.

174 Z Chaudhry, 'The Myth of Misogyny: A Reanalysis of Women's Inheritance in Islamic Law', 61 *Albany Law Review* 511, 527–536.

the deceased's estate.[175] In general, on each level the woman only receives one half of what her male counterpart receives. For example, the son receives a portion equal to that of two daughters.[176] For surviving spouses, the widowed husband would receive one fourth of the wife's estate, if she left behind a child and one half if there were no surviving children, whereas the surviving wife would receive only one eighth of her deceased husband's estate if he had a surviving child and one fourth if he did not.[177] It is also important to note that the surviving child must be either a direct child or an agnatic grandchild (grandchild through a son) however low, to affect the husband's inheritance. Meanwhile, the husband's surviving child does not have to be from that particular marriage.[178]

The Convention on the Elimination of all Forms of Discrimination Against Women (CEDAW) promotes the unrestricted equality of men and women.[179] Its comprehensive scope covers all areas of rights for women: civil, political, social, cultural, economic, public and private.[180] Article 15 requires that women be accorded with status equal to that of men under the law[181] and equal legal capacity in civil matters, such as the administration of property or in court proceedings.[182] The devaluation of female testimony in comparison to male testimony within Islamic law contradicts the principle of equality with respect to legal capacity in civil matters. Moreover, Articles 14 and 26 of the ICCPR ensure the equality of all persons before the law, courts and tribunals.[183] The double witness rule directly counters this anti-discriminatory principle.

With respect to family life, Article 16 of CEDAW mandates that State Parties take appropriate measures to eliminate discrimination against

[175] See W Coggins, 'Succession in Traditional Islamic Law', 60 *Journal of the Missouri Bar* 180, 181.

[176] Qu'ran 4:11: Allah (thus) directs you as regards your children's (inheritance): to the male, a portion equal to that of two females: if only daughters, two or more, their share is two-thirds of the inheritance; if only one, her share is a half.

[177] Qu'ran 4:12: In what your wives leave, your share is a half, if they leave no child; but if they leave a child, ye get a fourth; after payment of legacies and debts. In what ye leave, their share is a fourth, if ye leave no child; but if ye leave a child, they get an eighth; after payment of [bequests] and debts.

[178] Z Chaudhry, 'The Myth of Misogyny: A Reanalysis of Women's Inheritance in Islamic Law', 61 *Albany Law Review* 511, 535.

[179] See generally Bharati, 'Venkatraman, Islamic States and the United Nations Convention of the Elimination of all Forms of Discrimination Against Women: Are the Sharia and the Convention Compatible?' 44 *American University Law Review* 1949 (elaborating on the compatibility of Sharia and CEDAW).

[180] UN Convention on the Elimination of All Forms of Discrimination Against Women, opened for signature Mar 1, 1980, 1249 UNTS 13 [hereinafter CEDAW]. CEDAW was adopted by the General Assembly of the United Nations on December 18, 1979, and it entered into force on September 3, 1981.

[181] CEDAW art 15(1).

[182] CEDAW art 15(2).

[183] ICCPR, art 14, 16 http://www.unhchr.ch/html/menu3/b/a_ccpr.htm.

women in all matters relating to marriage and family relations. CEDAW calls for equality to be ensured with respect to certain rights, including: (1) the same right to enter into marriage; (2) the same right freely to choose a spouse and to enter into marriage only with both parties' free and full consent; (3) the same rights and responsibilities during marriage and at its dissolution; (4) the same rights and responsibilities as parents, irrespective of their marital status, in matters relating to their children; (5) the same rights and responsibilities with regard to guardianship, wardship, trusteeship and adoption of children; and (6) the same rights for both spouses in respect of the ownership, acquisition, management, administration, enjoyment and disposition of property, whether free of charge or for a valuable consideration.[184]

Furthermore, allowing unilateral divorce for men and not women contradicts equality at dissolution. In rights relating to children, article 16 calls for the principle of 'sameness' to be observed; however, Islamic law prefers the father with respect to custody of children. Furthermore, the Convention on the Rights of the Child states that decisions in respect of children must be made with primary regard to the child's best interests. The mechanism of affording custody within Islamic law is based on the child's age and does not generally take into account the best interests of the child, nor does it necessitate an opportunity for the child to be heard in the judicial and administrative proceedings.[185]

In matters of inheritance, the widowed father will only lose a portion of his inheritance if the surviving child is a direct child (or agnatic grandchild); however, the surviving wife would lose a portion of her inheritance for any legitimate child—whether from their marriage or not. In addition, though no single article within CEDAW exclusively addresses women's right of inheritance, by affording women equality with men before the law with respect to civil matters such as contractual capacity and the control of property, CEDAW obliges State Parties to ensure non-discrimination in the acquisition and administration of real property.[186] Therefore, the gendered system of inheritance also conflicts with established international human rights norms.

CONCLUSION

Despite the fact that Islam brought with it a raft of significant reforms in respect of the penal system within Arabian society, there were also a

184 CEDAW art 16.

185 CRC, art 12(2), available at: http://www.unhchr.ch/html/menu3/b/k2crc.htm.

186 A N Behrouz, 'Transforming Islamic Family Law: State Responsibility and the Role of Internal Initiative', 103 *Columbia Law Review* 1136.

number of customary laws and traditions that were retained. If it is argued that Islam has had a positive impact in relation to expelling some cruel and discriminatory practices from the pre-Islamic era, it must also be contended that the existence of some normative Islamic standards cast into serious doubt the extent of the religion's compatibility with some very basic human rights standards as embodied in various international human rights conventions. Unfortunately, the increasing concern and criticism levelled at certain Muslim States in regard to various substantive norms in the Islamic tradition appears to be legitimate. However, and as we shall see below, the practice of Muslim States is usually determined through the manner in which Sharia is implemented at the domestic level.[187] To conclude this section, contextualized Islamic law does show an improvement from pre-Islamic Arabian society. However, there still exist numerous contentious provisions that are in need of further theoretical clarification or reform in order to increase Islamic law's compliance with international human rights norms.[188]

Section Two The Status of Islamic law within the Legal Systems of Muslim States

The importance placed on the substance of Islamic law must not overshadow the significance of the status given to Sharia law by the State. Indeed, its status constitutes a determinant factor that measures the true extent of the role accorded to the religion within the legal 'cogs' of the State's internal system. It is our position that the challenge posed to human rights in various Muslim States is not derived directly from Islamic doctrine but rather from the integration of its provisions into the substantive law. For instance, the Quran cites provision for the institution of slavery in more than 29 verses, which would seem to indicate the acceptability of owning slaves. In practice, however, the human rights implications of these provisions is now a redundant issue as the concept of slavery has been rejected by all Muslim States and any provisions sanctioning it have been repealed from substantive law. Some States have taken these measures a step further and actually forbidden slavery, as in Saudi Arabia where Islam is the exclusive source of law. In 1936, during the course of implementing the provi-

[187] See below, 37 et seq.

[188] See Javaid Rehman, The Sharia, 'Islamic Family Laws and International Human Rights Law: Examining the theory and practice of polygamy and Talaq', International Journal of Law and the Family, volume 108, April 2007.

sions of Article 7 of the Treaty of Jeddah[189] between Saudi Arabia and the United Kingdom, the King of Saudi Arabia signed a decree which had the effect of significantly restricting the importation of slaves into the country. This was then followed by the eventual prohibition of the practice.[190] Therefore, it is evident that Muslim States can take steps to limit the implementation of older Sharia-based norms which conflict with modern legal, social and political practice. In other words, the State can prevent the national implementation of those interpretations of Sharia which violate human rights norms.

This study adopts the position that the tension between Islam and human rights is derived from a State's illegitimate interference with individual freedoms, which is then justified through Islam and a misguided application of Sharia law. Here, the human rights issues raised do not concern the personal conviction of believers who might deliberately limit their own 'rights' in applying their own interpretation of the religious texts. Rather, the analysis centres on the restrictions of rights imposed by the State. Therefore, the limitation of movement, acts and speech as an expression of a self-restriction that reflects the exercise of a personal belief, which represents a right in and of itself, should be distinguished from a systematic and repressive State policy that imposes harsh limitations on human rights. An illustrative example is the headscarf customarily worn by Muslim women. The imposition of a severe dress code for women in Iran and Saudi Arabia in particular, which is enforced ruthlessly by the State, is considered contrary to human rights. However, where women freely choose to adopt the same style of dress as a reflection of their personal understanding of Sharia, they are then exercising their right to practise their religious belief. A voluntary, personal, and independent decision to limit one's own personal freedom should be supported and enabled as an expression of personal autonomy, a concept that is the very backbone of human rights. Furthermore, it allows for the celebration of different cultural practices. Therefore, limitations placed on the right of individual choice in this matter amounts to a violation of international human right norms.

The difference between these two approaches may be appreciated through the following example that was cited in a study on Islamic law and international human rights:

> A Muslim woman who agrees to consider only Muslim males as a prospective spouse—based on her free religious conviction that to marry

[189] Treaty of Friendship and Good Understanding Between His Brittanic Majesty and His Majesty the King of the Hejaz and of Nejd and its Dependencies, Signed at Jeddah 20 May 1927 (No 1658). *League of Nations Treaty Series* (1928): 152.

[190] Levy Reuben, *The Social Structure of Islam* (Cambridge University Press, UK, 1957), 85.

a non-Muslim spouse would be sinful, even if a Muslim male is permitted to marry certain non-Muslim women—does not raise a concern for human rights law; it is only when a State would prohibit her from marrying a non-Muslim on the grounds that such a marriage is invalid under Islamic law that a human rights violation occurs.[191]

Sharia law can demand formal obedience and create social conditions for the 'righteous path', but actually choosing that way should be an individual choice and not that of the State. Even if religion were to become a matter for the State, the degree of conformity to Sharia should remain optional.

Among Muslim countries themselves, Islam is not accorded the same status within the legal system of the State. As a consequence, the impact of Islam on the internal set of laws, notably on legislation, jurisdiction and the rules defining the organization and the functioning of power, varies drastically and arbitrarily from one Muslim country to another. Accordingly, the interaction between Islam and human rights law varies arbitrarily depending upon the Sharia-based context of each individual State.

In order to understand the relationship between State and religion, the following section will analyse it in three subsections: (1) the position of Islam and its role within the Constitutions of Muslim States; (2) the place accorded to Islam in the normative pyramid forming the substantive law in each context; and (3) the way Sharia manifests itself in the Personal Status Laws of the respective States. This constitutes a preliminary and incontrovertible step which enables a stronger understanding of the specificities of each legal public system with regard to Islam. This in turn enables a more accurate analysis of the contours of the relationship between Islam and the provisions of the international instruments on human rights.

SUBSECTION ONE: THE CONSTITUTIONAL DETERMINATION OF THE RELATIONSHIP BETWEEN ISLAM AND THE STATE

There are significant differences in the way Islam is treated in the Constitutions of Muslim countries,[192] 'especially in terms of its relationship

191 Mohamad Fadel, Public Reason as a strategy for principled reconciliation: the case of Islamic law and international human rights, University of Toronto Legal studies series, Research paper No. 981777, April 2007, pp. 1–16, p.2 available at: http://papers.ssrn.com/sol3/papers.cfm?abstract_id=981777.

192 See Ted Stahnke and Robert C Blitt, *The Religion–State Relationship and the Right to Freedom of Religion or Belief: A Comparative Textual Analysis of the Constitutions of Predomintly Muslim Countries (USCRIF 2005)*, available at : http://www.uscirf.gov/countries/global/comparative_constitutions/03082005/Study0305.pdf (last accessed Friday 18 January 2008).

to the state and public life'.[193] This in turn reflects the various levels of the implementation of Islam within the public institutions. The Constitutions of Muslim States do not always expressly refer to Islam as the State religion, and often when they do, the designation may have no tangible impact on the organization of power within the State.

There are no definite criteria by which to determine a Muslim State. The Organisation of the Islamic Conference (OIC) consists of 57 States. Being a member of the OIC would certainly be based upon a definite relationship between the State and Islam; but it could be that the State is purely and constitutionally an Islamic State, or that it defines Islam as the religion of the State, or merely that a significant number of the population are Muslim. The countries selected for this comparative study are all members of the OIC, but their constitutional acknowledgment of Islam varies significantly. These relationships will be illustrated below, beginning with (A) Constitutions where Islam is not constitutionally privileged; followed by (B) those Constitutions where Islam is constitutionally acknowledged.

A. Constitutions in which Islam is not constitutionally privileged

Lebanon

A notable example of where the Constitution does not assign a privileged status to Islam, is the Constitution of the Republic of Lebanon. Although Lebanon is a member of the OIC, Islam does not enjoy a particular assigned status in the political structure of the State. Lebanon has been conceived as a multi-confessional ('con-sociationalist') State since its creation and, as a consequence, the Constitution adopts and maintains the same distance towards the different religions in the country. The specificities of the Lebanese system have had significant repercussions on the power structure of the State. It is stated in Article 95 of the Constitution that the Chamber of Deputies will be elected on the basis of equality between Muslims and Christians; that in the formation of the Cabinet the religious groups are to be represented in a just and equitable manner; and that 'grade one posts' and their equivalent in the public system must be distributed equally between Christians and Muslims.[194] This power structure is not in any way

193 Abdullahi A An-Na'im, Human Rights in the Arab world: A regional perspective, 23 Human Rights Quarterly 23 (2001) (Johns Hopkins University Press) 707.

194 Article 95 of the Lebanese Constitution provides the following:

'(1) The first Chamber or Deputies which is elected on the basis of equality between Muslims and Christians takes the appropriate measures to realise the abolition of political confessionalism according to a transitional plan. A National Committee is to be formed, headed by the President of the Republic, including, in addition to the President of the Chamber of Deputies and the Prime Minister, leading political, intellectual, and social figures.

the result of Islamic doctrine, nor is it attributable to the implementation of Islamic principles into the Lebanese Constitution. Rather, it is the consequence of the multi-confessionalism that is in force in Lebanon's public law structure.

At the time of Lebanon's independence from France in 1943, the National Pact agreement consecrated this confessional formula upon which the President of the Republic was to be a Maronite Christian, the Prime Minister a Sunni Muslim, and the Speaker of Parliament a *shia* Muslim. Other lower political posts were also assigned according to this formula. Representation in Parliament was set according to a ratio of 6:5 in favour of Christians. The Taif Agreement of 1989 which was followed by the amendment of the Lebanese Constitution in 1990, reasserted the confessional formula but changed parliamentary representation to a 50:50 Christian/Muslim ratio, as encapsulated in the constitutional provisions mentioned above. However, the amended Constitution specifies that confessionalism is to be implemented only during a transitional phase, at the end of which political confessionalism would be abolished. Hence the preamble of the Constitution makes it clear that 'the abolition of political confessionalism is a basic national goal and shall be achieved according to a gradual plan'. In principle, the Lebanese institutions are to be founded on a non-religious basis at some point in the future. In the meantime, however, the religious implications on the constitutional system results from the multi-confessional composition of the Lebanese people, also reflecting the fear of each sect of being politically evicted by another.

Turkey

Similarly in Turkey, the organization of power is independent of Islam. Religion is not acknowledged in the Constitution, and its terminology is not dependant upon Islamic standards. Islam is not acknowledged in any context within the Turkish Constitution. Article 2 provides solely that:

> The Republic of Turkey is a democratic, secular and social State governed by the rule of law; bearing in mind the concepts of public peace, national solidarity and justice; respecting human rights; loyal to the nationalism of Atatürk, and based on the fundamental tenets set forth in the Preamble.[195]

Countries outside the scope of this study, including Djibouti and Somalia, have also refrained from acknowledging Islam within their Constitutions or as an influencing factor on the power structure or functioning of public

[195] Databank of the constitutional texts available to view at: http://www.anayasa.gen.tr/english.htm (last accessed 17 January 2008).

institutions. While recognising that almost all the population is Muslim, Somalia's Constitution instead emphasises the principle of separation between the State and the national religion, and refuses to reflect any Islamic constitutional principle with respect to the organisation of power.

B. Constitutions in which Islam is constitutionally acknowledged

It is possible to divide the States that acknowledge Islam in their Constitutions into two distinct categories. The first comprises the States where the constitutional acknowledgment of Islam has not dramatically affected the structure and organization of power within those States. The second group includes those States in which the express recognition afforded to Islam within their Constitutions has, in contrast, led to significant internal constitutional consequences. As highlighted by Stahnke and Blitt, the practical ramifications of a declaration of Islam as the religion of the State vary from State to State.[196]

1. *Limited acknowledgment with limited consequences on the organisation of power*

The classical constitutional formulation includes the acknowledgment of Islam as the religion of the State.[197] This may be demonstrated by the constitutions of Algeria,[198] Egypt,[199] Jordan[200] and Yemen.[201] The ubiquitous and simply worded 'Islam is the religion of the state' is to be found in Article 2 of the Algerian, Jordanian and Yemeni Constitutions, with references to Arabic as the official language. However, of the aforementioned countries, Egypt is the only one to include actionable language relating Islam to the legal structure of the country in the same article as a declaration of State religion: 'the principal source of legislation is Islamic Jurisprudence'. However, despite this formulation, it is important to note that the reference to Islam as the religion of the State does not have significant repercussions on the organization of power within the State or on the

196 Tad Stahnke and Robert C. Blitt The Religion–State Relationship and the Right to Freedom of Religion or Belief: A Comparative Textual Analysis of the Constitutions of Predominantly Muslim Countries, p. 7.

197 For the reference to Islam in Constitutions of Arab States, see Blanchi Gilles and Rycx Jean-Francois, 'Références à l'Islam dans le droit public positif en pays arabes', Pouvoirs, n 12, 1979, pp. 57–69.

198 Available at: http://www.algeria-un.org/default.asp?doc=-const (last accessed 08/01/08).

199 Available at: http://www.misr.gov.eg/english/laws/constitution/index.asp (last accessed 08/01/08).

200 Available at: http://www.kinghussein.gov.jo/constitution_jo.html (last accessed 08/01/08).

201 Available at: http://www.al-bab.com/yemen/gov/gov.htm (last accessed 08/01/08).

functioning of the public institutions. The proclamation of Islam as the formal religion of the State, therefore, does not lead to the establishment of an Islamic regime.

The principle of the separation of powers is not admitted in the Islamic constitutional system, but the Constitutions of some Muslim countries appear to be in conflict with the Islamic constitutional ideology. For example, the acknowledgment of Islam as Tunisia's State religion in Article 1 has a very limited effect on the structure of the Tunisian constitutional powers. Article 38 of the Constitution specifies that the Head of the State should be Muslim.[202] Article 2 paragraph 1 of the Constitution of Egypt declares that Islam is the religion of the State.[203] But this declaration has no practical impact on the organization of power in Egypt. However, in practice the head of State has been a Muslim since Egypt became an Islamic State 10 centuries ago.

With regard to Malaysia, the Federal Constitution, as it stands today, determines the status of Islam in Malaysia. Article 3 provides that 'Islam is the religion of the Federation; but other religions may be practiced in peace and harmony in any part of the Federation'. Moreover, it declares that the rulers in each State are considered by the Constitution as the head of religion of Islam.[204]

2. *A deep acknowledgment with strong constitutional consequences on the organization and functioning of power*

In this category, the acknowledgement of Islam as the religion of the State implies a status of privilege. There is an adjustment of the structure of the State, modifying significantly the organization of power and its functioning in a way to fit with the political and structural requirements of Sharia. Upon a strong Islamic approach, the Qur'an not only lays down principles of morality and ethics, but also gives guidance in the political, social and economic fields. It prescribes punishments for certain crimes and enunciates principles of monetary and fiscal policy. These cannot be translated into practice unless there is a State to enforce them. And herein lies the necessity of an Islamic State.'[205]

[202] The Constitution of the Republic of Tunisia, adopted 1 June 1959 and amended in 1988 and 2002.

[203] See below.

[204] Arts 3(3) & (5) Rulers of States declared heads of religion of Islam by State Constitutions; in absence of Muslim rulers (States of Malacca, Penang, Sabah and Sarawak) or in Federal Territories (Kuala Lumpur and Labuan) *Yang di-Pertuan Agong* (Head of State) is declared head of religion of Islam.

[205] Sayyid Abul A'la Maududi, 'The Islamic Law and Constitution' (4th edn, Islamic Publications, Lahore, 1969) 158.

This would mean, as explained by Maududi, 'that religion does not merely mean prayers, and fasting and *Hajj* and *zakat*, it also includes the law of the land and the institutions of the State'. Maududi adds:

> [I]f we want to establish religion of God, the objective will not be achieved by merely establishing the institutions of *Saum* (fast) and *Salat* (prayer). We shall have to establish side by side with them the Divine Law and make the Sharia the law of the land. If the latter is not established, then even if the institutions of *salat* etc... are in force, it will not amount to the establishment of din. It would only be a partial enforcement of it and not a total one. And if instead of God-given laws some other laws are adopted, it means nothing short of rejection of the din as such.'[206]

Iran, Pakistan and Saudi Arabia belong to the category in which the Islamic affiliation is reflected in the saturation of the constitutional Islamic regime, as defined in the text of the Constitution. The organization of power in these countries reflects an interpretation of the Islamic constitutional system, or simply Islamic principles in which there is no separation between the State and religion.

The following section aims to describe the Islamic implications within the constitutional legal system in Bahrain, Iran, Pakistan, and Saudi Arabia.

Bahrain

Bahrain provides an interesting example of the consequences of the institutionalization of Islam within the constitutional structure of the State. Bahrain's political and constitutional system combines two different models within its structure: the Islamic concept of the organization of power and the foundations of certain modern political thought. This combination is reflected in the Bahrani political and legal structures: Article 1 of the Constitution declares Bahrain as an 'independent Islamic Arab State'. The preamble of the Constitution declares Bahrain as a constitutional monarchy founded on a counsel (*shura*), in which the Ruler, in his perspicacity, chooses certain experienced people to form the Consultative Council (Majlis al-Shura). The electorate—the aware, free and loyal people—choose through elections those who will comprise the Chamber of Deputies (*Majlis al-Nuwwab*). Together, the two chambers achieve the popular will, as represented by the National Assembly (*Al-Majlis al-Watani*). Bahrain's constitutional system therefore appears to be a mixture of secular and Islamic structures.

[206] Sayyid Abul A'la Maududi, ibid 159.

The Islamic Republic of Iran

The Islamic Revolution of 1979 founded the new Iran based on Islamic principles. The Constitution defines the Islamic Republic as a State ruled by Islamic jurists. As demonstrated in Asghar Schirazi's work on the constitution of Iran,[207] the Iranian Constitution presents the following characteristics which are of an Islamic nature: (1) the creation of an Islamic State with goals and tasks in accordance with its Islamic character; (2) the requirement that legislation is bound to Sharia;[208] (3) the position of leadership is reserved for Islamic jurists; (4) restrictions that have been defined with an Islamic construction are put on the democratic rights of individuals, of the nation and of ethnic groups; and (5) institutions are set up with the task to ensure the Islamic character of the State.

The Islamic revolution established an Islamic State ruled by Islamic law and founded on the theory of *Wilayat al-faqih*[209]as mainly identified through Ayatollah Khumayni's several lectures to his students in the city of Najaf.[210] He outlined that in a true Islamic State those holding government posts should have knowledge of Sharia. Moreover, the country's ruler should be a *faqih,* those who 'surpass all others in knowledge' of Islamic law and justice. Finally, the ruler must be capable of providing political and spiritual guardianship over his people, as well as the necessary intelligence and administrative ability.[211]

In the context of this doctrine, Article 5 of the Iranian Constitution[212] provides that an individual jurist who is endowed with all the necessary qualities, or a council of jurists, has the right to rule and exercise leadership in the Islamic Republic. Provisions set out in Articles 57 and 110 specify the precise extent of a ruling jurist's power in supervising the three branches of government; appointing the jurists to the Guardian Council; appointing the highest judicial authority in the country; holding supreme command over the armed forces; signing the certificate of appointment of the President

[207] Asghar Schirazi, The Constitution of Iran, Politics and the State in the Islamic Republic (translated by John O'Kane, IB Tauris, 1997) 8.

[208] See below.

[209] *Wilayat al-Faqih* is or *Guardianship of the Islamic Jurists* is a concept in *Shi'a* Islam which holds that Islam gives *faqih* or *fuqaha* (Islamic jurist or jurists) custodianship or guardianship over those in need of it. This doctrine has been introduced by Ayatollah Khomeini to the Iranian consitutional system. Accordin ot it, in the absence of the 12th Imam, the Islamic society should have a supreme leader to guide them. This leader is appointed for life and would have supreme power over the legislature, executive and judiciary.

[210] Islam and Revolution, Imam Khomeini, Islam and Revolution, Berkeley 1981, translated by H. Algar.

[211] ibid 59.

[212] Iranian Constitution, available to view online at: http://www.iranonline.com/iran/iran-info/Government/constitution.html (last accessed 17 January 2008).

after the latter's election by the people;[213] and granting amnesty or reduction of sentence in accordance with Islamic principles.

Pakistan

Islam is inherent to the creation of the State of Pakistan. As mentioned by Niaz Shah,[214] 'Pakistan emerged as an independent Muslim State on the world map on 14 August 1947,' and 'Islam played a vital role in its creation'. The author cites Muhammad Ali Jinnah, the founder of Pakistan, who said in 1943 that the aim of Pakistan is to promote a base for the Islamic renaissance.

GW Choudhury's classification of Pakistan as a 'laboratory of constitutions'[215] is indicative of the country's stuttering approach to the codification of Islam in its constitutional structure.[216] Successive Constitutions in Pakistan have tried to define and demarcate the boundaries in which Islam is to be applied.[217] The 1956 Constitution omitted any reference to Islam's role as an official religion, deeming it unnecessary given the implicit undertaking to adhere to Islamic principles and the explicit text of Articles 19 and 25 to preserve the nation's cultural heritage and an Islamic way of life. Thus, Islamic scholars consider the Islamic provisions in the Constitution as being merely symbolic in nature.[218] 1958 even saw the word 'Islamic' temporarily expunged from the title of the Republic, and it was only in the constitution of 1973 that Islam was codified as the State religion of Pakistan.[219] The President and the Prime Minister of the Country must be Muslim, they should take a 'specific form of oath declaring their faith in the unity and oneness of Allah (God), the books of Allah and the finality of the Prophethood of Muhammad.'[220] The impetus for this was no doubt the inclusion of religious figures in the constitutional committee for the 1973

213 The Leader has also the prerogative to dismiss the president in case the Supreme Court declares that the president has violated his legal duties or in case the Parliament (*Majles-e-showra-ye Melli*) judges that he is politically incompetent.

214 For a description of the role of Islam in the creation of Pakistan, its stats in the successive constitutions and the factors/motives behind the process of Islamisation of the legal system, see Niaz Shah, *Women, the Koran and International Human Rights Law: The Experience of Pakistan* (Martinus Nijhoff Publishers, Leiden/Boston, 2006, 91–107.

215 GW Choudhury, *Constitutional Development in Pakistan* (Longman, 1969).

216 Muhamamd Ali Jinnah's view that India would be 'divided or destroyed' set the political agenda for partition, whereupon the State of Pakistan could enjoy official recognition as an Islamic Republic. See Alan Gledhill, *Pakistan—The Development of its Laws and Constitution* (Stevens & Sons, London, 1967) 12.

217 See Siobhan Mullally, 'Women, Islamisation and Human Rights in Pakistan: Developing Strategies of Resistance', in *Religion, Human Rights and International Law*, Javaid Rehman and Susan Breau (Brill, 2007) 382.

218 R. Mehdi, The Islamisation of the Law in Pakistan (Curzon Press Ltd, 1994) 87.

219 Constitution of Pakistan, Article 2: Islam shall be the State religion of Pakistan.

220 Shah, Niaz, *Women, the Koran and International Human Rights Law: The Experience of Pakistan* (Martinus Nijhoff Publishers, Netherlands, 2006) 99.

Constitution as well as pressure from religious parties in government. Indeed, the Pakistan People's Party agreed not to oppose the measure, and it was widely regarded as understandable in light of the nation's heritage, though not by any means necessary.[221]

Saudi Arabia

In Saudi Arabia, the State is mandated with the mission to protect 'the rights of the people in line with the Islamic Sharia' (Saudi Arabia – Basic System (Decree A/90) Art 26.

The Basic Law of 1992 heralded a codification of Saudi Arabia's legal structure, with Article 1 affirming the inherent role of Islam in the Kingdom.

> The Kingdom of Saudi Arabia is a sovereign Arab Islamic State with Islam as its religion; God's Book and the Sunnahh of His Prophet, God's prayers and peace be upon him, are its constitution.

This is a view receptively shared by Saudi, Wahhabi jurists and the Qur'an, which expounds: 'Unto every [community] of you We appoint a law and way of life...'[222] Indeed, the entire premise of constitutional law and the very existence of the State is based upon the notion of treating the Kingdom as a means to an end; the end in this case being the absolute rule of Islam and adherence to it by all Saudis, not merely the promulgation and institutionalization of a State religion. This is made evident throughout the text of the Basic Law.

For example, Article 5(a) of the Basic Law states the system of government in the country to be a monarchy and demands fealty of all subjects to the King. Contemporary western notions such as separation of powers are ignored, with legislative and executive branches of government 'understood as extensions of the King's power'.[223] However, power itself is neither held by the King, nor is his authority absolute. His mandate to rule is actually severely restricted by numerous provisions in the Basic Law, the most prominent of these being Article 5(b) and Article 6 which restrict his powers 'in accordance with the holy Qur'an and the tradition of the Prophet'.[224] Both articles serve to introduce a concept of subsidiarity to the exercise of the King's powers. Essentially, the King is not to interfere in areas of law patently administered by the Qur'an.

[221] Syed Shabbar Raza Rizvi, *Constitution of the Islamic Republic of Pakistan* (Nadeem Law Book House, Lahore 1992) 32.

[222] Qur'an 5:48.

[223] F.E. Vogel, *Islamic Law and Legal Systems: Studies of Saudi Arabia* (Brill, Leiden, 2000) 170.

[224] Basic Law of Saudi Arabia, Article 6.

This has created a conflict between what Vogel describes as 'microcosmic judicial *ijtihad*[225] [and the] macrocosmic ruler's *siyasa*'.[226] Article 1 of the Basic Law has ensured a dogmatic interpretation of governance and constitutional law, as the natural source of authority is not legislation or precedent, but the *ijtihad* of past and present religious-legal scholars (*ulema*).[227] Thus any *fiqh* opinion authoritatively rooted in the Qur'an and Sunnahh is Saudi Law, for it is a statement of Sharia. Conversely, *nizams*[228] emanating from the King are only followed to the extent that they comply with *fiqh*.

By using religious law as a basis for a legal system, Saudi Arabia necessarily relocates power to religious interpretative organs, entrenching the substantive and procedural law surrounding the Constitution. Article 7 elucidates this point best, stating 'Government in Saudi Arabia derives power from the Holy Koran and the Prophet's tradition'.

In essence, the effect of Article 1 of the Basic law is merely to provide a written explanation of what is regarded as *a priori* knowledge—that the Saudi Constitution and system of governance is not based on Islamic principles. Rather, it is the embodiment of Islam. The codified provisions of Islam as a State religion are superfluous.

SUBSECTION TWO: THE PLACE ACCORDED TO ISLAM IN THE NORMATIVE PYRAMID FORMING SUBSTANTIVE LAW

The influence of Islam as a normative set of provisions on the national set of laws has varied widely in practice. This influence exists where Islam is considered a source of legislation capable of directing the entire legal structure within a State. The variation in the degree of application accorded to Sharia in Muslim countries occurs on a very large and diverse spectrum.

The following section aims to analyse the place of the Sharia within the substantive law of the different Muslim countries that are subject to this study. Section A will analyse cases where States adopt a 'radical' position with regard to the place of Sharia within the State. This will be done by distinguishing between the liberal models in which Sharia is not considered to be a source of national law and the conservative models in which Sharia law constitutes the quasi-unique source of legislation. Section B will analyse the cases between these two extremes where the Sharia occupies a varied, albeit important, source of substantive law.

225 The process of making a legal decision by independent interpretation of the Qur'an and Sunnah.

226 The ruler's perspective of law and legal theory.

227 See FE Vogel, *Islamic Law and Legal Systems: Studies of Saudi Arabia* (Brill, Leiden 2000), also http://servat.unibe.ch/icl/sa__indx.html (last accessed 15/01/08).

228 Decrees, laws or regulations.

A. Radical Positions with Regard to the Place afforded to the Sharia within Internal Legal Systems

1. States in which Sharia is not a Source of Legislation: Turkey

Among the Muslim countries subject to this study, secular Turkey's system may be found at one end of the spectrum.

Turkey

Despite the fact that 99.8 per cent of the population is Muslim, the legal system in Turkey is completely secular. As has been shown previously, religion is not mentioned in the Constitution at all and is not afforded the status as a source of law for the relevant legislative bodies nor in respect of judicial reasoning by the national tribunals.

The preamble of the Constitution strongly underlines the fact that Islam does not have any normative impact within the State as it provides '*as required by the principle of secularism, there shall be no interference whatsoever of the sacred religious feelings in State affairs and politics.*'

2. Sharia as the Only Source of Legislation

In complete contrast, at the other end of the spectrum are: the Islamic Republic of Iran,[229] where ultimate legislative authority rests with religious clerics; and Pakistan and Saudi Arabia, where the Quran is itself considered to be the Constitution.

Iran

The Constitution of the Islamic Republic of Iran places Islamic principles at the pinnacle of the normative hierarchy within the constitutional, legal, and political framework of the State. Article 4 paragraph 1 of the Constitution enshrines this approach. It stipulates that '[a]ll civil, penal, financial, economic, administrative, military and political law and other laws and regulations, shall be based on the Islamic standards'.

It is clear from the formulation of this provision that Islamic principles are to prevail over all other laws and regulations in the Islamic Republic of Iran. It is possible to infer from this Article that Sharia embodies the Constitution itself. However, the second paragraph of Article 4 establishes a hierarchy among the constitutional provisions, upon which Islamic law prevails. Paragraph 2 specifies that the principle that all laws comply with Islamic criteria 'applies absolutely and generally to all articles of the Constitution as well as to all other laws and regulations'. Consequently, the

[229] In Iran, the Islamic Revolution of 1979 caused an extensive attempt to build an Islamic constitutional order.

positioning of the Iranian set of norms (at least in theory) appears to follow thus: Islamic principles are positioned at the top of the hierarchy, followed by other constitutional provisions and then other sets of laws, namely ordinary legislation and regulations. In practice, however, the premises of this principle are not exhaustive or clear-cut. In modern times, the acceptance of various laws within the Iranian system that are in fact alien to the principles of Sharia have been unavoidable and attests to the existence of an ability, on the part of Muslim States where they are willing, to override Islamic provisions that stand in flagrant violation of human rights norms.[230]

In any case, the task of reviewing the decisions of the *Majlis* (the Iranian Parliament) in order to bring them into conformity with the principles of Sharia law belongs to the Guardian Council. Article 91 of the Iranian Constitution provides that:

> The Guardian Council shall be established with a view to safeguarding the rules of Islam and the Constitution and to see that the decisions of the *Majlis* are not inconsistent with them.

Article 72 gives the Guardian Council the power to decide whether a decision needs to be reviewed or not. It provides that:

> The Islamic Consultative Assembly cannot make laws that are contradictory to the principles, official religion of the country or the constitution. Discretion on whether such contradictions exist, as stated in article 96, is assigned to the Guardian Council.

Pakistan

In Pakistan, the chapter of the Constitution governing the Islamic Provisions places the Quran and the Sunnahh above all normative authority, with Article 227 clearly stipulating that 'all existing laws shall be brought in conformity with the injunctions of Islam as laid down in the Holy Quran and the Sunnahh ... and no law shall be enacted which is repugnant to such injunctions'. The Islamic Council was created with the mission to advise authorities as to whether a proposed law is or is not repugnant to the tenets of Islam, and to make recommendations for measures that would bring existing laws into conformity with the injunctions of Islam and the stages by which such measures should be brought into effect (see Article 230 of the Constitution of Pakistan governing the functions of the Islamic Council).

The Eighth Constitutional Amendment created a new institution, the Federal *Shariat* Court, which has the power to examine and decide whether

[230] cf II. A. etc.

or not any law or provision is contrary to the Sharia, as laid down in the Quran and Sunnahh. In cases where the court does find a law to be in conflict with Islamic injunctions, it may ask the concerned governmental department to present its point of view and make submissions to the court. If the law or provision is nevertheless held to be repugnant to the injunctions of Islam, the President or the governor will be required to take steps to amend the law so as to bring it into conformity with Islam.

Saudi Arabia

In a State where the Constitution consists solely of the Quran and the Sunnahh, the sphere of influence that Islam has over the legal structure is naturally very large, and almost unlimited. Article 9 of the Royal decree specifies that the implementation of the law must be carried out in accordance with the stipulations of the Islamic faith. Moreover, the State has a constitutional duty to implement Sharia (Article 23), and the courts will apply the rules of Sharia in the cases that are brought before them and in accordance with what is indicated in the Quran and the Sunnahh.

The majority of Islamic States have not as yet made legislative enactments in respect of personal status law. Instead Sharia law, as compiled in the traditional legal manuals, is still formally applied in its entirety in most Arab Gulf States. Although this trend is widespread, it is not a common trait to all Islamic countries: Iran and Pakistan have codified Sharia into a comprehensive and very large set of laws. Maintaining Sharia law as the sole source of legislation has been an unrealistic aim in practice, and these principles have faced some degree of moderation in Iran, Pakistan and Saudi Arabia.

B. States in which Sharia is an Important But Not Exclusive Source of Legislation

Between the two extremes where, on the one hand, Sharia does not have any normative or legal impact on legislation and where, on the other hand, Sharia comprises the sole source of law, sit a number of cases which accord Sharia different degrees of status as a normative source of law. These generally include (1) where Sharia is a significant source of the substantive law in general; (2) where Islam is declared as the religion of the State.

It is necessary to analyse the range of roles Sharia plays within a State's legal system in order to draw attention to certain inconsistencies that arise. Often, the sometimes ambiguous nature of the connection maintained between Islamic law and substantive law allows the State concerned to found or justify its acts or behaviour on the premise that it is obliged to observe Sharia even where Sharia is not expressly defined as being the exclusive source of legislation in the text of the Constitution.

1. *Sharia as part of the substantive law in general*

Aside from Iran, Pakistan and Saudi Arabia, Sharia is considered an important normative source of law in other Muslim countries such as Bahrain, Egypt, Morocco and Syria. But the influence of the religion on the substantive law is not identical in each of these countries. The status of Islam as a normative source varies slightly from one legal system to the other. The terminology used in the original Arabic texts of the Constitutions of these Muslim countries, refers generally to the importance that is assigned to Islam as *a source of law* within the internal legal system. When a constitutional provision considers 'Sharia as a source of legislation' as in Bahrain, or 'Islamic jurisprudence as a main source of legislation', as in Syria, this means that Islamic law constitutes just one amongst a possible variety of legislative sources, and that other sources are envisaged which, together with the substantive law, could legitimately found the adoption of legislative rules. However, Egypt's formulation that considers Sharia as 'the main source of legislation' is significantly more extensive.

Egypt

The legal implication of the difference between the two alternative formulations, *Sharia* as *a source of law* and *sharia* as *the main source of law*, was seen clearly when Egypt's Constitution was amended in 1980 changing the former to the latter. Bowing to the rising pressure of Muslim groups that were seeking a more integral role for Islamic law within the internal legal system, the Government amended the Constitution, altering the wording of Article 2. Subsequent to that amendment, Article 2 of the Egyptian Constitution now provides that 'Islamic jurisprudence is the principal source of legislation'.[231] The 1971 Constitution, before the amendment, did not require that all legislation adopted by the Parliament (People's Assembly) be consistent with Sharia principles.

The significant legal consequences of this amendment have been reflected in the jurisprudence of the Supreme Constitutional Court (SCC) of Egypt. The SCC decided in 1985 that the requirement that all legislation be consistent with Sharia principles was to have prospective effect only from the date of adoption on 22 May 1980. This means that all legislation adopted after this date should be in accordance with the provisions of Sharia.[232]

The jurisprudence generated by Article 2 has been developed fairly

231 In the Arabic version: *'al-sharia el-islamiyya al masdaru al-raisiyu lil-tashri'*.

232 See on this controversy: John Murray and Mohammad el-Mollah, 'Islamic Sharia and Constitutional Interpretation in Egypt', in Eugene Cotran and Adel Omar Sherif, Democracy, the Rule of Law and Islam (CQ Press, USA, 1999) 507–524; Frank E Vogel, 'Conformity with Islamic Sharia and Constitutionality under Article 2: Some Issues of Theory, Practice and Comparison', in Eugene Cotran and Adel Omar Sherif, *Democracy, the Rule of Law and Islam*, 525–544.

consistently by the Egyptian Supreme Constitutional Court since the amendment took effect. It can be summarized by the stance of the court in a particular matter that came before it, a stance that derived from the culmination of many previous decisions that had been issued by the court on this legal matter:

> The principles of the Islamic Sharia are the major source of legislation. This imposes a limitation curtailing both the legislative and executive power, through which they are obliged that whatever laws or decrees they enact, no provision contained in them may contradict the provisions of Islamic law which are definite in terms of their immutability and their meaning. (...) Whatever legislative enactment contravenes them must be declared null and void'.[233]

In light of the above, it is evident that the jurisprudence of the SCC reflects the extent to which the Egyptian judiciary plays a role in shaping the scope of human rights in the internal legal system.[234]

Yemen

The Constitution of Yemen includes a relatively ambiguous provision which states that 'Islamic Sharia is the source of all legislation'.[235] The provision provokes some interesting legal questions which invite further analysis. For instance, does this provision imply that Sharia is the exclusive source of legislation or does it simply mean that it represents one amongst many? Although Yemen does not feature in this comparative study, it is worth mentioning that the relatively high importance given to Sharia in its substantive law has not prevented the country from ratifying several international human rights treaties without having to enter reservations on the grounds of religious considerations.

2. *Islam as the religion of the State*

Libya

The Constitution of Libya stipulates in Article 2 that 'Islam is the religion of the state'; however, the Constitution fails to indicate any legal consequences that may flow from this. Islam is also mentioned at two other points. First, Islam is cited in the final paragraph of Article 8 as being the sole source of norms for the specific issue of inheritance—'inheritance is a right which will be governed by the Islamic Sharia'. The terminology

233 Appeal no 5257/43 on 28 December 1997.
234 We will be assessing this issue in Part 2 which follows.
235 The Constitution of the Republic of Yemen, 1991, Article 3 as amended in 1994.

employs '*a* right' and not '*the* right', and this could imply that other rights may also be included within the scope of the Islamic principles. Regardless, the other mention of Islam is in Article 6, which states: '[Libya's] inspiration is its Arabic and Islamic heritage.' This ambiguous stipulation has kept the way open for the use of Islam in the interpretation and application of law. This has been evidenced by Libya's general reservation to CEDAW in 1995 that stated 'accession cannot conflict with the laws on personal status derived from the Islamic Sharia'.[236] Libya's further reservations to Article 2 and Article 16(c) and (d) of CEDAW stated that, with regard to Article 2, 'the Convention shall be implemented with due regard for the peremptory norms of the Islamic Sharia' (in relation to inheritance) and that 'the implementation of paragraph 16(c) and (d) of the Convention shall be without prejudice to any of the rights guaranteed to women by the Islamic Sharia.'[237]

Malaysia

As will be illustrated later,[238] Malaysia is a federation of 13 States where both federal government and State government exercise executive and legislative powers. Civil law (and family law as a subset of civil law) comes under the federal legislature's jurisdiction. The federal Constitution under the Ninth Schedule divides matters into 'Federal Lists' and 'State Lists'. Islamic law in Malaysia applies to Muslim citizens only and is confined to the matters specified in the State List of the Federal Constitution. The State List contains Muslim personal laws which include matrimonial law, charitable endowments ('*awqaf*'), bequests and inheritance. The list also includes offences that are not governed by federal law, such as matrimonial offences, '*khalwat*' (intimate proximity between a Muslim male and a female, regardless of whether she is a Muslim or not, to whom he is not married), and offences against religion as well as native personal law and custom. These are regulated by State enactments and the power to legislate on these matters is vested in both the State legislature and the Sultan.

Morocco

The status of Islam in the Constitution of Morocco is particularly interesting to note. Article 6 of the Constitution provides that 'Islam is the religion of the State which guarantees to all freedom of worship' which may at first sight appear similar to the Constitutions of other Muslim States. It could seem that Islam does not wield any normative power over or benefit from

[236] Government of the Socialist People's Libyan Arab Republic, notification to Secretary General, 5 July 1995: http://www.un.org/womenwatch/daw/cedaw/reservations-country.htm#N38.
[237] Reservations by Libyan Arab Jamahiriya: http://www.un.org/womenwatch/daw/cedaw/reservations-country.htm.
[238] See below, 53–54.

a privileged legislative status within Morocco. However, a closer analysis of the provision of the Constitution reveals that Islam does play an important role in the normative hierarchy of Moroccan law.

Following the assertion that 'Islam is the religion of the State', it appears to derive from this assertion that, as a consequence of this, the State 'guarantees to all freedom of worship'. Inferring such a guarantee from the acknowledgment that Islam is the religion of the State may presumably be founded on principles of Sharia which protect and guarantee this liberty. In this manner, applying the stipulations of Islam concerning this specific point of freedom of religion has led Morocco's constituents to acknowledge as a constitutional principle, the liberty of worship. From this provision of the Moroccan Constitution, Sharia appears not only to form a part of substantive Moroccan law but also to enjoy a high position in the hierarchy of norms as a foundation for the constitutional principles. This apparent normative influence of Sharia is not evident in the provisions of Malaysia, for example, where it states in Article 3: 'Islam is the religion of the Federation; but other religions may be practised in peace and harmony in any part of the Federation'.

The constitutional recognition of Islam as the religion of the State also has direct effect within the Moroccan legal system. The status of Islam as a normative source is evidenced by the declaration that it entered to Article 14 of the Convention on the Rights of the Child where it stated that the Government would interpret the provision related to the freedom of religion of the child in accordance with both Article 6 of the Constitution which 'provides that Islam, the State religion, shall guarantee freedom of worship for all', as well as the Family Code (Article 24, Act 70-03) which provides that 'parents owe their children the right to religious guidance and education based on good conduct'.[239] Previously, the same provision had been reserved against 'in view of the fact that Islam is the State religion'.[240]

Article 19 of Morocco's Constitution also appears to support the high normative status accorded to Islam. Article 19 governs the King's prerogatives, and accords to him the right and duty to ensure 'the observance' of both Islam and the Constitution. Ensuring the observance of Islam presumably means ensuring that the provisions of Islam are respected and applied in domestic practice, just as ensuring the observance of the Constitution would mean ensuring that the provisions of the Constitution are respected and implemented within the legal system. Taking this into consideration, we could reasonably conclude that Islam rests at the top of the hierarchy of norms, even at the same level as the Constitution. As a consequence, it is

[239] Convention on the Rights of the Child, Reservations of Morocco: http://www2.ohchr.org/english/bodies/ratification/11.htm#reservations.

[240] http://www2.ohchr.org/english/bodies/ratification/11.htm#N31.

inevitable that Islam would influence the substantive law of the State. As we shall see below, this implied construction of Islam's status within the Moroccan system, together with the power of the King ('Commander of the Faithful') with regard to the respect of religious norms, has enabled significant progress towards the improvement of the human rights record in the country.[241]

Tunisia

Article 1 of the Constitution of Tunisia stipulates that the religion of Tunisia is Islam. This general provision does not appear to have had any constitutional consequences as a source of legislation. The attitude of the Tunisian Government on this matter seems somewhat paradoxical and ambiguous. For example, on the one hand, the Tunisian Government declares that Sharia is a source of rights and progress within the State but it is not a part of the positive law.[242] Yet, on the other hand, when reporting to the committee of the ICESCR in 1989, Tunisia confirmed that the law abolishing polygamy had the consent and approval of Islamic jurists, clearly demonstrating that Sharia has a role to play within the sphere of positive law. The Tunisian representative reported to the CEDAW Committee in 1995 that Tunisia has 'adopted a dynamic interpretation of Islam' and has modelled its common legislation 'within the framework of the modern Islam, gradually abandoning the static models of thought inherited'.[243] Generally and with the exception of personal status law, Tunisian legislation does not refer explicitly to Islam, although it may be argued that Islamic considerations and values play a role in devising certain legal norms.

SUBSECTION THREE—THE WAY THE SHARIA MANIFESTS ITSELF IN THE FAMILY LAW OF MUSLIM STATES

If the status of Sharia law within any given Muslim country remains at the top of the substantive law hierarchy as an incontrovertible norm, the real extent of its impact is de facto weakened by the concurrent secular legislation that is typically established in almost all fields of law. However, if Sharia still has a noteworthy but restricted impact on laws in modern-day Muslim countries, its ubiquitous presence remains incontrovertible in

241 See below at 121.
242 See Report of Tunisia to the Human Rights Committee (A/42/40 1987).
243 See Concluding Observations of the CEDAW Committee, UN Doc. A/50/38 (1995) at para. 221 Cited in Mashood Baderin, 'A Macroscopic Analysis of the Practice of Muslim States Parties to International Human Rights Treaties: Conflict or Congruence,' Human Rights Law Review, 1 (2), 274.

family matters. Indeed, family law in most Muslim countries has resisted nearly all attempts at secularization and still remains a body of law that is almost completely in compliance with Islamic standards. This area of law is relevant to all of the countries that are within the scope of this study, with the sole exception of Turkey where the Swiss Family Code plays a major role in the legal system. Therefore, apart from Turkey, which has completely abandoned Islamic law, a general overview of family law matters and its articulation of the Sharia will provide the necessary foundation for a deeper analysis later in this study.

Family law takes shape in various forms throughout the world, ranging from the civil code tradition of continental Europe and the common law system of England, Australia and Canada, to the Islamic law system applied in Muslim countries. The latter refers to Islamic norms which apply to family relations that revolve around marriage, divorce, marital rights and duties, and custody of children. Islamic family law is formally recognized under the denomination of personal status law, '*Kanoun Al Ahwal Al-Shakhssiya*'. This term[244] was first coined in Egypt and then later adopted by numerous other Muslim countries including Iraq, Tunisia, Lebanon and Syria.

In the first group of those States in which Islam affects all fields of legislation, family law falls naturally within the scope of religious considerations. It is possible to identify two trends in this category: States which have codified the Islamic family law in total harmony with the injunctions of Islam, and States which have allowed Islamic family law to remain an uncodified set of norms.

In the category of States previously identified where the Sharia still has some impact on the legal system, the Sharia is generally perceived to be a strong and quasi-unique normative source in family matters, while it seems to have been deeply tampered with if not completely abandoned in other fields of law. This category is by itself very broad and diverse, and it is possible to divide the countries subject to this study into two different groups: (A) where the State communalizes religion by according religious authorities the privilege of applying their own sets of laws in family matters (these countries are generally characterised by a diverse population); and (B) where the State incorporates Sharia principles into the national legal system. The latter are usually Islamic States where Muslims from the same Islamic school of thought constitute a majority of the population and where Islam is recognized as the official religion. In both groups Islamic principles have an impact on the internal system, either directly or indirectly.

244 This legal Arabic term has been adopted by Islamic States referring to family matters (in this regard see: Jamal J Nasir CVO, *The Islamic Law of Personal Status* (3rd ed, Kluwer Law International, 2002) 34–40. The expression Ahwal Al-Shakhssiya is currently used in Arabic for family matters in many Muslim countries and includes marriage, divorce, maintenance, custody, filiations and in some legal systems succession.

An analysis of the evolution of the substance of family law as applied within these two trends will demonstrate that the nationalization of Islamic family law together with the abolition of the Sharia court has proven to be an efficient mechanism towards reforming the substance of the law within the framework of Sharia. In other words, the delegation of family legislation to the religious authorities impedes the reform of the substantive law and renders legally impossible the intervention of the State in this field. This situation puts the State in a very politically sensitive position, as experienced by Lebanon where the State has undertaken to abide by the international conventions whilst, in reality, being incapable of controlling this area of law on the internal level.

A. Group of countries where family law is the national law adopted by the legislator

We can identify two main subgroups within this group. The first subgroup is composed of countries such as Egypt, Morocco and Tunisia which have 'nationalised' their family law, so family law is the national law adopted by the legislator in these countries. In this group, the law is drafted by the State but remains an adaptation of Islamic law. Reforms undertaken by governments confirm that the passage of family law from Islamic law to 'national' family law is certainly inspired by Sharia and based on *fiqh*. However, these laws are significantly transformed by the impact of codification and the different legislative procedures.

Egypt

The Egyptian family code is derived from Islamic law and is based on a series of legislative enactments that have been adopted since 1920 and throughout the last century. The most important laws on matters dealing with issues of personal status are Law No 25 of 1920, Law No 56 of 1923 and Law No 25 of 1929. These have been amended by Law No 100 of 1985 and recently by Personal Status Law No 1 of 2000. An in-depth analysis of the reform of some aspects of these laws will be carried out later in this study.[245]

Malaysia

The peculiarities of the Malaysian federal system and its resulting impact on legislation related to Sharia concerns, allows us to distinguish Islamic family law in Malaysia from the Moroccan, Tunisian or Egyptian illustrations. Islamic family law in Malaysia is a codified law based on Sharia. It is a 'national law' in the sense that it is set by the public authorities, but this prerogative is not exclusive to the federal State.

[245] See below, 125–129.

In Malaysia,[246] the administration of Islamic family law falls under the separate jurisdiction of different States where each State has its own command over matters relating to the family law governing Muslims. The federal Parliament can legislate only on matters dealing with Islamic law and religion that is specific to the federal territories of Kuala Lumpur, Putrajaya and Labuan. Therefore, it has no power to legislate for the rest of Malaysia. Article 76 of the federal Constitution thus stipulates that Parliament can legislate on matters pertaining to the State List only in order to realise 'uniformity of law and policy', or in matters of Islamic law and Malay custom 'if so requested by the legislative assembly of any state'. Even when Parliament enacts legislation on personal law matters at the request of the State legislative assembly, such law 'shall not come into operation in any state until it has been adopted by a law made by the legislature of that state'. Such a law is then deemed to be a State law and not a federal law, and 'may accordingly be amended or repealed by a law made by that legislature'. It is clear that even when Parliament passes a law on Sharia-related matters, the State legislature has powers to amend or repeal it as it deems fit. This could be a recipe for disparity and divergence, as can now be seen in the application of Islamic law in Malaysia. These disparities have prompted observers to note that 'there are various family laws practiced in Malaysia', and that 'Malaysia is the only country in the Muslim world where each state has independent jurisdiction over religion leading to inconsistencies and contradictions in the provisions of law, an interpretation and in implementation, state by state'. In response to the question as to why Malaysia should have 14 different religious authorities, another observer argued that religion provides the 'basis for [the] Monarch's legitimacy' and that religion was 'among the few things left' to indigenous Malay rulers who otherwise surrendered their powers to federal and state authorities. Thus, attempts to bring about uniformity of Muslim law throughout Malaysia have not been successful due to the understandable reluctance of the states to relinquish one of their remaining powers.[247]

Although the substantive provisions on marriage and divorce in the various enactments were somewhat similar as they were all based on the '*Hukum Syara*', what did exist were differences in administrative procedures that not only led to diversity and complexity but also to hardship and dissatisfaction.

[246] The Sharia Courts are an integral part of the court system in Malaysia and are distinct from the civil courts as to their function and jurisdiction. There are three levels of Sharia courts: Sharia Subordinate Courts, Sharia High Court and Sharia Appeal Court.

[247] Mohamed Hashim Kamali: Islamic Law in Malaysia: Issues and Developments, available at www.thefiqh.org under the heading Jurisprudence (last accessed 15 May 2008).

These inconsistencies between the laws of the various States pose a problem when it comes to enforcement. In 1984, the federal Parliament enacted the Islamic Family Law (Federal Territories) Act 1984 (Act 303) for the federal Territories. Many of the states have implemented slightly altered versions of this model, but several states, particularly the states in the northern part of the country, have adopted their own family law enactments which incorporate their own parameters of women's rights in marriage and divorce in contrast to the Federal Territories Act. The Islamic Family Law[248] (Federal Territories) Act was amended in 1994. The Islamic Family Law (State of Selangor) Enactment 2003 was introduced as a potential blue-print of efforts to standardise the provisions on Islamic law among the States.

The 176th Conference of Rulers Meeting held on 1 August 1997 agreed with the Government of Malaysia's proposal to standardise the laws pertaining to Sharia law in Malaysia. Pursuant to the same, the 188th Conference of Rulers Meeting held on 22 March 2001 agreed on 5 Model Laws relating to the Administration of Islamic Law, Islamic Family Law, Sharia Court Evidence, Sharia Criminal Procedure and the Sharia Court Civil Procedure.

Morocco

The Moroccan Personal code, or '*Moudawana*', was promulgated in 1957, a year after Morocco won full independence. It represents the only major area of the Moroccan legal system that is based on the Sharia. *Moudawana* was reformed for the first time in 1993, but this reform fell below expectations and in 2004, a major reform to the *Moudawana* was completed. It may be interesting to highlight that since the very first version of the *Moudawana* of 1957, the traditional positions of Islamic law have been altered. For instance, the Moudawana set the age of consent for marriage at 18 years for men and 15 years for women while traditional Islamic sources recognise puberty as the legal age for women to marry. Significant advances in the legal status of women have also been made in the new *Moudawana* of 2004.[249]

Tunisia

The Tunisian Code of Personal Status, or '*Majallah*', enacted on 13 August 1956 only six months after the independence is an affirmation of the modernist approach. It has then been amended many times. Its last major reform was in 1993. This code integrates certain fundamental principles that have prevailed despite the evolution of contemporary societies. The two most progressive features of this code are the abolition of polygamy

[248] See below, 49. [249] See below, 121.

and the consecration of the exclusivity of judicial divorce. Consequently, divorce outside a court of law is without legal effect in Tunisia.

B. Group of countries where family law is directly under the control of religious authorities

In the second group, to which Bahrain and Lebanon belong, family law does not fall within the competence of the public State institutions but is directly under the control of religious, notably Islamic, authorities.

Bahrain

In Bahrain, personal law remains un-codified, and is administered by the Sharia courts which are divided into *Shia* and Sunni departments applying Jaafari[250] and Shafii or Maliki[251] *fiqh*, respectively. These courts have jurisdiction over all disputes relating to Muslim personal status, except disputes over estates and there are no official publications of Sharia Court decisions.

Lebanon

The State of Lebanon has no official religion. It is usually put under the category of a multi-confessional State, but in reality, Lebanon is a secular State. Lebanon's complicated sectarian structure gives total autonomy to the religious authorities to act as legislators in family matters. The State refuses to interfere in this sphere where 18 recognised sects act as legislators when it comes to family law matters and they have their own established courts to enforce their sets of law.

The role of Sharia as a source of law is witnessed in the 'Personal Status' law of Lebanon, which is applied by Muslims of the Sunni, Shia and Druze sects. However, some areas usually considered as part of personal status are governed by the Lebanese common civil code. This guarantees women the right to own their businesses and it also accords to their testimony in court the same weight as that of men.

The significance of Islamic within the legal system and the place accorded to Islam within the normative pyramid forming subtstantive law, notably family law, are essential factors to consider when assessing the impact of religion on human rights. Nevertheless, these factors are not always determinant themselves. For example, even in Turkey, where secularism is constitutionally and legally established, human rights violations that could be seen to originate from 'Islamic culture' or related to patriarchal influences do still occur. This phenomenon led the Committee on the Elimination of Discrimination against Women to state in its concluding comments on Turkey that it is:

[250] See above, x. [251] ibid.

> ... strongly concerned about the pervasiveness of patriarchal attitudes and deep-rooted traditional and cultural stereotypes regarding the roles and responsibilities of women and men in society, and which continue to cast women in a position of inferiority. It expresses its concern that these attitudes contribute to the perpetuation of violence against women, including in the form of 'honour killings', and negatively affect women's enjoyment of their rights in many areas; they also impede the full implementation of the Convention, including in regard to education, employment, health and participation in decision-making. It is also concerned about the persistence of certain traditional and cultural practices that are discriminatory to women, such as early marriage, forced marriage and polygamy, notwithstanding the relevant provisions in the Civil Code.[252]

Additionally, there is no need to stress again the influence of political factors on the human rights records of the concerned States regardless of Islam, as discussed in the introduction of this study.

CONCLUSION

The above chapter has illustrated how Islam had a positive influence in humanizing pre-Islamic Arabia's laws, customs and norms. Indeed, the advent of Islam had an exceptional impact on improving the rights of women and children as well as fostering a sense of economic justice. However, as positive as these developments may have been at the time, the now traditional Sharia (whose rules and norms have changed little over the centuries) is currently engaged in a normative confrontation with contemporary human rights standards that are becoming increasingly internationalized. This normative confrontation is most easily observed and arguably most significant when it comes to the interaction of Muslim States with international human rights treaties. However, as the different Muslim States accord to the Sharia a distinct position within their hierarchy of norms, ranging from Saudi Arabia where Sharia is the backbone and constitution of the State, to Tunisia, where its role appears to be limited albeit at times ambiguous, generalizations as to the real role of Sharia (traditional and non-traditional) within this normative confrontation cannot be justified. Aware of the unique position that

[252] Committee on the Elimination of Discrimination against Women, 'Concluding Comments: Turkey, CEDAW/C/TUR/CC/4-5, Thirty-second session, 10–28 January 2005 (http://www.wwhr.org/files/Cedaw_ConcComments2005.pdf).

Sharia occupies in each of these States, their Constitutions and their legal systems, the next chapter will analyse what impact the Sharia really has on the respective Muslim States when it comes to their engagement with international human rights treaties.

CHAPTER TWO

The Impact of Sharia on the Ratification of International Human Rights Treaties

An analytical overview of the degree to which Muslim countries adhere to the main international human rights treaties, particularly with regard to the reservations that are entered against them in the name of Sharia law, reinforces the fact that religious considerations certainly have an influence on the level of engagement with human rights by Muslim States. However, in the majority of cases, this impact remains artificial. The key justifications typically put forward for selectively adhering to human rights commitments on the grounds of Sharia, often serve political motivations.

The purpose of this chapter is two-fold. In the first section it demonstrates that Sharia has a direct impact on the ratification of international human rights instruments and that this influence tends to limit the scope of the engagement of Muslim States at the international level. In the second section, an in-depth analysis of the use of Islamic considerations by Muslim States shows that the influence of Sharia on the ratification process remains relatively small.

Section One **The Direct Influence of Sharia on the Ratification of Major International Human Rights Treaties**

Sharia is an important factor in determining whether Muslim States will adhere to international human rights treaties. Indeed, the seemingly inherent normative conflict between Sharia and human rights is often considered to be behind the State's reluctance to be part of international human rights instruments.[1] The following section will discuss the *use* of Sharia by States

[1] It should be noted that a number of Islamic scholars/academics believe that Sharia can be reconciled with international human rights norms through the application of jurisprudential techniques which are themselves integral to Sharia. These include: *ijtihad; maslaha; maqasid al-Sharia* ; or even a reversal of abrogation. The application of such techniques, particularly *ijtihad* have been widely used amongst the modern Islamic Feminist movement as summarised by Margo Badran: 'Islamic feminism: what's in a name?' Al-Ahram Weekly Online, 17–23 January 2002, Issue No. 569. Available at: http://weekly.ahram.org.eg/ 2002/569/cu1.htm See

to (1) abstain from voting on or ratifying human rights treaties; and (2) persistently limit their observation of the obligations stipulated in the international conventions.

SUBSECTION ONE: RELIGIOUS CONSIDERATIONS AS A DETERMINANT FACTOR IN THE DECISION OF SOME MUSLIM STATES TO ABSTAIN FROM VOTING ON HUMAN RIGHTS TREATIES

On 10 December 1948, the UN General Assembly proclaimed and adopted the Universal Declaration of Human Rights. There were no dissenting votes. The 48 affirmative votes approving the Declaration included those of eight Muslim States which were then members of the United Nations: Afghanistan, Egypt, Iran, Iraq, Lebanon, Pakistan, Syria and Yemen. Saudi Arabia (along with South Africa and six other members of the Communist bloc) was the only Muslim State to abstain from the vote. The main reason behind this abstention was the alleged violation of certain provisions of the Sharia that the implementation of the Declaration would entail. According to Saudi Arabia's representative, the Declaration reflected Western culture and was 'at variance with patterns of culture of Eastern states' and that furthermore, the Declaration's provision on religious freedom was at odds with Islamic law.[2] The Saudi ambassador to the United Nations, Al Barudi, objected specifically to Article 18:

> Everyone has the right to freedom of thought, conscience and religion; this right includes freedom to change his religion or belief, and freedom, either along or in community with others and in public or private, to manifest his religion or belief in teaching, practice, worship and observance.[3]

The ambassador insisted that the Quran forbids a Muslim to change his faith[4] and that a right to change religion would be an affront to Muslims and encourage missionary activity in the Arabian Peninsula.[5] Evidently,

generally: Abdullahi Ahmed An-Naim, Toward an Islamic Reformation. Civil Liberties, Human Rights and. International Law, Syracuse, Syracuse University Press, 1990.

[2] John Kelsay, 'Saudi Arabia, Pakistan, and the Universal Declaration of Human Rights', in *Human Rights and the Conflict of Cultures: Western and Islamic Perspectives on Religious Liberty*, David Little, John Kelsay, and Abdulaziz Sachedina ((eds), University of South California Press, Columbia, 1988).

[3] Article 18, Universal Declaration of Human Rights 1948. Adopted and proclaimed by General Assembly resolution 217A (III) of 10 December 1948.

[4] See M Ganji, International Protection of Human Rights, 1962 (n 48) 145, n 12.

[5] See 3.UN GAOR C.3 (127 mtg.) at 391–392, UN Doc. A/C.3/SR.127 (1948).

Saudi Arabia's objection was 'ostensibly based on Islamic religious grounds.'[6]

Michael Ignatieff states in his article, 'The Attack on Human Rights', that the Saudi delegate to the Committee that examined the draft of the Universal Declaration posited an argument that has resonated ever since in Islamic encounters with human rights theory. The argument was that:

> [T]he authors of the draft declaration had, for the most part, taken into consideration only the standards recognised by Western civilisation and had ignored more ancient civilisations which were past the experimental stage (and whose institutions such as marriage) had proved their wisdom through the centuries.[7]

Religious considerations were also put forward by other Muslim countries in what was a futile attempt to modify the controversial paragraph in Article 18. Lebanon was the only Muslim country to vote in favour of this provision and was duly criticised for this by other Muslim countries.[8] Eventually Egypt, Iran and Pakistan voted in favour of the Declaration and only Saudi Arabia abstained. Two factors could explain why the other Muslim countries did not object to a positive vote on the UDHR. First, the UDHR is a non-binding document and their adherence to this international instrument would not necessarily require any 'concrete' measures to be made to their domestic legal systems. Secondly, the positive votes were accompanied by reservations, as was the case with Egypt.[9]

Eighteen years on, if it could be said that two other key international conventions[10] have garnered a widespread consensus of opinion (evidenced by 105 votes for the ICESCR and 106 for ICCPR with no votes made against the text), it is probably because these two instruments have reconsidered many of the controversial provisions present in the UDHR, notably taking into consideration the specificities and sensitivities of Islam. Accordingly, references to religious matters in both Article 23 concerning the right to marry and to found a family and Article 18 concerning the right to change one's religion were removed. It is of great significance that the

[6] See An-Naim, 'Religious Minorities under Islamic Law and the limits of Cultural Relativism', 9 Human Rights Quarterly 1.7 & n 17.

[7] Michael Ignatieff, 'The Attack on Human Rights', Foreign Affairs, November/December 2001, Vol 8, Number 6, 103.

[8] See M Ganji, International Protection of Human Rights, 1962 (n 48) 145, n. 12. On Lebanon and the UDHR see also Mary Anne Glendon, *A World Made New: Eleanor Roosevelt and the Universal Declaration of Human Rights* (Random House, 2001).

[9] In this regard see A. Verdoodt, Naissance et signification de la Declaration Universelle des droits de l'homme (Nauwelaerts, Louvain-Paris) 168–182.

[10] The two international conventions are:
1) International Covenant on Economic, Social and Cultural Rights
2) International Covenant on Civil and Political Rights

controversial provisions in the UDHR have disappeared from the ICCPR. Consequently, Article 18 acknowledges freedom of thought, conscience and religion, the right to have or adopt a religion or belief and to manifest one's religion or belief, without a specific citation on the right to change one's religion. Following the same trend, Article 23 of ICCPR recognises the right to marry and found a family but omits sensitive stipulations which would most likely lead to reservations from Muslim countries on this point.[11]

Despite the changes that have been made to these sensitive provisions, Saudi Arabia has not ratified either of the two international conventions. It has already been highlighted that during the debates on these two instruments, Saudi Arabia's objections were maintained on the grounds of Islamic considerations. With regard to Article 18 of ICCPR, Al Barudi argued that 'it would raise doubts in the minds of ordinary people to whom their religion [is] a way of life'. With regards to the ICESCR, the Ambassador for Saudi Arabia objected to Article 9 which guarantees 'the right of everyone to social security including social insurance'. He asserted that Sharia goes beyond what he deemed as inferior Western requirements,[12] and accordingly refused to make his country a party to the international instrument.

Iran

Unlike Saudi Arabia, Iran has signed and ratified all three instruments. However, Iran is not a party to CEDAW, which was adopted in 1979 by the UN General Assembly, coinciding with the abdication of the Shah and the commencement of the Islamic Revolution. The Islamic Republic of Iran's persistent refusal to ratify the convention, which seeks to safeguard the rights of women,[13] mainly finds its justifications in Islamic considerations.

In 2003, the Guardian Council[14] rejected a bill that was approved by the Parliament allowing the ratification of the international women's treaty CEDAW. Iranian scholars have reported that 'the reformist-dominated Sixth *Majles* (2000–2004) passed many bills in women's favour, though most—including the proposal to ratify the CEDAW treaty—were rejected by the Guardian Council, the unelected clerical body constitutionally empowered to vet legislation for their adherence to "Islamic" principles.'[15] According to the *New York Times*, Ibrahim Azizi, the Council's spokesper-

[11] ICCPR: http://www.unhchr.ch/html/menu3/b/a_ccpr.htm.

[12] Piscatori, 'Human Rights in Islamic Political Culture', in the Moral Imperatives of Human Rights 139, 150 (K. Thompson ed. 1980) at 151.

[13] CEDAW is the most comprehensive instrument for the protection of women's rights.

[14] See above, 40 and 45; see below, 107.

[15] See Ziba Mir-Hosseini, 'Is time on Iranian women protesters' side?', Middle East Report, 16 June 2006, available at: http://www.merip.org/mero/mero061606.html (last accessed 6 July 2007), Ziba Mir-Hosseini, 'The Conservative Reformist Conflict over women's rights in Iran', International Journal of Politics, Culture and Society, Vol. 16, No 1, Fall 2002, 37–53.

son, claimed that the bill was rejected because it went against Islamic law and was therefore unconstitutional.[16]

Pakistan

Pakistan is yet to ratify ICCPR or the Convention Against Torture (CAT), and although it is a signatory party to the ICESCR, it has yet to ratify it. The weight of the Islamic considerations cited as justification for Pakistan's abstention to the main human rights core instruments can be assessed through its 1993 Initial Report on the Convention on the Rights of the Child (CRC) in which the Government expressly linked the decision to ratify and to implement the CRC was because of the convention's compatibility with both Islam and the Constitution. It is stated in paragraph 177 of the report that 'as most of the articles of the Convention do not come into conflict with any provisions of the Constitution of Pakistan and Islamic precepts, efforts have been made to implement these provisions to the extent possible within Pakistan's socio-cultural and economic milieu'.[17] Indeed, the existence of an institutional organ that is continuously devoted to ensuring the compatibility of all existing laws with the precepts of Islam reflects the significance that is accorded to Islamic considerations.[18]

The examples above illustrate the force that Islamic considerations have had in impeding the adherence of Muslim States to the major international human rights treaties. In the next section, another aspect of the limiting effect that Islamic considerations have will be examined, namely, the tendency of Muslim countries to agree to adhere to international human rights norms but then use Islamic considerations to restrict their impact and effectiveness.

SUBSECTION TWO: RELIGIOUS CONSIDERATION AS A CENTRAL JUSTIFICATION FOR LIMITING THE IMPACT OF INTERNATIONAL HUMAN RIGHTS CONVENTIONS IN MUSLIM STATES

This section aims to identify the key trends of adherence to human rights treaties that have emerged among Muslim States. In order to enunciate a definition of the term 'reservation', the Vienna Convention on the Laws of Treaties 1996 ('VCLT') consolidated the modern regime of reservations.

16 Fathi, Nazila, *Iran's Hard-Liners Reject Reforms Bills Approved by Parliament*, The New York Times, August 14, 2003.

17 Initial Reports of States parties in 1993, Pakistan 28/05/1993, CRC/C/3/Add.13 on 28 May 1993, section V. paragraph 177, available at http://tb.ohchr.org/default.aspx?country=pk (last accessed on 16 January 2008)

18 See above, 45.

The term has been defined in Article 2(d) as a 'unilateral statement, however phrased or named, made by a state when signing, ratifying, accepting, approving or acceding to a treaty, whereby it purports to exclude or modify the legal effect of certain provisions of the treaty in their application to that state.' Article 19(c) of the VCLT provides that a state may not formulate a reservation that is incompatible with the object and purpose of the treaty. This provision reflects the view taken by the International Court of Justice in the *Reservations to the Convention on the Prevention and Punishment of the Crime of Genocide (Advisory Opinion)*,[19] where the court established a standard for ascertaining whether a reservation may be permitted, or rather prohibited, in circumstances when a treaty remains silent on this issue.

It is usually open to the drafters of an international human rights treaty to pre-arrange the regime for reservations, either by excluding the possibility of any reservations being entered at all,[20] expressly permitting them,[21] limiting their scope by imposing strict requirements of form,[22] or imposing substantial restrictions on their content.[23]

Reservations to the ICERD are permitted by Article 20 on the condition that they are not incompatible with the object and purpose of the Convention and do not inhibit the effective operation of any of the bodies established by the Convention. The Convention gives a two-third majority of the States opposing to the reservation (the 'objecting States') the power to determine when a reservation should be considered incompatible or inhibitive. Accordingly, a reservation shall be considered incompatible or inhibitive if at least two-thirds of the States parties to the Convention object to it. With regards to the ICCPR and the ICESCR, these core human rights instruments are silent on the admissibility of reservations.

CEDAW adopts the 'impermissibility principle' contained in the Vienna Convention on the Law of Treaties, where reservations are concerned. Article 28(2) states that 'a reservation incompatible with the object and purpose of the present Convention shall not be permitted'. Although the Convention does not prohibit the entering of reservations, those entered which undermine the fundamental principles of the Convention are regarded as contrary to the provisions of the Convention and international law in general. As such, other States parties may challenge them.

19 (1951) ICJ Rep 15 '*Reservations Case*'.

20 For example : Supplementary Convention on the abolition of slavery, the slave trade and institutions and practices similar to slavery, 266, U.N.T.S. 3, art.9 (1957).

21 For example: Convention on the Political Rights of Women, 193 R.T.N.U. 135, art. VII (1954).

22 For example: The European convention on Human Rights, 213 R.T.N.U. 221, Eur T.S. No 5, art. 64, (1955).

23 For example International Convention on the Elimination of All Forms of Racial Discrimination and CEDAW.

Article 28 of the CAT states that it is possible for State parties to make reservations with respect to certain articles of the Convention, provided the reservations are made at the time of ratification or accession. However, such reservations must not be incompatible with the object and purpose of the Convention.

Article 51 of CRC governs the regime of reservations and it expressly provides for the possibility of entering reservations whilst still specifying in paragraph (2) that 'a reservation incompatible with the object and purpose of the present convention shall not be permitted'.

It is important to describe the nature of the reservations made by Muslim countries to each of the relevant international instruments addressed in this study. An analysis focused on the actual substance of the reservations made by Muslim States required the consideration of two legal points: (1) the extent to which this practice undermines the legislative function of the treaties; and (2) the extent to which Islamic considerations invoked to justify the reservations constitute a genuine ground for these limitations.

This section focuses on the practice of entering reservations to the main human rights instruments as undertaken by Muslim countries with the aim of identifying the different patterns in the formulation of those reservations, and measuring the extent to which Islamic considerations represent the ultimate justification of such limitations. In this regard, an overview of the different patterns of citing Sharia law in the reservations will be described in Part A, and an assessment of its use by Muslim States as justification for not fully observing their obligations will follow in Part B.

A. Trends in the use of reservations

It is possible to identify three distinct trends when it comes to the entering of reservations to international human rights instruments by Muslim countries. First is acceding to treaties without entering reservations at all; second is acceding to treaties by entering a general reservation of very broad scope; and third is finally acceding to treaties by lodging precise reservations made to exclude certain provisions of the treaty.

1. Acceding to treaties without entering reservations

The first trend occurs where Muslim countries adhere to their human rights commitments under the international conventions without entering any reservations to them. It is often possible to isolate two patterns that occur within this category. The first occurs where States adhere to an international convention without restricting its legislative impact because they deem the provisions contained in that instrument as reflective of an aim that they wish to pursue or support. In this case the State in question will endeavour to take all appropriate measures necessary to align their domestic practice with the convention standard, even if this requires a review of the internal set of norms. The second pattern depicts States that adhere to human rights treaties without imposing any a priori limitations to their undertaking, but this act does not correspond with a genuine will to implement the treaty. Rather, it can be seen as a mechanical approach of acceptance of the international provision without a sincere consideration of the real implication of this engagement. Usually, in this category the implementation of the treaty never takes place and adherence to it would be considered a merely symbolic and diplomatic gesture, and this would attest to the fragility and difficulty of imposing international law on States generally.

The first pattern may be illustrated by the following examples. Bahrain has ratified ICCPR without formulating any reservations limiting the scope of its engagement with these conventions; Egypt to CERD and CAT; Iran to ICERD, ICCPR and ICESCR; Lebanon to ICCPR, ICESCR, CAT and CRC; Morocco to ICCPR and ICESCR; Pakistan to ICERD; and Tunisia to ICERD, ICCPR and ICESCR. These States do not always adhere to human rights conventions without entering reservations against them but have done so, at least, for the conventions stated above.

The second pattern depicts those States that almost always adhere to these instruments although with some exceptions. Because this second pattern is widespread in the practice of Muslim countries generally, it is important to highlight a few examples. Some countries that have adhered to the ICERD, ICCPR, ICESCR, CEDAW, CAT and CRC without reserving any provisions include Benin, Burkina Faso, Cote d'Ivoire, Chad, Kyrgyzstan, Nigeria, Tajikistan, Togo, Sierra Leone, and Senegal. Yemen has made technical and political reservations that do not affect the substance of the norms in these international instruments. For this topic it is appropriate to analyse the extent to which the observation of human rights conventions that are ratified without the entry of reservations culminates in a precise application of these instruments on the internal level, with a view to comparing the legal implications of the different State practice in both the accession phase as well as in domestic practice and implementation. The sub-Saharan African countries have signed CEDAW without entering any reservations against it. However, it has been argued that this willingness to accede to the Convention without fettering its effectiveness has not, generally speaking, translated into the African governments taking a more activist stance on matters of women's rights.[24]

The Nigerian experience in this area, as exemplified by the numerous reports conducted by international organizations on the human rights violations occurring in this country, demonstrate that these accessions to

[24] see Callaway and Greevy, 1989.

the international conventions in reality often pay little more than lip-service to the intention behind the norms contained therein. The internal practice of the State reflects the gap[25] between the text itself and the reality of the text's implementation, simultaneously exposing the weakness of enforcement measures in international law generally.[26] The establishment of Sharia courts in 12 of the northern states[27] which exercise jurisdiction over criminal matters and impose harsh punishments, undermine some of the most basic rights of citizens. Punishments include amputations and flogging for theft or alcohol consumption and the death penalty for extra-marital sexual relations.[28] The furore that surrounded the recent presidential elections that were held in April 2007 is another example of the fundamental civil and political rights of citizens being violated. The election was marred by reports of violence and fraud, and reported incidents in the Dutsi municipality included voting stations being closed early while queues of people still remained and ballot boxes and papers being re-diverted to the home of the local government chairman.[29]

In his study on the impact of international human rights treaties on State practices, Hathaway[30] explains that a country's expression of commitment to the treaty's goals need not be consistent with the country's actual course of action. In fact, he contends that the process of treaty ratification might even sometimes be associated with worse human rights practices than otherwise expected. For the author, countries that take the relatively uncompromising step of treaty ratification may thereby offset the pressure of having to make costly changes in policies, with monitoring and enforcement usually being minimal.

2. *Acceding to treaties by entering a general reservation of generally broad scope*

The second category in this section refers to Muslim States which adhere to human rights treaties but compromise their effectiveness with the

25 See below, 102 et seq.

26 ibid.

27 Human Rights Watch report, ' Nigeria, Under Islamic law, rights still unprotected', 21 September 2004, available at http://hrw.org/english/docs/2004/09/21/nigeri9364.htm (last accessed 4 July 2007).

28 Human Rights Watch report, 'Political Sharia?' Human Rights and Islamic Law in Northern Nigeria, Vol. 16, No. 9(A) September 2004, available at http://www.hrw.org/reports/2004/nigeria0904/index.htm (last accessed 4 July 2007).

29 In this regard, see Chris Albin-Lackey and Ben Rawlence, 'What's Next for Nigeria? The Whole Concept of African Democracy is at Risk', *Guardian Unlimited*, 8 May 2007, available at http://commentisfree.guardian.co.uk/chris_albinlackey_and_ben_rawlence/2007/05/whats_next_for_nigeria.html (last accessed 4 July 2007).

30 Oona A Hathaway, 'Do Human Rights treaties make a difference', Yale Law Journal, 26 April 2002, 1941.

implementation of very broad and sweeping reservations. Before we consider this trend in depth, it is important to assess the role of reservations in international law.

Theoretically presented as a legitimate means by which to account for the diversity that occurs across the international community, the concept of reservations, and particularly reservations to human rights treaties, is a controversial one. They raise the fundamental problem of whether such limitations in international law are desirable, or indeed, lawful. The issue of the general legitimacy of reservations, particularly with regards to human rights treaties, does not fall within the scope of this study though a considerable volume of academic debate has been generated in this field.[31] A significant number of scholars have devoted their attention to this topic and have addressed the issue of reservations in relation to the different international human rights instruments, particularly the women's convention[32], the child's convention[33] and the Covenant on Civil and Political Rights.[34]

The Vienna Convention on the Law of Treaties does not distinguish between different categories of treaties. It establishes rules on reservations to treaties without taking into consideration the very specific nature of human rights treaties, which aim to create an objective and normative regime for the protection of human rights in which, according to Clark, 'the obligations incumbent upon a State party are not reciprocal obligations owed to the other States parties but unilateral obligations owed to citizens of that state party'. [35] The vague and broad nature that characterise some of the most notorious reservations is an issue that has been addressed by many scholars. Although the human rights instruments being considered here do not explicitly prohibit general reservations, as is the case with the

[31] Catherine Logan Piper, 'Reservations to multilateral treaties: the goal of universality', Iowa Law Review, October 1985.

[32] In this regard, see notably Rebecca J Cook, 'Reservations to the Convention on the Elimination of All Forms of Discrimination against Women', Virg. JIL, volume 30, (1990), 643–716 at 644; Belinda Clark, 'The Vienna Convention reservations regime and the convention on discrimination against women', 85 AJIL 281–321 (1991), Jane Connors, 'The women's convention in the Muslim world', in Human Rights as General Norms and a State's Right to Opt Out (BIICL, 1997, 85–103; Cook & Stoot, Memorandum: Re Reservations to the Convention on the Elimination of all forms of discrimination against women, International women's rights action watch (Jan 5, 1987).

[33] In this regard, see Lawrence J Leblanc, 'Reservations to the Convention on the Rights of the Child : A Macroscopic View of State Practice', The International Journal of Children's Rights 4, 357–381 (Kluwer Law International, 1996); D O'Donnell, 'The Reservation Generation', International Children's Rights Monitor 1992 (9), 8–14; William A Schabas, 'Reservations to the Convention on the Rights of the Child', Human Rights Quarterly 18 (1996) 472–491 (Johns Hopkins University Press, 1996) 478.

[34] In this regard see Konstantin Korkelia, 'New Challenges to the Regime of Reservations under the International Covenant on Civil and Political Rights', European Journal of International Law, April 2002.

[35] Belinda Clark (n 32) 287.

European Convention on Human Rights as entrenched in Article 64, it may be conceivably argued that these reservations affect the application of every provision of the Convention and deprive other parties, States, committees and, most importantly, the individuals that they seek to protect, from being able to accurately define the obligations of the reserving States.

As shall be shortly demonstrated, Muslim States often employ reservations that are far too general and subsequently have a drastic limiting effect on their obligation to international human rights treaties. This in turn casts doubt on the sincerity of their commitment to the object and purpose of the international instrument, an issue that persists in the different objections to such reservations. Some scholars have not hesitated in criticising such reservations as effectively constituting a total absence of ratification[36] or even making a legal nonsense of ratification.[37]

An illustration of this practice includes Djibouti's reservation to the CRC. It is a very broad reservation and it states that 'the government of Djibouti shall not consider itself bound by any provisions or articles that are incompatible with its religion and its traditional values.'[38]

Similarly, the reservation made to this Convention by Indonesia begins by asserting that the Constitution guarantees the fundamental rights of the child irrespective of their sex, ethnicity or race and prescribes those rights to be implemented by national laws and regulations. Following these clarifications, the Indonesian reservation then broadly states that 'the ratification of the Convention on the Rights of the Child by the Republic of Indonesia does not imply the acceptance of obligations going beyond the constitutional limits nor the acceptance of any obligation to introduce any right beyond those prescribed under the constitution'.

Other States such as Iran in its accession to the CRC asserted that it 'reserves the right not to comply with any provisions or Articles of the Convention that are incompatible with Islamic laws and the internal legislation in effect.'[39] Similarly, Pakistan's reservation to CEDAW which provides that 'the accession of the government of the Islamic Republic of Pakistan to the said convention is subject to the provisions of the Constitution of the Islamic Republic of Pakistan',[40] is also extremely broad. Equally are Pakistan's initial reservations to the Children's Convention which states that 'provisions of the convention shall be interpreted in the

36 William A. Schabas, 'Reservations to the Convention on the Rights of the Child', Human Rights Quarterly 18 (1996) 472–491, by the John Hopkins University Press, 1996, p. 478.

37 Jenny Kuper, 'Reservations, declarations and objections to the 1989 Convention on the Rights of the Child', in Human Rights as general norms and a state's right to opt out (BIICL, 1997) 108.

38 http://www2.ohchr.org/english/bodies/ratification/11.htm#reservations.

39 http://www2.ohchr.org/english/bodies/ratification/11.htm#reservations.

40 Available to view online at http://www2.ohchr.org.org/english/bodies/ratification/8.htm (last accessed 17 January 2008).

light of the principles of Islamic law and values'.[41] The expression, 'Islamic laws and values', is so vague and potentially infinite that it is difficult to define exactly what the parameters of Pakistan's obligations under the CRC are.

The nature of Saudi Arabia's reservations also illustrates the trend of formulating far-reaching reservations attributed to Sharia which affect the entire set of rules in the treaty, thus making it impossible for other actors to identify the scope of its adherence to the international instrument. An example of this is Saudi Arabia's reservation to ICERD[42] which states that 'the government of Saudi Arabia declares that it will implement the provisions of the above convention, providing these do not conflict with the precepts of the Islamic Sharia'.[43] Saudi Arabia limits its engagement to the CRC by providing that it enters 'reservations with respect to all such articles as are in conflict with the provisions of Islamic law'. Finally, the same attitude ought to be noted with regard to CEDAW, where Saudi Arabia makes it very clear that 'in case of contradiction between any term of the convention and the norms of Islamic law, the Kingdom is not under obligation to observe the contradictory terms of the convention'.

Furthermore, the legal implications of these broad and vague reservations to the applicable scope of the elementary and incontrovertible norms of public international law permits a grave uncertainty over the sincerity of these countries when they claim to adhere to the international conventions to which such reservations are entered. Yet, certainty and good faith are of the most fundamental principles of international law and constitute an indivisible and indispensable part of its rules.[44] The principle of good faith is enshrined in Article 2(2) of the Charter of the United Nations and states that 'all Members, in order to ensure to all of them the rights and benefits resulting from membership, shall fulfil in good faith the obligations assumed by them in accordance with the present charter'. It has been defined in Article 26 of the Vienna Convention as a guiding principle to the interpretation and implementation of treaties, stating that 'every treaty in force is binding upon the parties to it and must be performed by them in good faith', and further still in Article 31, which stipulates that 'a treaty shall be interpreted in good faith in accordance with the ordinary meaning to be given to the terms of the treaty in their context and in the light of its object and purpose.'

41 Available to view online at http://www2.ohchr.org/english/bodies/ratification/11.htm (last accessed 17 January 2008).

42 Committee for the Elimination of Racial Discrimination.

43 http://www2.ohchr.org/english/bodies/ratification/2.htm#reservations.

44 In this regard, see E Zoller, Bonne foi en droit international public, Paris, 1977; H. Thirlway, 'The Law and Procedure of the International Court of Justice', 60 BYIL, 1989, 3, 7; G Fitzmaurice, The Law and Procedure of the International Court of Justice (CUP, Cambridge, 1986), vol. I, p. 183 and vol. II, p. 609.

Just as the principle of *pacta sunt servanda* in the law of treaties is based on good faith,[45] the adherence of States to treaties is naturally governed by the same principle. Malcolm N Shaw[46] states that the principle of good faith is a background principle informing and shaping not only the observance of existing rules of international law, but also setting a framework for the adherence to new rules of international law whilst also constraining the manner in which those rules may legitimately be exercised.

Eminent legal academics have declared that a State's action of ratifying a treaty while attaching an illegal condition to it constitutes a 'patent contradiction'.[47] Furthermore, even if the practice of making reservations to treaties has been tolerated and become legally acceptable—in recognition of the 'important and legitimate role for reservations to treaties'[48]—the systematic use of vague and sweeping reservations would not be considered a proper exercise of a legitimate right but rather, an abuse of that right (*abus de droit*). It has been argued that 'the principle of good faith which governs international relations controls also the exercise of rights by states'.[49] This indicates that the exercise of a right 'for the purpose of evading either a rule of law or a contractual obligation will not be tolerated'.[50]

The International Court of Justice has clarified that good faith as a concept is 'not in itself a source of obligation where none would otherwise exist'.[51] However, the principle of good faith has been acknowledged by the UN-appointed 'Committee for the Elimination of all kinds of Discrimination against Women' which considered in its statement on the subject that those State parties that have entered reservations to the Convention have certain options open to them. According to the Special Rapporteur appointed by the International Law Commission to report on the law and practice relating to reservations to treaties, a State party may either, (a) after having examined the finding *in good faith*, maintain its reservation; (b) withdraw its reservation; (c) 'regularise' its situation by replacing its impermissible reservation with a permissible reservation; or finally (d) renounce its intention of being a party to the treaty.'[52]

[45] See Nuclear Test cases, ICJ Reports, 1974, 253, 267; 57 ILR, 398, 412.

[46] See Malcolm N Shaw, International Law (4th edn, Cambridge University Press, 1997) 82.

[47] Derek W. Bowett, 'Reservations to Non-Restricted Multilateral Treaties', 48, British Yearbook of International Law 67 (1976–1977) at 76.

[48] See Effective implementation of international instruments on human rights, including reporting obligations under international instruments on human rights, UN Doc. A/47/628, paragraph 60 (1992).

[49] See Bin Cheng, General Principles of Law as Applied by International Courts and Tribunals (Stevens & Sons Ltd, london, 1953) 121.

[50] ibid 123.

[51] See *The Border and Transborder Armed Actions case* (Nicaragua v. Honduras), ICJ Reports, 1988, 105; 84 ILR, 218.

[52] See Report of the Committee on the Elimination of Discrimination Against Women,

The third trend includes Muslim countries that adhere to human rights treaties but limit their engagement by entering precise reservations.

3. *Acceding to treaties with precise reservations made to exclude certain provisions*

The focus on specific provisions of a convention not only indicates that an effort has been made to identify precisely the obstacles impeding the full implementation of the convention by the State, but it also puts the other protagonists—individuals, NGOs, States, committees, and the United Nations, in a position where they may establish the basis on which to deal with the concerned States and their reservations.

Bearing in mind that the ultimate status of the reservation is meant to be temporary and give the State time to align its internal system with the requirements of the reserved provisions before they are withdrawn, an analysis of these reservations reveal that those that are broad in nature, as previously considered,[53] are significantly more difficult to remove or withdraw than those that are definite and precise.[54]

This third trend is not in itself homogenous as it encompasses two kinds of practices. In the first group, reservations are demarcated and precise in form but their impact remains very broad, while in the second, reservations are precise not only in form but also in substance.

(i) A formal delimitation

We ought to distinguish between two further patterns within this group. The first incorporates a precise reservation which affects the core subject of the treaty and therefore whose validity is thrown into doubt. The second represents an accumulation of seemingly innocuous reservations but whose cumulative effect is problematic.

An apt illustration of the first pattern may be seen with the reservations that have been lodged by some Muslim countries to provisions in CEDAW, namely Articles 2 and 16 of the Convention. Article 2 condemns discrimination against women in all its forms and provides that State parties should 'agree to pursue, by all appropriate means and without delay a policy of eliminating discrimination against women', by undertaking constitutional, legislative, administrative, and other measures. Article 16 is dedicated to the institution of marriage and family relations and seeks to establish equality between men and women in entering into marriage, during marriage,

Eighteenth and Nineteenth sessions, United Nations, New York, 1998, A/53/38/Rev. 1, p. 49, paragraph 18, available at http://www.un.org/womenwatch/daw/cedaw/reports/18report.pdf (last accessed 6 July 2007).

[53] See above 67.

[54] See below 77.

and upon the dissolution of marriage. For the latter, Article 16 stresses that the same rights be afforded to both parents in all matters relating to their children. The countries that have entered reservations to Article 2 and Article 16 of CEDAW include Bahrain, Egypt, Lebanon, Malaysia and Morocco.[55]

Several Western States have objected to these reservations on the grounds that they are incompatible with the object and purpose of CEDAW. Taking as an illustration the objections made to Bahrain's reservations, it is worth highlighting the reactions of some European States. For example, the Government of Finland noted in its objection that the reservations concerned targeted some of the most essential provisions of the Convention and had the effect of excluding some of the fundamental obligations owed under it, therefore contradicting the object and purpose of the Convention. In the same sense, the government of the Netherlands, recalling that Article 28(2) of CEDAW provides that a reservation which is incompatible with the object and the purpose of the Convention shall not be permitted, considered:

> ... that the reservations with respect to Articles 2 and 16 of the convention, concerning the Islamic Sharia of Bahrain, reservations which seek to limit the responsibilities of the reserving State under the convention by invoking the Islamic Sharia, may raise doubt as to the commitment of this State to the object and purpose of the convention and moreover, contribute to undermining the basis of international treaty law.[56]

It would be cumbersome to recall all of the objections that were made, but they all followed the same rationale and were large in number. Some of the notable objections included that of Mexico to Egypt's reservations to Articles 2 and 16 of CEDAW, along with Sweden to Egypt, and the Netherlands to Morocco.[57]

The Committee's taking of a firm and forceful stance on the matter of reservations and the resulting problems caused has been very gradual. In the first years of CEDAW's entry into force, the committee failed to directly address the issue of reservations and this enabled the continuance of the de facto ambiguity and obscurity surrounding them. The existence of much tension and protest on this subject, notably between Muslim and Western States, has obliged the Committee to avoid issuing an unequivocal condemnation of this practice. Instead, it has called for strict compliance of

55 On 6 February 1998, the Government of Malaysia withdraws its reservation in respect of article 2(f), 9(1), 16(b), 16(d), 16(e) and 16(h). But it is still reserving on Article 16 (1) (a) (c) (f) and (2).

56 http://www2.ohchr.org/english/bodies/ratification/8.htm#declarations.

57 http://www2.ohchr.org/english/bodies/ratification/8.htm#declarations.

the Convention in its report of 1986.[58] The Committee went a step further in 1987 when it expressed its concern about 'the significant number of reservations that appeared to be incompatible with the object and purpose of the convention'.[59] In 2004 the Committee finally took a firm position on the validity of reservations, stating that those entered with regard to Articles 2 and 16 of CEDAW are impermissible and should be withdrawn.

With regards to Article 2, the Committee states that:

> It is central to the objects and purpose of the Convention. State parties which ratify the Convention do so because they agree that discrimination against women in all its forms should be condemned and that the strategies set out in Article 2, subparagraphs (a) to (g), should be implemented by State parties to eliminate it.[60]

Where Article 16 is concerned, the Committee stated that 'neither traditional, religious nor cultural practice or incompatible domestic laws and policies can justify violations of the Convention'. The Committee also 'remains convinced that reservations to Article 16, whether lodged for national, traditional, religious or cultural reasons, are incompatible with the Convention and therefore impermissible and should be reviewed and modified or withdrawn'.[61]

Therefore, it is the Committee's view that reservations to these two articles should be considered as incompatible with the object and purpose of the Convention.[62] In light of this statement, the validity of reservations entered against Article 2 or Article 16 by Morocco, Malaysia,[63] Lebanon, Bahrain and Egypt are considered as impermissible reservations, despite being specific reservations which targeted precise provisions in the Convention. The same observation could be made of Turkey's ratification before it withdrew its reservations on Articles 15 and 16. The statement of the Committee is currently very clear with regard to the validity of reservations to both articles.

[58] GA Res. 41/108 (Dec. 4, 1986).

[59] General recommendation 4, Report of the Committee on the Elimination of discrimination against women, Sixth Session, 42 UN GAOR Supp. (No 38), para. 579, UN Doc. A/42/38 (1987).

[60] http://www.un.org/womenwatch/daw/cedaw/reservations.htm.

[61] http://www.un.org/womenwatch/daw/cedaw/reservations.htm.

[62] See Committee on the Elimination of Discrimination Against Women, 'Statement to commemorate the twenty-fifth anniversary of the adoption of the Convention on the Elimination of All Forms of Discrimination against Women', 13 October 2004, United Nations, available at: http://www.un.org/womenwatch/daw/cedaw/cedaw25anniversary/statement/CEDAW%20statement%20E.pdf (last accessed 9 July 2007).

[63] On 6 February 1998, the Government of Malaysia withdraws its reservation in respect of article 2(f), 9(1), 16(b), 16(d), 16(e) and 16(h). But it is still reserving on Article 16 (1) (a) (c) (f) and (2).

It also happens that an accumulation of many reservations to an international instrument could render them incompatible with its object and purpose.[64] Although each reservation when considered separately would not present any suspicion, the cumulative use of reservations by the State within one convention would generate concerns as to their validity. On this matter, Belinda Clarke argues that 'a larger number of limited, specific reservations (that singly do not create major conflict with the provisions of the convention) might produce so many derogations from the treaty that, taken as a whole, they would be incompatible with its object and purpose'.[65]

Generally, the reservations entered by Muslim countries either do not belong to this category for they are so general that they target the entire set of provisions in the treaty, or the reservations apply to articles which constitute the core subject of the instrument. However, it is debatable whether the reservations of Algeria to the Convention on the Rights of the Child would fall into this category. Upon ratification on 16 April 1993, Algeria made reservations on the following provisions: Article 13, Article 14 (1) and (2), Article 16 and Article 17. The formulation of a reservation on any one of these articles individually would not have been problematic. However, by simultaneously reserving against articles related to freedom of expression, freedom of thought, conscience and religion, the right to privacy, family, home and correspondence, the right to the protection of the law, and the right of the child to have access to information, provokes doubt over the Algerian government's real intention of acceding to this instrument. Similarly, cumulative reservations to the ICESCR made by Bangladesh and affecting the provisions of Articles 1, 2, 3, 7, 8, 10 and 13, belong to this same category.

The following section will demonstrate that reservations can be very specific in their substance, thus constituting a material delimitation of very definite scope.

(ii) A material delimitation of definite scope

This category of reservations targets the precise provisions of international instruments. They have a specific scope which does not go beyond the articles targeted by the State's limitations. These reservations do not affect the entire set of norms assessed in the instrument, they remain relatively

[64] In this regard see Belinda Clark, 'The Vienna Convention Reservations Regime and the Convention on Discrimination against Women', American Journal of International law, April 1991, 22, para 7.

[65] Belinda Clark, The Vienna Convention Reservations Regime and the Convention on the Elimination of Discrimination against Women', April 2001, American Journal of International Law, 22, para 7.

limited, and they do not erode the substance of the international human rights instruments.

Typically, all technical reservations belong to this category, but it is much more interesting to analyse the substantive reservations that could be considered more precise. Formulating limited and precise reservations usually puts other State parties and the UN institutions and committees to the instrument in a better position to deal with the reserving State: they can usually set their own positions with respect to the reservation in full knowledge of its scope, content and implications. Hence, theoretically, this category is the most politically correct amongst all the different forms of limitations to international human rights instruments. The World Conference on Human Rights that was held in Vienna in June 1993 encourages States to consider limiting the extent of any reservations they lodge to international human rights instruments, and to formulate any reservations as precisely and narrowly as possible. This is to ensure that none are incompatible with the object and purpose of the relevant treaty, while also regularly reviewing any reservations with a view to withdrawing them.[66] The CEDAW Committee has also emphasized that reservations must be formulated as precisely and as narrowly as possible, and regularly reviewed with a view to withdrawing them.[67]

It has been argued that any reservation entered against a provision of a human rights treaty is unlawful on principle because the entire set of provisions in the treaty is essential to its 'object and purpose'. This stream of thought usually employs the argument that the reservations that were tolerated in the ICJ's advisory opinion[68] on the Convention for the Prevention and Punishment of the Crime of Genocide were very precise and very technical. The reservations subject to the controversy concerned the competence of the ICJ to consider complaints made by one State against another with respect to violations of the Convention, which were not of a substantive nature at all. A more hard-line approach rejects the use of reservations in any instance, whether substantive, technical or administrative. In his individual dissenting opinion to the ICJ's advisory opinion, Judge M Alvarez took an even stricter approach to the issue of reservations, expressing his dissatisfaction with the view that reservations may be valid if accepted by all Contracting States, as well as the view adopted by the Court, that reservations would be inadmissible if contrary to the object and purpose of the treaty. He argued that:

66 Vienna Declaration and Programme of Action, U.N. Doc. A/CONF.157/24ch.III (1993), Pt 1 (1994), reprinted in 14 Hum Rts LJ 352, 357.

67 See the Committee's statement on reservations, A/53/38/Rev.1, 47–50.

68 *Advisory Opinion on Reservations to the Convention on the Prevention and Punishment of the Crime of Genocide* 1951 ICJ 15, 28 May 1951.

> States making reservations could argue that their reservations were not in conflict with the aim of the Convention, while States objecting to the reservations might allege the opposite. And, when one realizes that in this event it would be the duty of the International Court of Justice to settle the dispute, this tribunal will find itself so overburdened with controversies of this nature that its functions would be utterly distorted. The best solution would be to establish plainly that reservations are inadmissible in the four categories of multilateral conventions which have been mentioned ...[69]

He also laid emphasis on the 'universal character' of certain types of multilateral treaties[70] that 'impose obligations upon States without granting them rights, and in this respect are unlike ordinary multilateral conventions which confer rights as well as obligations upon their parties.'[71]

In any respect, the reservations that fall into this 'legitimate' category as described above do not tend to be the sort of reservation relied upon by Muslim countries. As seen above, the large majority of reservations made by Muslim States are usually either conceived in such broad terms that they affect the entire set of norms in the treaty or they target limited provisions which undermine the main subject and purpose of the human rights convention. However, reservations belonging to this category can be seen in the practice of a few Muslim countries, for example as with the reservations to Article 20 of the Convention on the Rights of the Child that were entered by Egypt[72] and Jordan on the ground of the specificity of Sharia, namely the incompatibility of the institution of adoption with Islamic precepts.

Articles 20 and 21 of the CRC address the institution of adoption. The first Article governs cases where children are deprived of a family environment and obliges State parties to ensure alternative care for those children, stipulating that such care could include adoption. The second Article is more direct in assessing the institution of adoption, providing that children have the right to care and protection when they are adopted and that the first concern should be the best interests of the child. In addition, it states

69 1951 I.C.J. 15, 32.

70 Judge Alvarez listed the four following types of multilateral treaties possessing universal character: '(a) those which seek to develop world international organization or to establish regional organizations, such as the European organization which is of such great present-day interest; (b) those which seek to determine the territorial status of certain States; such conventions have existed in Europe since the beginning of the XIXth century, and have constituted what may be called 'European public law'; (c) conventions which seek to establish new and important principles of international law; (d) conventions seeking to regulate matters of a social or humanitarian interest with a view to improving the position of individuals.'

71 1951 I.C.J. 15, 29.

72 Withdrawn in July 2003 This is important to note in the body because it shows that the more liberal Muslim states are reconsidering their reservations and can be held up as a example to those states that are more belligerent with their use of reservations.

that the same rights and safeguards should be ensured whether the adoption takes place in the country where the children are born or they are taken to live in another country.

Although having the same scope, these two reservations have not been received in the same way by other non-Muslim States. While Egypt's reservations to the provisions on adoption have not been echoed by any objections from other States, the reservations formulated by Jordan to the same articles have been objected to by Finland, Ireland and Sweden. The Egyptian reservation reads as follows:

> Since the Islamic Sharia is one of the fundamental source of legislation in Egyptian positive law and because the Sharia, in enjoining the provision of every means of protection and care for children by numerous ways and means, does not include among those ways and means the system of adoption existing in certain other bodies of positive law, the government of the Arab Republic of Egypt expresses its reservation with respect to all the clauses and provisions relating to adoption in the said convention, and in particular with respect to the provisions governing adoption in articles 20 and 21 of the convention.[73]

The reservation formulated by the Government of Jordan provides that:

> [T]he Hashemite Kingdom of Jordan expresses its reservation and does not consider itself bound by articles 14, 20 and 21 of the Convention, which grant the child the right to freedom of choice of religions and concern the question of adoption, since they are at variance with the precepts of the tolerant Islamic Sharia.[74]

While Egypt has taken the time to clarify the reason behind its reservation, Jordan has kept its reasons vague.

On 9 June 1993, the Secretary-General received the following communication from the Government of Finland:

> The Government of Finland has examined the contents of the reservation made by Jordan [...]. In the view of the Government of Finland's communication, this reservation is subject to the general principle of treaty interpretation according to which a party may not invoke general principles of national law as justification for failure to perform its treaty obligations. For the above reason the Government of Finland objects to the said reservations. However, the Government of Finland does not

[73] http://www2.ohchr.org/english/bodies/ratification/11.htm#reservations.
[74] http://www2.ohchr.org/english/bodies/ratification/11.htm#reservations.

consider that this objection constitutes an obstacle to the entry into force of the said Convention between Finland and Jordan.

This kind of precise reservation has the advantage to facilitate correspondence between the reserving State and the international human rights monitoring bodies because it localises it in a specific and well-delineated framework.

Following this illustration of the three main patterns evident in treaty reservations, the following section will analyse and assess the use of Sharia as a justification for the lodging of such reservations.

B. Assessing the use of the Sharia as a justification for reservations

States that have used Sharia as a justification for their reservations have been criticised by both objecting States and a number of scholars. Critics have mainly called into question these reservations because of the seemingly vague nature of Sharia law itself. In this regard, France has complained that the Government of Bahrain's reservation to CEDAW grounded in the Sharia was of 'general and indeterminate scope', such that it is not possible to ascertain which obligations under the Convention were going to be effected. Denmark made it clear that the reason they objected to Bahrain's and Pakistan's reservations to CEDAW was due to 'the provisions of Islamic Sharia [which] is of unlimited scope and undefined character.' Norway's objection to the reservations made by Saudi Arabia, which provides that the norms of Islamic Law shall prevail in the event of conflict with the provisions of CEDAW, also expressed concern with the characteristics of Sharia. The same grounds can be identified in the objections of Western countries to the reservations made by Muslim States to the provisions of the CRC. This was the case in the objections made by Finland[75] and Germany to the reservations made by Iran.[76]

It is the habitual practice of Muslim States to cite Sharia as justification for their limited acceptance of international human rights instruments without

[75] The government of Finland objected to Iran's reservation to the Convention on the Rights of the Child on 5 September 1995. The objection reads as follows: 'In the view of the Government of Finland this reservation is subject to the general principle of treaty interpretation according to which a party may not invoke the provisions of its internal law as justification for failure to perform a treaty. For the above reason the Government of Finland objects to the said reservation.'

[76] Germany notified the Secretary General of its objection to Iran's reservation on 11 August 1995. The objection reads as follows: 'This reservation, owing to its indefinite nature, does not meet the requirements of international law. The Government of the Federal Republic of Germany therefore objects to the reservation made by [Iran (Islamic Republic)].' Objection entered on 11 August 1995. Available to view at the Office of the United Nations High Commissioner for Human Rights: http://www2.ohchr.org/english/bodies/ratification/11.htm#reservations (last accessed on 23 January 2008).

isolating and identifying the specific Islamic norm that is perceived to be in conflict with the reserved provisions. Referring to Sharia in general without giving any substantive indications as to its content puts all the protagonists (other States parties, UN Committees, International Human Rights bodies, Human rights advocates, etc.) in a difficult position in knowing how to deal with this broad and undefined subject. In this regard, the reservations made by the Government of Saudi Arabia to CEDAW and the objections of the Government of Ireland reflects the perplexity of international actors when faced with such claims:

> *(...) the Government of Ireland is of the view that a reservation which consists of a general reference to religious law without specifying the content thereof* and which does not clearly specify the provisions of the Convention to which it applies and the extent of the derogation therefrom, *may cast doubts on the commitment of the reserving State to fulfil its obligations under the Convention.* The Government of Ireland is furthermore of the view that such a general reservation may undermine the basis of international treaty law.[77]

States that objected to the reservations made by the Government of Iran to the CRC included: Austria, Denmark, Finland, Germany, Ireland, Italy, Netherlands, Norway, Portugal and Sweden. The Austrian government was very precise and specific in its objection, but none of these States went so far as to remove itself from treaty relations with Iran, the reserving State. The Government of Austria's objection demonstrates the extent of the unease State parties feel towards reservations being made based on Islamic Sharia, which is of indefinite scope, and feels incapable of assessing the admissibility of such broad reservations without further clarification from the reserving State. The Austrian objection provides that:

> Under Article 19 of the Vienna Convention on the Law of the Treaties which is reflected in Article 51 of the Convention on the Rights of the Child, a reservation, in order to be admissible under international law, has to be compatible with the object and purpose of the treaty concerned. A reservation is incompatible with the object and purpose of a treaty if it intends to derogate provisions the implementation of which is essential to fulfilling its objects and purpose.

[77] This objection was entered on 2 October 2001 by Ireland in response to the reservation entered by Saudi Arabia to the Convention on the Elimination of All Forms of Discrimination Against Women. Available to view online at the Office of the High Commissioner for Human Rights: http://www2.ohchr.org/english/bodies/ratification/8_2.htm (last accessed on 23 January 2008).

> The Government of Austria has examined the reservation made by the Islamic Republic of Iran. Given the general character of this reservation a final assessment as to its admissibility under international law cannot be made without further clarification.
>
> Until the scope of the legal effects of this reservation is sufficiently specified by the Islamic Republic of Iran, the Government of Austria considers this reservation as not affecting any provision the implementation of which is essential to fulfilling the object and purpose of the convention.
>
> Austria, however, objects to the admissibility of the reservation in question if the application of this reservation negatively affects the compliance by the Islamic Republic of Iran with its obligations under the convention essential for fulfilment of its object and purpose.
>
> Austria could not consider the reservation made by the Islamic Republic of Iran as admissible under the regime of Article 51 of the Convention and Article 19 of the Vienna convention on the Law of treaties unless Iran, by providing additional information or through subsequent practice ensures that the reservation is compatible with the provisions essential for the implementation of the object and purpose of the convention.[78]

Belinda Clark elucidates further:

> There is considerable scope for different judgments about the nature and extent of conflict between the Sharia and the convention, their interpretation or application of the Sharia may differ considerably from that of the reserving state. Only the reserving state knows what its reservation means. It is not a stated requirement that a reservation be specific, but ex post facto demonstrations of incompatibility mean that imprecise reservations 'cheat' the requirements of the Vienna Convention since the Article 19(c) test cannot be applied. This consequence undermines that regime in general, as well as the particular treaty to which reservations pertain.[79]

[78] Austria's objection to the reservation entered by Iran to the Convention on the Rights of the Child was made on 6 September 1995. Available to view at the Office of the United Nations High Commissioner for Human Rights: http://www.bayefsky.com/html/austria_t2_crc.php (last accessed on 23 January 2008).

[79] Belinda Clark, The Vienna Convention Reservations Regime and the Convention on Discrimination Against Women , *The American Journal of International Law*, Vol. 85, No. 2 (Apr., 1991), 310–311.

CONCLUSION

Whilst three main patterns of Muslim State practice on reservations to human rights treaties have been identified, the same incoherencies and paradoxes exist as those in relation to the very ratification of treaties themselves. This is especially so when it comes to general reservations of broad scope, which certainly raises suspicions as to the real intentions of the State party. The same causes for concern also arise in relation to both specific reservations which limit the core subject of the treaty, and an accumulation of individually innocuous reservations which result in compromising the very object and purpose of the treaty. Unfortunately, the only types of reservation that are truly responsible, ie those that target precise provisions of definite scope, are the least common among Muslim States. Moreover, as demonstrated above, when Sharia is used to justify certain reservations, it too fails to provide any real insight into the reasoning behind reservations or the scope of their effect.

Section Two The Relative Impact of the Sharia on the Ratification Process of International Human Rights Treaties

The influence which Sharia wields during the phase of acceding to human rights treaties is neither exclusive nor exhaustive. However, Sharia is not solely accountable for all of the possible reasons that justify Muslim countries relinquishing their obligations under human rights law. Furthermore, regardless of Sharia's influence on the ratification process, some ambiguous aspects as to the *reasons* behind the reservations entered by Muslim States remain. More generally, an analysis of the domestic human rights practices of certain Muslim States reveals that reservations made on the basis of adhering to the principles of Sharia are hardly convincing. The following section will first address the alternative considerations used by Muslim States to justify limitations to human rights treaties and second, the incongruity in the use of Sharia-based reservations to human rights instruments.

SUBSECTION ONE: ALTERNATIVE CONSIDERATIONS USED BY MUSLIM STATES TO JUSTIFY LIMITATIONS TO HUMAN RIGHTS INSTRUMENTS

The following section will briefly illustrate the two types of reservations that are often made by Muslim States which are *not* related to Islamic considerations. These include (A) reservations of a political nature; (B) reservations of an administrative nature.

A. Reservations of a Political Nature

A recurrent reservation found in international treaties signed by Muslim States, refers generally to the Israeli-Palestinian conflict. Muslim States have consistently underlined their particular stance towards the conflict in declarations which are presented as reservations and which are made against the international treaty concerned in order to prevent any eventual obligation to the State of Israel arising from the international engagement.[80] This kind of statement is not in any way founded on Sharia. Rather, it is a political consideration, deeply rooted in diplomatic and foreign policy matters.[81]
An example of a political declaration which affects the actual substance of human rights treaties include Morocco's declaration against Article 2 of CEDAW which states that the article will apply where it is 'without prejudice to the constitutional requirement that regulate the rules of succession to the throne of the Kingdom of Morocco'.[82] An example of a political reservation affecting the substance of the CRC includes that of Algeria against article 13, 16 and 17 where the provisions will be interpreted in light of its 'Information Laws'.[83] The UAE made a similar reservation against Article 17 stating that with respect to mass media, 'it shall be bound by its provisions in the light of the requirements of domestic statues and laws and, in accordance with the recognition accorded them in the preamble to the Convention, such a manner that the country's traditions and cultural values are not violated.'[84]

80 http://www2.ohchr.org/english/bodies/ratification/2.htm#reservations.

81 The most formal and grave declaration on this matter is the Government of Iraq's declaration upon signature of the ICERD on the 18 February 1969 in which the Government of Iraq was defining the limit of the adherence to the international treaty not only on Iraq as a state but on Arab states in general. 'The Ministry for Foreign Affairs of the Republic of Iraq hereby declares that signature for and on behalf of the Republic of Iraq of the Convention on the Elimination of all forms of Racial Discrimination, which was adopted by the General Assembly of the United Nations on the 21 December 1965, as well as approval by the Arab States of the said convention and entry into it by their respective governments, shall in no way signify recognition of Israel or lead to entry by the Arab States into such dealings with Israel as may be regulated by the said Convention'.

82 http://www2.ohchr.org/english/bodies/ratification/8.htm#declarations.

83 For example, Article 26 of the Information Code which provides that "national and foreign periodicals and specialized publications, whatever their nature or purpose, must not contain any illustration, narrative, information or insertion contrary to Islamic morality, national values or human rights or advocate racism, fanaticism and treason. Further, such publications must contain no publicity or advertising that may promote violence and delinquency." (http://www.unhchr.ch/html/menu3/b/treaty15_asp.htm).

84 http://www.unhchr.ch/html/menu3/b/k2crc.htm.

B. Reservations related to the administration of the treaty

A common reservation amongst most of the States falling within the scope of this study, are those of a purely technical nature which relate to the administration of the treaty concerned.[85] Although common among Muslim States, this kind of reservation is not founded upon the Sharia, and neither is its use exclusive to Muslim States alone.

Article 29(1) of CEDAW provides that:

> ... any dispute between two or more States Parties concerning the interpretation or application of the present Convention which is not settled by negotiation shall, at the request of one of them, be submitted to arbitration. If within six months from the date of the request for arbitration the parties are unable to agree on the organisation of the arbitration, any one of those parties may refer the dispute to the International Court of Justice by request in conformity with the Statute of the Court.

Muslim States like Egypt, Indonesia, Kuwait, Lebanon, Morocco, Pakistan Saudi Arabia, Tunisia, Turkey and United Arab Emirates have formulated reservations to the Convention's dispute settlement provision, as have non-Muslim States, such as France, Monaco, Thailand and Venezuela. The reasoning behind these reservations finds its roots in the principle of sovereignty. The provision could potentially enable one State to hold another State accountable in a court of law without their prior agreement, significantly affecting State sovereignty.

Although technical reservations are not founded on Sharia, they are sensitive to the fragile relationship between human rights standards and Islamic considerations. As a result, this tenuous relationship could be a reason behind the decision of Muslim States to avoid being brought before a court without their prior consent. Indeed, with regard to these specific countries, this type of reservation could be considered a rampart that protects the State and their own conceptions of Sharia from being challenged without their consent.

SUBSECTION TWO: INCONGRUITY IN THE USE OF SHARIA-BASED RESERVATIONS TO HUMAN RIGHTS INSTRUMENTS

The adherence of Muslim countries to international human rights instruments does not seem to follow any consistent rationale. Many factors arouse the suspicion that the reservations made by Muslim States are

[85] Iran is not a party to CEDAW.

indicative of a desire to maintain or increase their margin of power under the 'legitimate' cover of 'sacred' Islamic considerations. Two of these factors shall be considered in turn. Part A will illustrate and analyse the ambiguity in the general attitude of Muslim countries towards international human rights conventions and Part B will examine the use of other considerations as an excuse to conceal considerations of an essentially religious nature.

A. The Incoherence of Muslim State Practice when adhering to International Human Rights Conventions

The incoherence of Muslim State practice upon adherence to international human rights conventions is reflected in the following ways. First, the double standards or paradoxes that occur when ratifying international human rights instruments; second, the withdrawal of reservations grounded in Sharia; and third, the formulation of reservations on obscure grounds.

1. Paradoxes in the Adherence of Muslims States to Different Human Rights Instruments.

The process of ratifying human rights conventions does not appear to follow a logical path reflecting a coherent attitude. This is evidenced by the practices of the Muslim States subject to this study. As a result, it is necessary to analyse these processes and ascertain the reasons behind these inconsistencies.

Article 16 of the UDHR encompasses the issue of equality in family matters and it states that men and women 'are entitled to equal rights as to marriage, during marriage and at its dissolution'.[86] It is commonly acknowledged that many of the rights laid down in the UDHR have a binding authority over States and that the basic principles enshrined in this UN instrument are universal.[87] However, norms related to gender equality tend to divide scholars. Many of them argue that this category of norms is erected as a norm of customary international law. Simultaneously, many

86 Article 16 of the UDHR states that:

1. Men and women of full age, without any limitation due to race, nationality or religion, have the right to marry and to found a family. They are entitled to equal rights as to marriage, during marriage and at its dissolution.
2. Marriage shall be entered into only with the free and full consent of the intending spouses.
3. The family is the natural and fundamental group unit of the society and is entitled to protection by society and the State.

87 In this regard, see Anne F. Bayefesky, 'General approaches to the domestic application of women's international human rights law', in Human Rights of Human, edited by Cook (University of Pennsylvania Press, Philadelphia, 1994) 360; Louis Henken, *The Age of Rights*, (Colombia University Press, 1990) 181–193.

other commentators and the international community in general, seem to accept the idea that the norm of gender equality implicates culture and includes religion within the scope of the latter.[88] Moreover, this cultural exception to gender equality seems to encompass the category of family law in particular. Nevertheless, beyond the controversy over the status of gender equality norms as *jus cogens*, the responsibility upon States to observe and protect these rights still exist through their obligations under the international human rights conventions that they are party to.

Egypt, (which voted in favour of the UDHR in 1948), has not lodged any reservations to the ICCPR including the unequivocal provisions of Article 23 paragraph 4 which provides that 'states parties to the present Covenant shall take appropriate steps to ensure equality of rights and responsibilities of spouses as to marriage, during marriage and at its dissolution.' At the same time, Egypt refuses to adhere to Article 16 of CEDAW which governs the equality of rights for men and women within the family unit. It appears that the same right conflicts with Sharia principles when addressed in a specific convention dedicated to women, but does not supposedly pose any conflicting controversy if cited in the frame of a wider and more varied international human rights convention. This inconsistency might find one explanation in the Government of Egypt's failure to fully understand the scope of its intended engagement on the different subject matters at the time of ratifying the ICCPR. The representative from Egypt had not at the time given any explanation of this contradiction towards the two different human rights instruments.[89]

Sharia law emerged as a holy impediment, limiting the adherence of the Government of Egypt only when an entire convention was about to be devoted to women (there are other countries within the scope of this study who have behaved similarly, namely Iran). This arguably reveals not only that Egypt's concern with Sharia law surfaces only when the matter is particularly sensitive and given wide media coverage, but also that Egypt's willingness to enter into human rights agreements is based on an ability to distance the treaty from a strict application of religious considerations, particularly where the treaty's remit is not straightforward and does not risk offending the sensitivities of the masses. Once again this goes to the heart of the political realities at home where governments need to maintain popular opinion in order to preserve power and are therefore very conscious of how signing onto any new treaties might affect this.

As a result of this paradoxical attitude towards the rights of women in the family where having formulated a reservation reducing the effectiveness

[88] Joel R. Paul, 'Cultural Resistance to Global Governance' (November 5, 2000). Available at SSRN: http://ssrn.com/abstract=272637.

[89] (A/39/40–1984).

of CEDAW even though it has not done so in respect of the ICCPR, Egypt could be held accountable for the non-compliance of its domestic law on the grounds of Article 23(4) of the ICCPR. This demonstrates the 'swings and roundabouts' nature of international law where under one convention protection appears to be lost, domestic protection is in fact gained under another less politically sensitive instrument. After all, the main concern should be that women achieve equality and that their rights are protected. It may even be argued that the issue of where exactly this protection derives is unimportant as long as it is achieved.

Pursuing this logic further, considering that the Government of Egypt is bound by Article 23 of ICCPR, it appears that it would be legally correct if Egypt were required to reform its family laws in a way so as to harmonise them with the requirements of the relevant binding provisions of the ICCPR. Egypt is hence under an obligation to modify its family law, and particularly its personal status law, independent of the influence, requirements, or even existence of CEDAW. Indeed, this was clearly affirmed in the concluding observations of the 1994 Human Rights Committee report on Morocco. The Committee here firmly reminded the government of Morocco that it had a positive obligation to prevent and eliminate discriminatory attitudes and prejudices towards women by among other things, revising its domestic legislation with a view to bringing it into conformity with Articles 2, 3 and 23 of the Covenant. The report stated that 'although several reservations have been made by Morocco in acceding to the Convention on the Elimination of All Forms of Discrimination against Women, Morocco remains bound to the fullest extent by the provisions of Articles 2, 3, 23 and 26 of the Covenant.'[90]

In general, women's rights have constituted one of the major preoccupations of the Human Rights Committee. The UN Committee has utilised the ICCPR as a robust legal tool with which to promote and foster 'full legal and de facto equality for women in all aspects of society,'[91] but most notably concerning the 'status of married women and their equal rights in matters of child custody, the transmission of nationality and parental consent for the marriage of minor children.'[92]

The Egyptian case study reflects this incoherent trend as well as its implications, but Egypt is not the only State guilty of this conduct. Morocco,

[90] Comments of the Human Rights Committee: Morocco—Concluding Observations of the Human Rights Committee: Morocco. 23/11/94.CCPR/C/79/Add.44 at E /4; available at: http://www1.umn.edu/humanrts/hrcommittee/MOROCCO.htm (last accessed 22 April 2008).

[91] Comments of the Human Rights Committee, *Concluding Observations of the Human Rights Committee : Libyan Arab Jamahiriya. 23/11/94. CCPR/C/79/Add.45 at section 19.*

[92] Concluding Observations of the Human Rights Committee: Tunisia. 10/11/94. CCPR/C/79/Add.43.

Bahrain, Tunisia, Lebanon, and until very recently, Turkey,[93] have all at some point maintained a dualistic and paradoxical approach towards human right matters. Like Egypt, they have ratified the ICCPR without formulating any reservations[94] to Article 23(4) whilst simultaneously limiting their ratification of CEDAW, specifically with regards to Article 16, which addresses the same rights. Ironically, even though Saudi Arabia is commonly regarded as having made some of the most controversial and impermissible reservations to human rights treaties, the State has maintained a minimum degree of coherence in the scope and substance of its international engagement on human rights. Indeed, Saudi Arabia did not participate in the vote for the Universal Declaration, it is not party to the ICCPR nor the ICESCR, and it maintains very sweeping and broad reservations to CEDAW in the name of Sharia law, limitations that render the ratification of the treaty meaningless. However, although its approach is considered to be very negative from the perspective of human rights, Saudi Arabia's practice at least demonstrates a degree of coherency and consistency.

Contradictions abound where Muslim State practice is concerned in the human rights field. A comparative analysis between the adherence to CEDAW and the CRC accounts for this ambiguous and incoherent trend in which States have entered reservations on articles they purport to accept in the context of other human rights instruments.[95] Lebanon, Egypt, Bahrain and Morocco find themselves in the somewhat strange position where they accord rights to children until the age of majority, at which point they then start to deny adults those same rights, particularly adult women. By adhering to the CRC, States pledge to ensure that they will take all appropriate measures to protect the child from any kind of discrimination. Conversely, by stipulating reservations to Article 2 of CEDAW, the same States refrain from pursuing by all appropriate means the elimination of discrimination against women. Hence, in the continuation of this logic, girls are technically protected against discrimination until the day they reach the legal age of majority. On becoming adult women, they lose the rights they had enjoyed during their childhood. This legal absurdity is entrenched in the human rights systems of Egypt, Bahrain, Morocco, Tunisia, and Pakistan. Saudi Arabia, Iran and Pakistan (before 1997), avoided the contradiction described above by maintaining a systematic limitation of human rights as the result of their across-the-board reservations to both CEDAW and CRC.

The situation in the State of Lebanon is relatively complicated and

[93] Turkey withdrew its reservation to article 16 of CEDAW on 20 September 2000.

[94] The reservations of Turkey to ICCPR do not affect the engagement of the Turkish State on women's rights but concern mainly the territory issue with Cyprus and rights of minorities.

[95] See Florence Butegwa, 'International Human Rights Law and Practice: Implications for Women, in 'From Basic Needs to Basic Rights: Women's Claim to Human Rights', M Shuler (ed) (Women, Law and Development International, 1995).

deserves special consideration. Lebanon's engagement with international conventions reflects the State's fragile internal and external sovereignty as well as its inherent structural incapacity, which manifests itself in among other things, the lack of a coherent legal system.

At first, the position of Lebanon appears to be quite confusing. On the one hand, consent is given to the implementation of Article 2 of CEDAW in order for the principle of equality to be embodied in the State's internal legal system 'in all its forms'. This includes the obligation to prohibit all discrimination against women; 'to take all appropriate measures to eliminate discriminations against women by any person, organization or enterprise'; and 'to take all appropriate measures to get rid of discrimination'. Yet, on the other hand, Lebanon refuses to observe Article 16 of the same Convention, which is an application of Article 2 in the field of family matters. Although Lebanon agrees to take all measures necessary to abolish discrimination, it has formulated a reservation on the provision that requires the State to make specific efforts to ensure equality between men and women in the field of family matters. The simple and straightforward question that arises from the Lebanese attitude is how the State could possibly envisage combating discrimination in all fields when it begins by making reservations on family relations. It would have been a more coherent approach to formulate a reservation to both Articles 2 and 16 as they are indivisible. A deeper analysis of the Lebanese legal system affords an explanation for this incongruity though it fails to justify this attitude.

The problem is that although Lebanon officially ratifies international instruments with the view to implementing human rights standards in its internal legal system, it also gives total autonomy to the religious authorities to act as legislators in family matters and refuses to interfere in this field. This duplication of sovereignty puts Lebanon in a very delicate situation at the international level. For this reason, the Lebanese State entered a reservation on the specific field of family law because this section is completely beyond its control. However, the State maintained its full engagement with regards to a global set of norms that are under its sphere of competence.

Nevertheless, Article 2 of CEDAW, to which Lebanon has agreed to adhere, requires the State to take all appropriate measures to eliminate discrimination against women by 'any person, organization or enterprise', and to ensure that public authorities and institutions act in conformity with the obligation to refrain from engaging in any act or practice of discrimination against women. The religious authorities are public persons for the sake of this provision, established on the Lebanese territory. Therefore, monitoring the religious authorities' acts to make sure that they are not discriminatory against women falls within the scope of tasks to which the Lebanese State has agreed to concern itself.

The contradiction between treaty ratification and State practice also affects women's rights in matters related to their children. The countries that have entered reservations to Article 16(d) of CEDAW, which gives the same rights and responsibilities to both men and women as parents in matters relating to their children and irrespective of their marital status include Lebanon, Egypt, Bahrain, Morocco, Turkey, and Tunisia. Paradoxically, provisions in the CRC grant 'both parents' 'common responsibilities for the upbringing and development of the child'. This means that women, as one half of the marital union, were not considered problematic for the adherence of these same States to the CRC. Therefore, in the light of their engagements to the CRC and under the application of Article 18 of the said convention, States ought to ensure that the principle of common responsibility of parents is recognised. However, as a consequence of the reservations made against Article 16, these States deny equal rights to women with regard to issues involving their children.

2. *Withdrawal of Islamic reservations*

The withdrawal of reservations formulated in the name of Islam invites an examination of the legitimacy of the grounds upon which the reservations were formulated in the first instance. The request by international human rights bodies for States to limit the scope of their reservations is completely understandable if ratifying States are not inclined to withdraw them.[96] It is not the purpose of this study to criticise the withdrawal of reservations made by Muslim countries. On the contrary, these developments demonstrate an effort made by these States to reinforce human rights standards in their respective jurisdictions. However, when a Muslim State formulates a reservation and founds it on a sacred and immutable religious set of laws, and this same country subsequently withdraws that reservation, the extent to which the previous considerations were in fact authentically based on religious considerations may be legitimately questioned.[97] (This may reflect a change in government and political agenda.) Although this change of direction would be warmly greeted, it still reflects the possibility that the practice of citing Islamic considerations in the first place was an excuse to enlarge their margin of power even though Sharia did not impede a full accession to the rights addressed in the international instruments.[98] This kind of

[96] See above 76.

[97] See Ann Elizabeth Mayer, 'The Convention on the Elimination of All Forms of Discrimination Against Women. The Political Nature of 'Religious' Reservations', 9.

[98] See Jane Connors, 'The Women's Convention in the Muslim World', in *Human Rights as General Norms and a State's Right to Opt Out*, JP Gardner (ed) (BIICL, 1997) 100–102.

reservation appears not to be prescribed by Sharia law and is instead based on political motivations.[99]

The reason behind this stance is not always necessarily one of bad faith. It could be a tactic employed by governments to dampen or weaken the impact of human rights standards on its own people in deference towards national public sentiment on religiously or culturally sensitive matters, for instance, the matter of adoption in Egyptian society. Adoption goes to the heart of Islam, as a boy who has reached majority cannot live with sisters or a mother he is not related to. Similarly, a girl child cannot live with a father and brothers she is not related to regardless of whether she is a minor or she has reached majority in Islam.

Pakistan and Egypt have both withdrawn reservations to the CRC that were originally entered into in the name of Islam. Egypt had previously entered reservations to the CRC with respect to Articles 20 and 21, on the grounds that they were incompatible with the institution of adoption as enshrined within the principles of Sharia.[100] On 31 July 2003, the Government of Egypt withdrew its reservation for both articles of the Convention. Following the withdrawal, the Committee praised Egypt and 'noted with satisfaction that there were different interpretations of some aspects of the application of *Sharia* (Islamic law) and that Egypt had adopted an attitude consistent with the spirit of human rights in that regard'.[101] Egypt's withdrawal thus demonstrates that Sharia is not inherently divergent from human rights and that it is actually reconcilable.

Following a similar pattern, on 23 July 1997, the Government of Pakistan informed the UN Secretary-General that it had decided to withdraw its reservation that had originally been made upon signature on later ratification, which read as follows: 'Provisions of the Convention shall be interpreted in the light of the principles of Islamic law and values'. Pakistan is the only State to withdraw a general reservation against the treaty and stated that it found nothing in the Convention that conflicted with 'the major precepts of Islam, barring the matter of adoption for which an appropriate provision has already been made'.[102]

99 See AE Mayer, 9.

100 The initial reservation reads as follows: 'Since the Islamic Sharia is one of the fundamental sources of legislation in Egyptian positive law and because the Sharia, in enjoining the provision of every means of protection and care for children by numerous ways and means, does not include among those ways and means the system of adoption existing in certain other bodies of positive law. The government of the Arab Republic of Egypt expresses its reservation with respect to all the clauses and provisions relating to adoption in the said convention, and in particular with respect to the provisions governing adoption in articles 20 and 21 of the convention.'

101 *Committee on the Rights of the Child: Consideration of Reports*, Concluding Observations, 2001 (Egypt), U.N. Doc. CRC/C/15/Add.145 (21 Feb. 2001).

102 *Committee on the Rights of the Child: Consideration of Reports*, 1994 (Pakistan), ¶ 5, U.N. Doc. CRC/C/SR.134 (11 Apr. 1994).

The withdrawal of reservations on international human rights conventions seem less religiously sensitive and reflect a normal and expectant legal practice when the reservations are founded instead on the domestic secular law. The example of the Government of Kuwait's withdrawal of the reservation against Article 7 (a) of CEDAW is an interesting illustration. The Government of Kuwait informed the UN Secretary-General in 2005 of its decision to withdraw the reservation which read as follows: 'The Government of Kuwait enters a reservation regarding Article 7(a), inasmuch as the provision contained in that paragraph conflicts with the Kuwaiti Electoral Act, under which the right to be eligible for election and to vote is restricted to males.'[103] The Kuwaiti example does not allow for the assumption that when other countries found their reservations on a 'secular' law, it is indistinguishable from the religious law. Pakistan does allow for this assumption as 'secular' law (often the constitution), is used as an excuse to place limitations to CEDAW which are really motivated by Sharia. This will be discussed further.

3. *Formulation of reservations on obscure grounds*

The ambiguous motivations behind the reservation against the right of women to grant nationality to their own children contained in Article 9 of CEDAW provides for the most explicit prohibition on gender discrimination in nationality laws compared to any other human rights treaty. Article 9 requires State parties to grant the same rights to men and women when it comes to the acquisition, change or retention of nationality. It states that neither marriage to an alien nor a husband's change of nationality, will alter the nationality of the wife thereby rendering her stateless, nor force her husband's nationality on her. It would be useful to pay further attention to this article's provisions which grant women equal rights with men with respect to their children's nationality. Muslim countries have systematically formulated reservations on Article 9 of CEDAW, notably against paragraph 2, which reads as follows: 'States Parties shall grant women equal rights with men with respect to the nationality of their children'.

Within the spectrum of countries subject to this comparative study, almost all the countries concerned have made reservations on this provision (with the exception of Iran, which is not a party to CEDAW). The formulation of the reservations on this matter seems ambiguous. They appear to be founded on inconsistent arguments, reflecting the will of Muslim States to remain vague on the subject but at the same time, distinguish it clearly from any considerations related to Sharia law. An example of this is the Government of Saudi Arabia's general reservation affecting Article 9 on the

[103] Withdrawn on 9 December 2005.

grounds of Islamic law. Yet, in a separate paragraph, Saudi Arabia stated that it considered itself not to be bound by paragraph 2 of Article 9, without giving any justification for this reservation. A similar attitude was adopted in the reservation formulated by the Government of Bahrain with respect to this Article.

Bahrain specified the articles of CEDAW which it deemed incompatible with the provisions of the Sharia, however, no justification was made for the reservation entered against Article 9(2). Tunisia also stipulated a reservation with regard to the provisions of this article, asserting that the provisions contained in Chapter VI of the Tunisian Nationality Code. Even secular Turkey, which withdrew its reservations to CEDAW in 1999 maintained its reservation against Article 9 on nationality.[104] Lebanon has also entered reservations to Article 9(2) without providing any explanation on this matter. Further reservations made by the Governments of Egypt, the United Arab Emirates and Malaysia demonstrates the widespread use of these limitations and invites us to look for a more solid reason behind this widespread attitude and practice of Muslim States.

The United Arab Emirates made a reservation to the nationality provision on the grounds that it considers the acquisition of nationality to be an internal matter, the conditions and control of which are established and governed by national legislation. This argument is problematic as it assumes that CEDAW has requested legislative powers over nationality or that the principle of sovereignty exclusively concerns legislation related to the rights of women to pass on nationality to their children which is why this provision is 'an internal matter' while others are not.

Egypt's attempts to justify its reservation to Article 9 demonstrates the State's uneasiness with the reservation, which it tried to base on social and policy arguments as opposed to genuine legal arguments. Egypt tried to defend its position by claiming that 'this [stance] is in order to prevent a child's acquisition of two nationalities where his parents are of different nationalities, since this may be prejudicial to his future', and underlines that 'it is clear that the child's acquisition of his father's nationality is the procedure most suitable for the child and that this does not infringe upon the principle of equality between men and women'.[105] Egypt's ambiguous arguments on this matter continue in the final paragraph of this unusual reservation: 'it is customary for a woman to agree, upon marrying an alien, that her children shall be of the father's nationality.' Markedly, the Government of Egypt's explanation failed to provide evidence of the proffered prejudicial effects, or reasons to explain why acquisition of the father's nationality is considered to be the 'most suitable procedure' for the child.

104 And Article 29, para 1 as mentioned above.
105 UN Doc. CEDAW/SP/13/Rev. Add 1, 18.

Morocco has also entered a reservation to this article, and explains its decision in a relatively long paragraph:

> The government of the Kingdom of Morocco makes a reservation with regard to this Article in view of the fact that the Law of Moroccan Nationality permits a child to bear the nationality of its mother only in the cases where it is born to an unknown father, regardless of place of birth, or to a stateless father, when born in Morocco, and it does so in order to guarantee to each its right to a nationality. Further, a child born in Morocco of a Moroccan mother and a foreign father may acquire the nationality of its mother by declaring, within two years of reaching the age of majority, its desire to acquire that nationality, provided that on making such declaration, its customary and regular residence is in Morocco.[106]

It is common to justify the restrictions on the rights of women to grant nationality to their children in Muslim countries, specifically the Arab ones, on the political ground related to the existence of Palestinian refugees in these countries. There appears to be a fear of the potential and consequences of widely spread 'blank marriages' between Palestinian men and national women for the purpose of getting nationality, if not for themselves, at least for their children, as well as the political implications of Palestinians losing their identity.[107] However, it seems this issue goes beyond the political aspect of the Palestinian cause, for Muslim countries as geographically and politically as far away as Malaysia have formulated exactly the same reservations.

Possible reasons behind this common reservation could be discovered by analysing the circumstances and debates over the eventual reform of nationality laws in these States. Indeed, it is evident from the Jordanian and Egyptian experience that even if the specific issue of Palestinian refugees is a concern, Islamic considerations always emerge during the course of the debates.[108]

The Government of Malaysia notified the UN Secretary-General on 6 February 1998 of a partial withdrawal of its reservations, stating that with regard to Article 9 paragraph 2, 'the Government of Malaysia declares that its reservation will be reviewed if the government amends the relevant law'. In brief, the Government of Malaysia has formulated a sentence to say very little in substance.

106 http://www2.ohchr.org/english/bodies/ratification/8.htm.

107 See generally: Takkenberg, Lex, *The Status of Palestinian Refugees in International Law*, Oxford: Clarendon Press, 1998.

108 http://www.learningpartnership.org/citizenship/

Many State parties to CEDAW have lodged objections to these reservations and declarations, but none has gone so far as to indicate that the Convention is not in force between them and the reserving States. To cite a few examples, the Government of Denmark has objected to the reservations made by the Government of Saudi Arabia, stating that 'the Government of Denmark (furthermore) notes that the reservation to paragraph 2 of Article 9 of the Convention aims to exclude one obligation of non-discrimination which is the aim of the Convention and therefore renders this reservation contrary to the essence of the Convention.' Similarly, the Government of France objected to the reservations made by the Government of Bahrain with respect to Article 9, paragraph 2; and the Government of the Kingdom of the Netherlands went so far as to consider that the reservation made by Morocco regarding Article 9, paragraph 2 is of the same scope as the reservation formulated to Article 16 and that both are incompatible with the object and the purpose of the convention as stated in Article 28, paragraph 2. However, the Netherlands' objection did not go beyond this point of criticism.

The extent to which Islamic considerations are responsible for the widespread policy of preventing women from passing on their nationality to their children requires further analysis. This is difficult to ascertain, as Muslim States do not defend their reservations on the grounds that they are incompatible with Sharia and, as evidenced above, their justifications for these reservations are often too vague.

Some studies on the issue of nationality in Muslim countries show that there is no influence of Islam in this set of laws but rather, they are the product of Western influence especially during the colonial period.[109] As recalled in a recent study for UNESCO:

> Western women lacked nationality rights until the 1930s. It was only towards the second half of the twentieth century that Western countries reformed their laws to enable women who were married to non-nationals, to pass on their nationality to their children and their spouses.[110]

[109] See Nadia Hijab, 'Les femmes sont aussi des citoyennes: les lois de l'Etat, la Vie des femmes', report of an expert meeting organised by UNDP which was held in Casablanca in July 2002, UNDP RBAS, available at www.pogar.org/publications/gender/nadia/summaryf.pdf (last accessed 14 August 2007); Gihane Tabet, Women in Personal Status laws: Iraq, Jordan, Lebanon, Palestine, Syria, in SHS Paper in women's studies, Gender research, No 4, UNESCO, July 2005, available at http://portal.unesco.org/shs/en/file_download.php/273076fe9922d6d33343dba2c06a3edeWomen_in_Personal_Status_Laws.pdf (last accessed 14 August 2007).

[110] ibid., Gihane Tabet, Women in Personal Status laws: Iraq, Jordan, Lebanon, Palestine, Syria, in SHS Paper in women's studies, Gender research, No 4, UNESCO, July 2005.

B. The use of other considerations as an excuse to conceal considerations of a religious nature

Upon accession to CEDAW, Pakistan entered a general reservation which affected the entire body of the Convention. Interestingly, Pakistan did not invoke any Islamic considerations as grounds for its limitation. The reservation states: 'The accession by the Government of the Islamic Republic of Pakistan to the said Convention is subject to the provisions of the constitution of the Islamic Republic of Pakistan'.

The Government of Pakistan's reservation gives the impression of being founded on legal and constitutional grounds, but a quick look at the Constitution of Pakistan shows that Sharia is not only repeatedly acknowledged in the text of the Constitution but is also considered to be the supreme law of Pakistan.[111] The Constitution of the State of Pakistan makes the provision that the entire set of laws in Pakistan should be in conformity with the requirements of the Sharia thus revealing the quasi-uniqueness of the Sharia as a source of law in the substantive law of the State of Pakistan as a whole.[112] Hence, it is apparent that what is behind the reservation to CEDAW is not the Constitution but Sharia. This is the ultimate justification for Pakistan's limitation to the scope of the Women's Convention.

In the same trend, the reservation lodged by the Government of Malaysia to the CRC which was then partly withdrawn at a later stage, reads as follows:

> The Government of Malaysia accepts the provisions of the Convention on the Rights of the Child but expresses reservations with respect to articles 1,2,7,13,14,15, 28 paragraph 1 (a), 37 of the Convention, and declares that the said provisions shall be applicable only if they are in conformity with the constitution, national laws and national policies of the Government of Malaysia.

In light of the role of Islam in Malaysia as explained above,[113] it can be argued that religious considerations are at the source of the reservation.

It is also worth noting that references to specific national legislation is not always distinguishable from religious considerations and should be read as the implementation of Sharia into the substantive law. Morocco's declaration on Article 2 of CEDAW explains the spontaneous assimilation

[111] In this regard, see Ann Elizabeth Mayer, 'The Convention on the Elimination of all Forms of Discrimination against Women. The Political Nature of Religious Reservations', 7–8.
[112] See above 45.
[113] See above 49.

between both sets of laws as it provides that 'certain… provisions contained in the Moroccan Code of Personal Status according women rights that differ from the rights conferred on men may not be infringed upon or abrogated because they derive primarily from the Islamic Sharia'. Notably, the reservations formulated upon accession by the Government of Kuwait were more qualified where they distinguished between the two sources of justification: the secular substantive law and Sharia. While some reservations were based on the stipulations of Kuwaiti codes, one was based on Sharia, hence delimitating the terrain on which the Islamic law applies.

Within many Muslim States, there appears to be an intimate relationship between the provisions of national law and the Sharia where the former is most often an application of the latter.[114] Therefore, the rule forbidding reserving States from invoking general principles of national law should be interpreted and implemented through the prism of religious considerations in Muslim countries. Indeed, even secular Turkey has formulated a general reservation against CEDAW which originally states that the State reserves against 'the articles of the convention dealing with family relations which are not completely compatible with the provisions of the Turkish civil code'. This reservation was later withdrawn in 1999 after ratification of the international women's instrument.

It is surprising to notice that Muslim countries which have ratified CEDAW have all formulated reservations against Article 16 which governs marriage and family regardless of the status of Sharia in their constitutional system, and especially regardless of the status of Sharia in the substantive law. Moreover, it is highly interesting to note that Turkey where Sharia is definitely not a source of legislation, has reserved against the same provisions as other Muslim countries when it comes to family law, with the exception that other Muslim countries referred to Sharia (directly or indirectly) in order to justify their limitations whilst Turkey based them on different grounds. Turkey's reservations before being withdrawn in 1999 affected various paragraphs of both Articles 15 and 16 which it considered incompatible with the provisions of the Turkish Civil Code. The justification for this anomaly could be found in one of these two options: (1) either Sharia still constitutes an indirect normative source for family law in Turkey and it would be inexact to put Turkey in the category of countries who have abandoned Sharia and made a complete swift to secularisation; or (2) the alleged grounds of Sharia used by Muslim countries in order to limit their engagements to international human rights instruments does not reflect purely Islamic considerations but rather cultural and socio-cultural patterns. These two possibilities will be further considered in the next part of the study which will among other things, analyse the conformity of State

114 On the status of the Islamic Sharia in the substantive law, see above 43.

parties, their laws and practices, to the international conventions which they have ratified.

CONCLUSION

In light of the above, it is evident that Sharia is not the only motivating factor behind treaty reservations. Moreover, where Sharia is used to justify certain reservations, the incoherence of its use as reflected by contradictory practices, withdrawals of Sharia-based reservations, and the formulation of reservations on obscure grounds, raises doubts as to the true role of Sharia in limiting human rights provisions. An important example of this is the widespread reservation by Muslim States against Article 9 of CEDAW concerning women's rights to acquire, change and retain their nationality, as well as pass it on to their children. The widespread use of this reservation and the equally obscure justifications for its use among Muslim States, demonstrates that other factors such as culture, do play a role in adherence to human rights treaties and even that perhaps Sharia does have a role, considering the commonality of its presence among the Muslim States. Indeed, such obscure reservations make it difficult to reach any conclusion as to the true intentions and motivations behind the practices of a contracting Muslim State.

The fact that a State may ratify human rights treaties does not mean that the same State does not violate human rights. Indeed, as stated by the Commission of Human Rights in 2006, 'ratification is obviously only a starting point, and remains meaningless in the absence of effective implementation'.[115] In this regard, it is of great importance to recall that at the time of the Rwandan genocide in 1994, Rwanda had been a State party to the ICCPR, ICERD and Genocide Convention of 1975, the three international law instruments addressing the issue of racial hatred and genocide which call upon States to fully implement their provisions by taking concrete measures and adopting effective legislation. As shown above, even though many Muslim States accepted the entire set of human rights instruments without formulating any reservations to them, it would have been too good to be true if this fact implied a genuine implementation of the provisions contained in these documents at the domestic level.

Internal State practice could deviate considerably from a State's engagement on the international level, but this discrepancy between pledge and

[115] Commission on Human Rights, E/CN.4/2006/WG.21/BP.2 on January 9, 2006, 'Taking stock of the debates on complementary international standards to strengthen and update international legal instruments against racism, racial discrimination, xenophobia and related intolerance', consultation paper prepared by Professor Frans Viljoen and Mr Tshepo Madlingozi.

reality is not always negative. New trends in Muslim countries show that the internal practice goes beyond the apparent boundaries forged upon accession. The second part aims to look into the domestic practice, particularly with regards to the issue of implementing human rights standards as addressed in the international documents. Having tried to assess the impact of Sharia on the ratification of the main human rights conventions by Muslim countries, it is now possible to move swiftly to the implementation of these international documents by attempting to analyse the impact of Islamic considerations on the translation of Muslim countries' human right engagements into domestic practice.

The implementation of human rights standards into domestic practice goes beyond the internal affairs of the concerned countries. As admitted by the representative of Egypt to the Third Committee:

> [T]he competence of the United Nations in the question of human rights was positive, and the provisions of Article 2, paragraph 7 of the Charter, guaranteeing non-interference in the internal affairs of member States, could not be invoked against such competence when, by adoption of the declaration, the question of human rights was a matter no longer of domestic but of international concern.[116]

Syria's representative on the same committee added that there would be no point in committing the Universal Declaration of Human Rights principles to paper if they were not to be respected in international behaviour'.[117] It is this 'behaviour' which requires further analysis.

116 (UN Doc A/C.3/SR 92 at 12 quoted in N. Robinson, Universal Declaration of Human Rights: its origins, significance and interpretation 28 (1950) at 21).
117 (UN Doc A/C.3/SR 91 at 10 quoted in Robinson at 20).

CHAPTER THREE

The Impact of Sharia on the Implementation of Human Rights Standards into Domestic Practice

> *'To the extent that international conventions protect the same rights protected by Sharia, nothing impairs an Islamic or Muslim state from becoming a signatory to any international convention on the protection of fundamental human rights.'*
> *'Nothing in Islamic international law precludes the applicability of these international obligations to the domestic legal system of an Islamic state provided these obligations are not contrary to Sharia. . . . [International human rights] are subject to the purposes and objectives of a given society, subject to the due process of law.'*
>
> Cherif Bassiouni[1]

The following chapter will analyse the role of Sharia when it comes to the implementation of human rights standards into the domestic practices of the Muslim States subject to this study. The analysis will begin in Section One with an examination of how international human rights instruments are incorporated within the State, their position within the legal and constitutional framework of the State, and the processes undertaken in order to ratify international conventions by the State. Thereafter, Section Two will provide an analysis of legislative reforms subsequent to the ratification of international treaties in order to determine the extent of Sharia's role in helping or hindering the process. Following on from this, Section Three makes the argument that Sharia has the potential to improve domestic human rights within the State by virtue of reform mechanisms integral to Sharia and as evidenced by positive reforms in Egypt, Tunisia and Pakistan. Finally, Section Four will analyse the role of the courts in applying human rights norms and international treaties both in national secular and Sharia courts, with the added intention of determining the role of Islam where Sharia judges reside. Following the analysis it will be possible to conclude what impact Sharia has on the implementation of international human

1 C Bassiouni 'Sources of Islamic Law and the Protection of Human Rights in the Islamic Criminal Justice System', in C. Bassiouni (ed) *The Islamic Criminal Justice System* 3, 23 (London, 1982) 39.

rights norms and whether or not it has the potential to help the process at the levels of both the reform of legislation and the judicial application of law.

Section One The Incorporation of International Human Rights Instruments into the Domestic Law

This section examines the incorporation of international human rights conventions into the domestic law of selected Muslim States, namely Iran, Egypt, Saudi Arabia, Morocco, Tunisia, Turkey, Malaysia, and Bahrain. This includes a discussion on (1) how the mechanism of incorporation used is affected by the relationship between international law and the respective State; (2) the approaches used by some States in implementing international human rights treaties based on their respective legal and constitutional frameworks; and (3) the steps that are taken domestically prior to ratifying a treaty (3).

SUBSECTION ONE: MECHANISM OF INCORPORATION

International law is primarily of application to States.[2] A State's commitment to international human rights standards is secured by entering into treaties which are regulated by the 1969 Vienna Convention on the Law of Treaties (VCLT). Treaty-making can be understood as a process of contract-making as it involves States voluntarily entering into a binding agreement.[3] This is done in international law through signature, exchange of instruments, ratification, acceptance, approval or accession.[4]

Authors have shown that the principle of *pacta sunc servanda* (ie good faith in contractual obligations) is paramount in the Islamic legal tradition, 'because it is God Who is the witness of all contracts'.[5] It follows that when signing international treaties, Muslim States are expected to ensure that all of their contractual obligations are clearly set out because contracts are

[2] Universal Declaration on Human Rights 1948 art 8, International Covenant on Civil and Political Rights 1976 art 2(3), International Convention on the Elimination of all forms of Racial Discrimination 1965 art 6, Convention Against Torture 1987 art 14(1), American Convention on Human Rights 1969 art 25, European Convention on Human Rights 1950 art 13, African Charter on Human and People's Rights 1986 art 7.

[3] Hilary Charlesworth and Christine Chinkin *The Boundaries of International Law: a Feminist Analysis* (Manchester University Press, 2000) 97.

[4] Vienna Convention on the Law of Treaties 1969 article 2(1)(b).

[5] Powell and Mitchell 2007: Nemeth 2005; Rayner 1991.

considered sacred.[6] For example, recent research shows that while Mulim States are less likely to accept the jurisdiction of the International Court of Justice, they will have the most durable commitments because of strong norms of contractual obligations which are carefully and meticulously crafted.[7]

International human rights agreements such as the International Covenant on Civil and Political Rights ('ICCPR') require that State parties take the necessary steps to implement the international provisions in their national legal systems. The ICCPR does not explicitly state that it is self-executing, that is, directly and automatically incorporated into domestic law.

Implementation is therefore based on a State's subscription to either monist or dualist theories on international law. In *monist* States, international standards are automatically implemented into the domestic legal system. These States have a legislature which plays a constitutional role in ratifying treaties. Domestic affairs of the State are regulated pursuant to international law, which takes supremacy over national law. Therefore, no specific national legislation is needed.

For example, Morocco is a monist State. International treaties duly incorporated by publication in the Official Bulletin become an integral part of domestic law.[8] Hence, customary international law is considered to be the law of the land. The provisions of the international treaties ratified become an internal part of the internal public order from which no derogation is admissible. Its provisions have ipso facto legislative and statutory effect in both public and private law.[9] It is the settled judicial practice of the Moroccan Supreme Court that when there is a contradiction between a domestic law and an international law, the latter prevails, provided that it has been published in the Official Bulletin.[10]

Similarly, in Egypt, bringing legislation into conformity with international human rights instruments is governed by Article 151 of the Egyptian Constitution which states that all agreements ratified by the President and

6 E J Powell and S M Mitchell, 'The International Court of Justice and the World's Three Legal Systems' The Journal of Politics 69 No. 2 (2007) 397.

7 *Ibid.* 397.

8 See, on ratification of treaties, Constitution of Morocco article 31: (1) The King accredits ambassadors to foreign powers and international organizations. Ambassadors or representatives of international organizations are accredited to Him; (2) He signs and ratifies treaties. However, treaties relating to the State finances cannot be ratified without prior approval of the Chamber of Representatives; (3) Treaties inconsistent with the provisions of the Constitution are approved in accordance with the procedures necessary for the revision of the Constitution.

9 For a list of international human rights treaties to which Morocco is a party see Appendix A.

10 *See, for example,* Moroccan Supreme Court decisions No. 49 of 1 October 1976, No. 5 of 3 November 1972 and No. 162 of 3 August 1979; The Convention against Torture and Other Cruel, Inhuman or Degrading Treatment or Punishment, ratified on 21 June 1993, was published in the *Official Bulletin* (No. 4440 of 19 December 1996).

approved by Parliament will automatically become part of domestic law immediately after publication in the Egyptian Gazette. Accordingly, Article 151 ensures that all international treaties and conventions—if ratified by the President and approved by Parliament—supersede any conflicting domestic legislation.

In Lebanon too, international treaties ratified by the State become an integral part of domestic law upon exchange of or deposit of instruments of ratification or accession.[11] The automatic incorporation takes effect upon publication of the treaty in the Journal Officiel (Official Gazette). Customary international law is also part of the law of the land. Rules of international law that are binding as a matter of international treaty or customary law are self-executing and can be directly invoked in the course of legal proceedings if they are sufficiently specific and concrete.

In Iran, 'treaty stipulations, which have been, in accordance with the Constitutional law, concluded between the Iranian government and other governments, shall have the force of law', under Article 9 of the Iranian Civil Code. According to Article 77 of the Constitution, all international treaties, protocols, contracts and agreements shall be approved by the Islamic Consultative Assembly. However, the constitution also emphasizes the superiority of the Islamic Sharia over all others laws.

The Constitution of Tunisia, under Article 32, provides that treaties have normative rank superior to statutes and, therefore, when conflicts arise, treaties prevail over statutory rules. International instruments ratified by the State party take precedence over norms of the State party's domestic law, and may be invoked directly before the courts.

In contrast, in *dualist* States, treaty provisions must be transformed into national law through legislation. Dualist theory distinguishes between the system of international law and national law, neither of which can per se create or invalidate the other.

Under Islamic law, the legislative power of the State is not completely unlimited. It is theoretically proscribed by the philosophy that God is the ultimate legislator who has set out what is and is not lawful through revelation in the Qur'an.[12] According to Justice Iqbal:

> The legislature in an Islamic state has a restricted role; technically speaking, its authority is delegated and can be exercised only within the limits prescribed by the Qur'an and Sunnah . . . Generally speaking, there are three possible spheres for legislative activity in a Muslim state:

[11] Georges J Assaf, 'The Application of International Human Rights Instruments by the Judiciary in Lebanon', in E Cotran and A Omar Sherif (eds) *The Role of the Judiciary in the Protection of Human Rights*, (CIMEL Book Series No. 5, Kluwer Law International 2007) 85.

[12] Mahood A Baderin, *International Human Rights and Islamic Law* (Oxford University Press (3) Oxford 2003) 52.

(1) enforce laws which have specifically been laid down in the Qur'an and Sunnah;
(2) to bring all existing laws in conformity with the Qur'an and Sunnah; and
(3) to make laws as subordinate legislation which do not violate the Qur'an and Sunnah.[13]

While conscious of the general rule of non-violaton of the Sharia in enacting subsidiary legislation, many Muslim States often rely on Islamic legal principles such as *siyasah shar'iyyah* (legitimate governmental policy), *darurah* (necessity), and *maslahah* (welfare), to legislate for the realization of human welfare and State policy.[14]

Bahrain operates under a dualist approach. Under Article 37(1) of the Constitution, all international treaties to which Bahrain is a party automatically became domestic law.[15] However, Bahrain is not strictly a monist State because Article 37(2) further provides that certain treaties 'must be promulgated by law to be valid', including those relating to 'State territory ... rights of sovereignty, the public and private rights of citizens ... treaties which involve the State Exchequer in non-budget expenditure or which entail amendment of the laws of Bahrain.'[16]

In Turkey, Article 90 of the Constitution deals with ratification of international treaties. They 'shall be subject to adoption by the Turkish Grand National Assembly by a law approving the ratification'. This includes agreements resulting in amendments to Turkish laws. Exceptions include agreements regulating economic, commercial and technical relations, and covering a period of no more than one year, may be put into effect through promulgation, provided they do not entail any financial commitment by the State, and provided they do not infringe upon the status of individuals or upon the property rights of Turkish citizens abroad. Also excluded are agreements in connection with the implementation of an international treaty, and economic, commercial, technical, or administrative agreements

13 Justice J Iqbal 'The Concept of State in Islam' in Ahmad, M (ed), *State, Politics and Islam* (1986) 37, para 49–50.

14 Mahood A Baderin *International Human Rights and Islamic Law* (Oxford University Press (3) Oxford 2003) 52.

15 Constitution of Bahrain, article 37(1): *The King shall conclude treaties by Decree, and shall communicate them to the Consultative Council and the Chamber of Deputies forthwith accompanied by the appropriate statement. A treaty shall have the force of law once it has been concluded and ratified and published in the Official Gazette.*

16 Constitution of Bahrain, article 37(2): *However, peace treaties and treaties of alliance, treaties relating to State territory, natural resources, rights of sovereignty, the public and private rights of citizens, treaties pertaining to commerce, shipping and residence, and treaties which involve the State Exchequer in non-budget expenditure or which entail amendment of the laws of Bahrain, must be promulgated by law to be valid.*

which are concluded depending on an authorization given by law. Further, agreements affecting the economic or commercial relations and private rights of individuals are not put into effect unless promulgated.

The Turkish hierarchy of norms has not been finally clarified but most scholars appear to hold the view that international treaties are equal or above the Constitution. The constitutional amendment in 2004 of Article 90 ensured supremacy of international conventions, including CEDAW over all national laws. Article 90(5) of the Constitution states that:

> In the case of a conflict between international agreements in the area of fundamental rights and freedoms duly put into effect and the domestic laws due to differences in provisions on the same matter, the provisions of international agreements shall prevail.

As far as the application of treaties in Malaysia is concerned, analysis of the constitutional provisions indicates that in Malaysia, like in the United Kingdom, the Executive possesses the treaty-making capacity[17] while the power to give domestic legal effect to treaties rests in Parliament. With respect to the power of the Executive, Article 39 provides that '[t]he executive authority of the Federation shall be vested in the Yang di-Pertuan Agong and exercisable ... by him or by the Cabinet.' Under Article 80(1), the executive authority of the Federation extends to all matters with respect to which parliament may make laws. By virtue of the 'Federal List' matters with respect to which Parliament may make laws include 'external affairs' which in turn include 'treaties, agreements, and conventions with other countries.' The executive authority of the Federation therefore extends to the making or conclusion of treaties, agreements and conventions with other countries.

Article 76(1)(a) of the Federal Constitution of Malaysia enables the Federal Parliament to make laws for the purpose of implementing any Treaty, agreement or convention between the Federation and any other country or any decisions of an International Organisation of which the

[17] This has been reaffirmed by the case of *the Government of the State of Kelantan v. Government of the Federation of Malaya and Tunku Abdul Rahman Putra Al-Haj* (1963) M.L.J 355. Here, Kelantan challenged the constitutionality of the Malaysia Agreement, an international treaty signed by the UK, the Federation of Malaya, Singapore, Sabah, and Sarawak. The main argument made by the Kelantan government was that the consent of the individual States of the Federation of Malaya should have been obtained before the arrangements for Malaysia can be lawfully implemented. Referring to Articles 39 and 80(1) of the Constitution, the Court affirmed the constitutionality of the Malaysia Agreement as follows:

> The Malaysia Agreement is signed "for the Federation of Malaya" by the Prime Minister, the Deputy Prime Minister, and four other members of the Cabinet. There is nothing whatsoever in the Constitution requiring consultation with any State Government or the Ruler of any State.

Federation is a member. A treaty to be operative in Malaysia, therefore, needs legislation by Parliament.

Overall, Morocco, Egypt, Lebanon, Iran and Tunisia automatically incorporate international human rights into domestic law based on their ratification. Bahrain, Turkey and Malaysia require domestic legislation to implement international human rights law after ratification of a treaty.

SUBSECTION TWO: LEGAL AND CONSTITUTIONAL FRAMEWORK

International standards are meant to serve as models for the rights protected under the constitutions and other domestic laws in individual countries.[18] Accordingly, how States implement international human rights treaties depend on their respective legal and constitutional framework. Regarding States where the legal system is principally derived from the Sharia (eg Iran and Saudi Arabia), it is important to comprehend the concept of *ijtihad*, which is at the root of *fiqh* (jurisprudence). *Ijtihad* can be described as 'individual striving' to discover from the revealed texts the divine value for every action.[19] This creates 'an immediate and continuous link between the actions of each individual believer and the divine revelation'. It does not find general laws, but finds God's will in a particular situation or act. This is a 'vertical' form of law-making versus a 'horizontal' one, which is the method used by modern Western legal systems.[20]

In Iran, international human rights conventions were passed through two different legal processes, that before 1979 and that after 1979. Before the Islamic Revolution, the process was as follows: the Ministry of Foreign Affairs recommended ratification and laid a bill before the two houses of the Parliament, the National Consultative Assembly and the Senate which have both to pass to law. CERD, CESCR and CCPR were ratified following this procedure. After the Revolution, the Islamic Republic of Iran was established and a new Constitution was put into force. The process of ratification changed and was put under the control of the Guardian Council.

The status of international treaties in Iranian law[21] is still a matter of debate in post-revolutionary Iran.[22] In general, the Guardian Council

18 Louis Henkin 'International Human Rights as Rights,' J. Roland Pennock and John W. Chapman *Human Rights: NOMOS XX111* (New York: New York University Press, 1981) 258–259.

19 Frank E. Vogel 'The Rule of Law in Saudi Arabia: Exploring Contradictions and Traditions', 128–136 in E Cotran, M. Yamani *The Rule of Law in the Middle East and the Islamic World, I.B.* (Tauris Publishers, London, in association with CIMEL, 2000) 130.

20 ibid. 132.

21 See Appendix A.

22 See, regarding the process of reception of International Norms in the Iranian legal system, Beigzadeh, Ebrahim, "Intégration des Norms Internationales en Droit Iranien," in Delmas-

believes that the obligations of International law are valid only in so far as they are consistent with the criteria of Islamic law. The Islamic State can only ratify 'un-Islamic' international standards by virtue of the interest of the Islamic system as a necessity (Maslahat-e Nezam).[23] According to the Government, 'the legal department of the judiciary, which comprises a number of highly qualified judges, has issued an advisory opinion (No. 7/1669 dated 19 October 1992) arguing that direct reference to provisions of international instruments may be made in judicial proceedings'.[24]

In Saudi Arabia, the Basic Law of 1992, Article 1 declares the Qur'an as the constitution of the country, governed on the basis of Islamic Sharia Law. This has had an impact on Saudi Arabia's participation in international human rights treaties. For example, Article 18 of the ICCPR provides that '[n]o one shall be subject to coercion which would impair his freedom to have or to adopt a religion or belief of his choice.' During the debates on the covenants in 1954 and 1960, Saudi Ambassador al-Barudi reiterated his objection to the provision on the ground that 'it would raise doubts in the minds of ordinary people to whom their religion [is] a way of life'.[25]

Article 70 of the basic law provides that 'international treaties, agreements, regulations and concessions are approved and amended by Royal decree.' The terms of ratification and publication of the international treaties are not found in the text of the Saudi constitution for the simple reason that there is no Parliament to ratify. The absence of any formal legislative body has been explained by the fact that legislation (*tashri'a*) has been perceived as inconsistent with the concept of the Sharia-based legal system.[26]

The Federal Constitution of Malaysia, unlike the Constitutions of other States, does not contain any provision saying that international law shall be deemed part of the law of the land or that treaties shall be the laws of

Marty, Mireille (ed.), *Criminalité é conomique et atteintes à la dignité de la personne, Vol.VI, Europe- Pays d 'Islam*, (ed). (MSH, Paris, 1999) 286–298, and Christopher Harland 'The Status of the International Covenant on Civil and Political Rights (ICCPR) in the Domestic Law of State Parties: An Initial Global Survey through UN Human Rights Committee Documents' *Human Rights Quarterly*, Vol. 22, No.1, (2000) 225. *See* Annual Reports of Amnesty International and Human Rights Watch for this period.

[23] Constitution of the Islamic Republic of Iran, articles 110 and 112

[24] See United Nations International Human Rights Instruments, 'Core Document Forming Part of the Reports of State Parties—Islamic Republic of Iran', HRI/CORE/1/Add.106, 28 January 1999, at para. 82, available at: http://www.unhchr.ch/tbs/doc.nsf/0/bb5e6edae249b576802567d10033a0bb?Opendocument (last accessed 1 April 2008).

[25] 15 U.N. GAOR C.3 (125th mtg.), U.N. Doc. A/C.3/SR.1025 (1960) 214. See also, id. at 197–98, 202–3, 206, 222–23; 9 U.N. GAOR C.3 (566th mtg.), U.N. Doc. A/C.3/SR.566 (1954) 116–117, 145–46.

[26] In Saudi Arabia, this absence counterbalances the influence of the religious scholars in their *fatwas* (legal opinion based on the sources of Islamic law). There are only government ordinances in the form of decrees to supplement, not to contradict the Shar-iah. See Aba-Namay, Rashed 'The Recent Constitutional reforms in Saudi Arabia' *International and Comparative Law Quarterly*, Vol. 42 (1993) 298

Malaysia. Nevertheless, certain provisions of the Constitution deal with 'treaty-making capacity' in Malaysia.

In Malaysia, treaties are entered into on the executive authority alone.[27] A comprehensive federal competence is given by the Federal Constitution of Malaysia. Article 74(1) of the Constitution enables legislative competence of the Federal Parliament to cover a wide range of matters. Article 76(1)(a) provides the Federal Parliament with competence to enact legislation for the purpose of implementing treaties even if the subject matter would otherwise be within the sole competence of a state. Limitations to this power are set out at Article 76(2) of the Constitution:

> (2) No law shall be made in pursuance of paragraph (a) of Clause (1) with respect to any matters of Islamic law or the custom of the Malays or to any matters of native law or custom in the States of Sabah and Sarawak and no Bill for a law under that paragraph shall be introduced into either House of Parliament until the Government or any State concerned has been consulted.

SUBSECTION THREE: PROCESS OF RATIFICATION

In Egypt, the procedure of accession starts with the Ministry of Foreign Affairs which leads representatives of other ministries, particularly that of justice, in the negotiations of human rights treaties. An official of the Ministry of Foreign Affairs would be empowered to sign the treaty. The president of the Republic refers treaties to the People's Assembly for ratification (Article 151 of the constitution). Once the treaty is ratified by the People's Assembly, it is once again be sent to the President to sign, to order its publication in the Official Gazette, and in this way it becomes legally binding as part of domestic law.

In Lebanon, an amendment made in 1990 of Article 52 of the Constitution introduced a complex system of ratification by the executive

[27] According to Article 74(1) of the Federal Constitution, "Parliament may make laws with respect to any of the matters enumerated in the 'Federal List' or the 'Concurrent List'." The 'Federal List' in the Ninth Schedule includes External Affairs:

(a) Treaties, agreements, and conventions with other countries and all matters which bring the Federation into relations with other countries;
(b) Implementation of treaties, agreements, and conventions with other countries...

We can conclude from the wording of Article 74, read together with the Federal List, that the Federal Parliament has the exclusive power to make laws relating to external affairs (including treaties, agreements, and conventions) and that it has the power to implement international treaties and make them operative domestically.

power whereby the President of the Republic negotiates and ratifies international treaties in agreement with the Prime Minister and approval of the Council of Ministers.

Thus, in Lebanon, the conclusion of an international convention involves three stages: negotiation, submission to the legislative for ratification by a two-thirds vote, ratification and promulgation of the convention by the President of the Republic, followed by publication in the Official Gazette as a matter of Public notice. So, the question of an international treaty becoming binding upon the State is governed by its incorporation in the internal legal system which takes place by virtue of ratification by the Executive after consent of the Parliament.

This automatic incorporation, however, does not take effect until after publication, as is the case for law enacted by the Parliament or decrees issued by the Executive published in the Official Gazette. The jurisprudence of the Lebanese Courts is very strict with respect to the publication of national legislation and decrees in the Official Gazette but has held that the publication of an international treaty, whatever the means of publication, is enough to incorporate it in the national body of legislation and therefore to make it enforceable in the national legal system, as long as the ratification law is published in the Official Gazette.[28]

When the treaty norms are so incorporated, the courts may apply them to effectively realire the rights of the individuals as per article 2, paragraph (2) of the Lebanese Code of the Civil Procedure. Once the process is complete, an individual may invoke the provision of an international treaty before a national court, if the provisions of the national legislation contradict those of the treaty invoked.

Consequently, the latter will have precedence over domestic legislation; however, this will not result in an amendment to the law which will continue to apply until it is amended by the Parliament. Lebanese civil courts have ruled that the provisions of the international treaties have precedence over the provisions of internal legislation pertaining to the same subject.[29]

Under the current constitutional framework in Iran, Article 94 of the Constitution stipulates that the Guardian Council has to scrutinize and to approve the laws enacted by the Parliament or the Islamic Consultative Assembly for compatibility with Islamic Laws and the provisions of the Constitution. Furthermore, according to Article 77 of the Iranian Constitution, international treaties and agreements must be approved by

[28] See An nashra al qadaiyya (the judiciary Publication) 1950, 50:650; Fahras al ijtihadati (Index of Jurisprudence), 2379 IDREL, Beirut.

[29] See Lebanese Court of Cassation, decision No 59, 9/12/1973, Al'Adl periodic 1974, 277, and Court of Appeal , decision No 121, 26/4/1988, 692.

the Islamic Consultative Assembly, Majlis.[30] They become binding following approval by the Council of Guardians and the signing by the President.[31]

In Turkey, where agreements are subject to adoption by the Turkish Grand National Assembly by a law approving ratification under Article 90 of the Constitution, these agreements must be brought to the knowledge of the Turkish Grand National Assembly within two months of their promulgation.

CONCLUSION

The above section has demonstrated the various means by which international treaties are formally acceded to and incorporated into the domestic legal systems of the selected Muslim States. What is particularly interesting is the role Sharia can play in the process, particularly with regard to Iran and Saudi Arabia where a formal analysis of compatibility of the treaty with domestic and religious law is instrumental in determining the State's decision to ratify a treaty and how it chooses to do so.

Section Two **Brief Survey of the Compatibility of Legislation with Human Rights Norms**

The main idea of this chapter is to measure the impact of Sharia on the implementation of human rights standards as derived from the international human rights conventions. Sharia law is very often invoked at the international level as a justification for the impossibility of implementing these international norms into the domestic practises of Muslim States. For example, Iran systematically invokes Islamic considerations in order to justify its refusal to comply with the requirements of the international human rights instruments to which it is a party, notably UDHR, ICCPR, ICESCR and ICERD. As Meron puts it:

> Divergence does not emerge from the context, it rises from the very initial phase. Islamic law is founded on the very original concept that divinity reigns supreme and divine law is pre-eminent to human law. The Declaration is genuinely secular in its theme and essence an as such, differs from Islamic law in its origin. There may be similarities or even complete compatibility on some provisions, in particular those that meet

30 See Constitution of the Islamic Republic of Iran, article 72.
31 See Constitution of the Islamic Republic of Iran, article 125.

> the conditions of jus cogens, but the original perceptions remain widely apart.[32]

But the use of the same Sharia could lead to a harmonization between international standards of human rights and those in application in Muslim countries. Some comparative aspects of amendment to legislative texts in the Muslim world show that the conciliation of legislation with the international human rights standards do not necessarily imply a secular legal framework and could be carried out within the framework of Sharia. In fact, the inherent flexibility of Sharia encompassing different legal tools creates room for interpretation and adaptation to changes of context and circumstance. Prominent reformist Islamic scholars have written about this.[33]

As further recognition of the potential of legislative reform within Sharia, the CEDAW Committee:

> ... requested the United Nations system as a whole, in particular the specialized agencies of the United Nations, and the Commission on the status of women, to promote or undertake studies on the status of women under Islamic laws and customs in particular on the status and equality of women in the family on issues such as marriage, divorce, custody and property rights and their participation in public life of the society, taking into consideration the principle of ijtihad in Islam.[34]

Section three will highlight some major amendments to the legislation undertaken in the Muslim word using Sharia as the platform or tool allowing for the change in law. Examples chosen touch mainly upon women's rights in a wide variety of Muslim countries, from the semi secular Tunisia to the Islamic regime of Pakistan and also Egypt where Sharia is given significant prominence in the Constitution. However, before illustrating these reforms in section three, the following section will provide an introduction which assesses an example of the general conformity of legislation with international human rights standards within the selected countries.

The ratification by Muslim countries of international human rights treaties has generally enhanced the national legal systems of the concerned

[32] See 'Iran's Challenge to the International Law of Human Rights', 13 Human Rights Internet Report (1989) 8, cited by Shaheen Sardan Ali, 'The Twain Doth Meeet! A Preliminary Exploration of the Theory and Practice of as.Siyan and International Law in the Contemporary World', in Rehman, J and Breau, S (ed), Religion, Human Rights and International Law (Martinus Nijhoff Publishers, Leiden, Boston, 2007) 9.

[33] See Abdullahi An-Naim, *Toward an Islamic Reformation, Civil Liberties, Human Rights and International Law* (Syracuse University Press, 1999).

[34] Decision 4 of the Committee on the Elimination of Discrimination against Women, 6th session in *The Work of CEDAW. Reports of the Committee on the Elimination of Discrimination against women, Volume II 1986-1987 (New York: United Nations, 1990), 296.*

countries in many respects, thus creating a steady and progressive approach to the protection and promotion of human rights. Usually, when reporting to human rights committees such as CEDAW, governments articulate the steps that they should take or have taken to comply with the provisions of the international instruments. This reflects, as stressed by the Tunisian delegation, the willingness of States to consider reviewing their laws in light of international standards.[35]

It is important to mention that one of the reasons behind the effectiveness of international treaties is the obligation upon States to report to the relevant human rights committees, compelling governments to engage in a dialogue with the international community about their State's legislation and domestic practices. Even if this engagement does not significantly drive a better domestic implementation of human rights, it puts States on the path towards doing so and commits a State to at least evaluate, assess and justify its own set of legislation and its compatibility with international human rights standards. An example of this is with regard to the government of Lebanon which had acknowledged already in its initial report[36] to the CEDAW committee that some Lebanese laws regulating matters like adultery or honour crimes violated the equality guarantees in Lebanon's own Constitution and in the various international human rights instruments and therefore, required amendment. This auto-evaluation and public acknowledgement of the shortcomings of its national legislation is by itself a positive step towards better implementation of human rights. Once they have admitted a failure to comply, States would feel embarrassed to constantly justify the incompatibility of their laws.[37]

The following section aims to demonstrate the potential of legal reform following a State's accession to international conventions and the effects of the resulting commitments. It will be evident, however, that while the international conventions and human rights committees have a positive effect on legal reform, there remains in many States a significant need for improvement, a state of affairs also noted by the reports of the same committees. As noted earlier in the study, different Muslim States accord Sharia a different prominence within their respective constitutions and legal systems, with the 'Islamic' States of Saudi Arabia, Iran and Pakistan at one end, and multi-confessional Lebanon and secular Turkey at the other. In light of this, it

35 General Assembly, Department of Public Information Report, HR/CT/693, 17 March 2008 available at http://www.un.org/News/Press/docs/2008/hrct693.doc.htm (last accessed 1 April 2008).

36 UN Committee on the Elimination of Discrimination against Women 'Initial report of States Parties: Lebanon' CEDAW/C/LBN/1, 2004, Part II, chap. I.B available at: http://www.un.org/womenwatch/daw/cedaw/33sess.htm (last accessed 1 April 2008).

37 See UN Committee on the Elimination of Discrimination against Women 'Third periodic report of States Parties: Lebanon', CEDAW/C/LBN/3, 2006, available at: http://www.ohchr.org (last accessed 1 April 2008).

would also be interesting to analyse the reports of the human rights committees in order to gage what effect the status of Sharia has on the reform processes of the respective State, if any at all.

Saudi Arabia

Saudi Arabia signed and ratified CEDAW in 2000 and by 2008, the UN Committee on the Elimination of Discrimination against Women had congratulated Saudi Arabia for establishing institutional mechanisms which advanced the protection of women from violence, and for undergoing a process of drafting legislation both for the implementation of women's rights and a coherent compilation of the laws of personal status from Sharia.[38] Furthermore, it was found that CEDAW was taken into consideration when framing laws and regulations promulgated after the Kingdom's accession to the Convention and amending existing laws and regulations, including the Labour and Workers Law, Social Insurance Law and regulations on employee leave.[39]

While these appear to be positive developments, the Committee still noted with dismay the general reservations Saudi Arabia made against CEDAW which seriously compromises the object and purpose of the Convention, 'particularly in light of the fact that the delegation assured that there is no contradiction in substance between the Convention and Islamic Sharia.'[40] Moreover, the Committee proceeding to identify numerous impediments to the effective implementation of CEDAW, including most importantly, the non-existence of a definition of discrimination against women within the State's basic laws and constitutions and provisions for its prohibition, as required by Articles 1 and 2 of CEDAW. With reference to seemingly religious obstacles to the implementation of CEDAW, the Committee urged Saudi Arabia to do more to effectively address male guardianship over women (*mehrem*) and to be more proactive in implementing the goals of CEDAW and Beijing +5. Even where some positive steps were recognised by the Committee, such as advances in the protection of women from violence, the Committee still expressed concerns about the incidents of violence against women, the absence of specific laws relating to violence against women, and the lack of prosecu-

[38] UN Committee on the Elimination of Discrimination against Women 'Concluding observations of the Committee on the Elimination of Discrimination against Women: Saudi Arabia', C/SAU/CO/2, 2008 http://www2.ohchr.org/english/bodies/cedaw/docs/CEDAW.C.SAU.CO.2_en.pdf.

[39] UN Committee on the Elimination of Discrimination against Women 'Concluding observations of the Committee on the Elimination of Discrimination against Women: Saudi Arabia', C/SAU/CO/2, 2008, section II para. 3-4 available at http://www.ohchr.org (last accessed 1 April 2008).

[40] ibid, para 10.

tion and punishment of perpetrators of violence against women, including domestic violence.[41]

In light of the above summary, it is evident that while CEDAW and the Committee appear to have had some effect on law reform in Saudi Arabia, many challenges remain with relation to even the most basic and fundamental provisions of the Convention. What is interesting, however, is the statement made by the Committee which noted the Saudi Arabian delegation's assertions that the Convention was compatible with Sharia. Could it then be concluded that Sharia as law (as distinguished from local custom and tradition) has had no impact on the failure of Saudi Arabia to meet the international human rights standards articulated by CEDAW? According to the delegation this seems to be the case for as a delegate claimed, 'Saudi Arabia respected women and defended their rights and that the principles of human rights were reinforced by Islamic law'.[42]

Turkey

There has been significant law reform in Turkey since the Committee reports of 1997 which had aimed at promoting gender equality and elimination of discrimination against women and achieving compliance with the obligations of the convention.[43] By 2005, the Committee's conclusions praised Turkey for its 'rapid transformation' and importantly, 'the amendment of article 10 of the Constitution in May 2004, making the State responsible not only for ensuring non-discrimination between women and men, but also for taking the necessary measures to provide equal rights and opportunities in practice for women in every field.'[44] The Committee noted advances within substantive law, most notably the Civil Code of 2001 which ensures women's rights and equality between women and men in marriage and family relations; the Organizational Law on the Directorate General for the Status and Problems of Women (November 2004); the establishment of a Consultative Council for the Status of Women, to ensure more effective policy formulation and coordination; and legislation

41 UN Committee on the Elimination of Discrimination against Women 'Concluding observations: Saudi Arabia' CEDAW/C/SAU/CO/2, 2008, para.15 available at: http://www2.ohchr.org/english/bodies/cedaw/docs/co/CEDAW.C.SAU.CO.2.pdf, (last accessed 1 April 2008).

42 UN Committee on the Elimination of Discrimination against Women, 'Consideration of reports submitted by States parties under article 18 of the Convention,' CEDAW/C/SR.816, para. 80 http://daccessdds.un.org/doc/UNDOC/GEN/N08/232/02/PDF/N0823202.pdf?OpenElement.

43 UN Committee on the Elimination of Discrimination against Women 'Concluding comments by the Committee on the Elimination of Discrimination against Women: Turkey' C/TUR/CC/4-5, 2005, para.18 available at http://www.un.org/womenwatch/daw/cedaw/cedaw32/conclude-comments/Turkey/CEDAW-CC-TUR-0523813E.pdf (last accessed 1 April 2008).

44 http://www.un.org/womenwatch/daw/cedaw/cedaw32/conclude-comments/Turkey/CEDAW-CC-TUR-0523813E.pdf, para. 3.

combating domestic violence (The Law on the Protection of the Family 1998) and the criminalisation of marital rape, human trafficking and sexual harassment in the work place (the Penal Code of 2004).[45] The Committee also commended Turkey for sponsoring General Assembly Resolution 59/165 of 20 December 2004, entitled 'Working towards the Elimination of crimes against women and girls committed in the name of honour'.

While these appear to be positive advances, the Committee went on to note that Turkey's definition of 'discrimination' did not conform to the standards required by Article 1 of the Convention, echoing the state of affairs in Saudi Arabia. In the same vein, the Committee asserted that 'traditional values and customs continued to have an impact on the practical implementation of the new laws,'[46] which was also the case in Saudi Arabia. The Committee thus criticized Turkey for provisions of the Penal Code and Civil Codes which continue to discriminate against women and girls. In particular, the committee expressed concern that genital examinations of women (so-called 'virginity tests') could still be carried out under certain circumstances without the consent of the woman and that, significantly, that the term 'custom killing' instead of 'honour killing' in the Penal Code often resulted in less vigorous prosecution of, and less severe sentences for the perpetrators of such crimes against women.[47] The Committee went on to suggest that more needed to be done to address 'honour killing', and so it appears that despite being a secular State, similar cultural impediments as in Saudi Arabia, prevent the realisation of CEDAW—cultural impediments which both governments have failed to sufficiently address inside and outside of legal reform. A further example of this is evident from the comments made by CEDAW in relation to domestic violence in both States. Despite both States making attempts to criminalise domestic violence and advance the protection of women against violence, the Committee noted that in Turkey:

> [T]he pervasiveness of patriarchal attitudes and deep-rooted traditional and cultural stereotypes regarding the roles and responsibilities of women and men in society ... continue to cast women in a position of inferiority. It expresses its concern that these attitudes contribute to the

[45] UN Committee on the Elimination of Discrimination against Women 'Concluding comments by the Committee on the Elimination of Discrimination against Women: Turkey' C/TUR/CC/4-5, 2005, para.18 available at http://www.un.org/womenwatch/daw/cedaw/cedaw32/conclude-comments/Turkey/CEDAW-CC-TUR-0523813E.pdf (last accessed 1 April 2008).

[46] UN Committee on the Elimination of Discrimination against Women 'Concluding comments: Turkey, CEDAW/C/TUR/CC/4-5, 2005, para.19 available at: http://www.un.org/womenwatch/daw/cedaw/cedaw32/conclude-comments/Turkey/CEDAW-CC-TUR-0523813E.pdf, para. 19 (last accessed 1 April 2008).

[47] ibid, para 6.

> perpetuation of violence against women, including in the form of 'honour killings', and negatively affect women's enjoyment of their rights in many areas.[48]

Practically the same has been said by the Committee with regards to Saudi Arabia as agreed by the Saudi delegation to the Committee itself.[49]

It is evident from the above analysis of Committee reports on Saudi Arabia and Turkey that the failure of these two States to fully implement CEDAW has as much to do with law as it does with custom and culture (which includes religion), and the lack of political will to address the concerns they present. Indeed, this appears to be the case across the board. For example, the Committee on CEDAW in its report of 2008 reiterates concern about article 562 of the Lebanese Penal Code which allows mitigation of the penalty for crimes committed in the name of Honour and which continues to be in force.[50] The Committee was also concerned about other discriminatory provisions in the Lebanese Penal Code, in particular article 503 which tolerates marital rape. Similarly, Malaysia which places a higher normative value on the role of Islam in State and society has also drafted a Domestic Violence Act which does not criminalise marital rape.[51] In Egypt too, the Committee expressed concern that:

> [A]lthough efforts have been made, there is no holistic approach to the prevention and elimination of violence against women, including domestic violence, marital rape, violence against women in detention centres and crimes committed in the name of honour or the punishment of perpetrators. The Committee is also concerned at the high level of violence against adolescent girls, and young married women.[52]

48 ibid, para 29

49 See: UN Committee on the Elimination of Discrimination against Women 'Concluding observations: Saudi Arabia' CEDAW/C/SAU/CO/2, 2008; and UN Committee on the Elimination of Discrimination against Women, 'Consideration of reports submitted by States parties under article 18 of the Convention,' CEDAW/C/SR.816.

50 UN Committee on the Elimination of Discrimination against Women 'Concluding observations of the Committee on the Elimination of Discrimination against Women: Lebanon' CEDAW/C/LBN/CO/3, 2008, para.36 available at: http://www2.ohchr.org/english/bodies/cedaw/docs/co/CEDAW.C.LBN.CO.3.pdf (last accessed 1 April 2008).

51 CEDAW/C/MYS/CO/2 http://daccessdds.un.org/doc/UNDOC/GEN/N06/384/40/PDF/N0638440.pdf?OpenElement.

52 UN Committee on the Elimination of Discrimination against Women 'Concluding Observations of the Committee on the Elimination of Discrimination against Women: Egypt',CEDAW/C/SR/492, 2001, section I para 1–11 available at http://www.ohchr.org (last accessed 1 April 2008).

CONCLUSION

Evidently, the ratification of international human rights conventions is not enough to ensure the implementation and protection of human rights in State practice. Indeed, there are clear disparities between on the one hand, rights enshrined in the Constitution, international human rights instruments, and the guarantees provided by the law, and on the other hand, human rights norms implemented into the domestic law of these States.

The domestic situation of human rights in many States reflects a deep gap between the texts and the reality. Examples of this are also evident in the conclusions and recommendations of Committees for other Conventions, such as the UN Committee on Torture in response to State reports. For example, in its 2005 report on Bahrain, the committee expressed concern at 'the persistent gap between the legislative framework and its practical implementation with regard to the obligations of the Convention', and 'the lack of a comprehensive definition of torture in the domestic law as set out in article 1 of the Convention'.[53] This is despite clear provisions in Bahrain's Constitution and laws which relate to 'torture'.[54] The committee made similar statements with regard to both Egypt[55] and Tunisia.[56]

On 26 May 2004, Kofi Annan addressing the continuing violations of human rights in the frame of the Lecture Series 'Who is Afraid of Human Rights?', said:

> More than half a century after the United Nations adopted the Universal Declaration of Human Rights, it is very easy to feel disillusioned, and for millions around the world to wonder if the Declaration's words will ever be more than just that: words on a page.

Therefore, it would be deceptive to assume a State complies with human rights on the status of ratifications to and reservations from international

[53] UN Committee Against Torture, 'Conclusions and Recommendations of the Committee against Torture: Bahrain,' CAT/C/CR/34/BHR, 2005, para.2, available at www.ohchr.org (last accessed 1 April 2008).

[54] Article 19(d) of Bahrain's constitution provides : 'No person shall be subject to physical or mental torture, or inducement, or undignified treatment, and the penalty for so doing shall be specified by law. Any statement or confession proved to have been under torture, unducement, or such treatment, or the threat thereof, shall be null and void'. See also: UN Committee Against Torture, 'Consideration of Reports Submitted by State Parties: Bahrain', CAT/C/47/Add.4, 2004.

[55] UN Committee Against Torture, 'Consideration of Reports Submitted by State Parties: Egypt', CAT/C/CR/29/4, 2002, available at: www.ohchr.org (last accessed 1 April 2008).

[56] UN Committee Against Torture, 'Consideration of Reports Submitted by State Parties: Tunisia', CAT/C/20/Add.7, 1998, available at: www.ohchr.org (last accessed 1 April 2008).

human rights treaties alone, as practice always differs. For example, Qatar is one Muslim State with a poor status with regard to the ratification of human rights treaties and the formulation of relevant and very severe or strict reservations which render some of these treaties almost void. Nevertheless, we cannot conclude that the human rights record in Qatar is the worst among Muslim States and indeed, it is not.[57] Qatar's human rights record is far less damning compared to that of other Muslim States.

As the ratification of human rights treaties, the incorporation of human rights norms in constitutions and the reforms of domestic law are not entirely sufficient in implementing human rights into domestic practice, other means must be considered. In the case of Muslim States, a particularly important and psychologically powerful tool is the implementation of human rights within the framework of the Sharia. As it appears that 'custom' and 'culture' are among the reasons behind the failure of Muslim States to effectively implement international human rights norms, particularly in areas related to women's and child rights, it is arguable that my making legitimate and well publicised reforms within the framework of the highest norm in society—Islam—domestic practices within the State could improve considerably.

Section Three Implementation of Legislative Reforms within the Framework of the Sharia

The idea that the rules of Sharia are unchangeable is misleading. Rather, reform of law within the framework of Sharia is necessary in order to reflect the constantly evolving norms of society. Hence, the relation between human rights and Islam cannot be perceived as static but rather, constantly changing. Even in the context of the Islamic Republic of Iran, the theocratic regime cannot enact unchangeable and permanent laws set out in accordance with fixed principles of Sharia or congealed human rights policies. Mayer's analysis of Iran's official positions on the impact of Islam on

[57] US Department of State 'Country reports on Human Rights practices: Qatar' available at: http://www.state.gov/g/drl/rls/hrrpt/2001/nea/8292.htm (last accessed 1 April 2008):

> The Qatari Government generally respected the human rights of its citizens; however, its record was poor in some areas, particularly regarding citizens' right to change their government and the treatment of foreign workers. Citizens do not have the right to change their government peacefully. The Government severely limits the rights of assembly and association. The Government restricts freedom of religion although it continued to take some steps to ease restrictions on the practice of non-Muslim religions. Women's rights are restricted by law and social customs. Women have the right to vote. The Government severely restricts workers' rights. Domestic servants are mistreated and at times abused. Noncitizens, who make up more than 75 percent of the residents of the country, face discrimination in the workplace. The country also is a destination for trafficked persons.

human rights in Iran over the past decades reveals many noteworthy twists and turns.[58] This has resulted in some positive legislative developments, including amendments to Divorce Regulations enacted in 1992 which effectively reinstate the rejected elements of the Family Protection Law of 1967 which was in 1979 declared by Khomeini to be in contradiction with Sharia and then rendered null and void.[59] The amendments to the laws of divorce changed the divorce procedure by requiring all couples seeking divorce to go through a process of arbitration and where if the arbiters failed to reconcile the couple in dispute, then the court would allow the man to effect and register a divorce only after he had paid his wife what she has a legal right to receive.

Another positive development in Iran comes with reference to a statement made by a member of the Iranian delegation to the Committee of the CRC in 2005 with reference to reforming the minimum age of marriage. There, the Iranian delegate stated that 'relevant *Sharia* provisions were currently being reconsidered in the light of the need for children to have attained a certain level of maturity before entering into marriage. The Government was considering the preparation of legal provisions to formalize the reforms.'[60] Prominent Human Rights Lawyer and Nobel Prize winner, Sirin Ebadi, envisions a better human rights future for Iran based on the power of interpretation and reform within Sharia. She recognizes the need to adopt a more dynamic interpretation of the Quran in order to provide laws that guarantee equal rights for women and argues that 'a basic right for women could be guaranteed within an Islamic framework of governance, provided those in government were inclined to interpret the faith in the spirit of equality.'[61] Thus, activating the inherent mechanisms of Sharia and interpreting Sharia in order to reform the law is a possible path even to the most theocratic regimes. For example, recent activism in Saudi Arabia has led to talks about lifting the ban on the prohibition to Saudi women and their right to drive a car.[62]

[58] See Ann Elizabeth Mayer (2007) 'The Islam and Human Rights Nexus: Shifting Dimensions', *Muslim World Journal of Human Rights*: Vol. 4 : Iss. 1, Article 4 at p. 11, available at : Available at: http://www.bepress.com/mwjhr/vol4/iss1/art4 ; see also Ann Elizabeth Mayer, 'Shifting Grounds for Challenging the Authority of International Human Rights Law: Religion as a Malleable and Politicized Pretext for Governmental Noncompliance with Human Rights', in *Human Rights with Modesty: The Problem of Universalism*, Andras Sajo (ed) (Martinus Nijhoff, 2004) 349–374.

[59] Ziba Mir-Hosseini, *Islam and Gender: The Religious Debate in Contemporary Iran* (Princeton University Press, New Jersey, 1999) 8.

[60] Committee on the Rights of the Child: Consideration of Reports, 2005 (Iran), ¶ 68, U.N. Doc. CRC/C/SR.1016 (28 Jan. 2005).

[61] Shirin Ebadi, *Iran Awakening*, 191.

[62] 'Saudi Women Demand the Right to Drive,' 24 Sep 2007, Reuters UK (http://uk.reuters.com/article/worldNews/idUKL2442000020070924).

Upon Statehood, a number of post-colonial Muslim States promulgated codes of law which introduced the rules and norms of Sharia in a statutory form, largely in areas of personal status and family law. Some of the laws within these codes have since been amended by legislative bodies in order to bring them further in line with the needs of a changing socio-economic reality and the demands of special interests groups/civil society and international standards. These reforms demonstrate the potential of a State's legislature to bring about reforms within the framework of Sharia, which also accommodate international human rights standards. Perhaps the most comprehensive of all recent legislative reforms is that of Morocco's personal status code of 2004—the *Moudawana*—this will be discussed in (A). Further examples of such reforms include (B) Law No. 1 of 2000 in Egypt concerning the woman's right to divorce; (C) Article 18 of the Tunisian Code of Personal Status 1956 concerning the abolition and criminalization of polygamous marriage; and (D) the reform of rape law in Pakistan through the Protection of Women (Criminal Laws Amendment) Act 2006.

A. The Moudawana *of Morocco*

Morocco's first code of personal status (Moudawana) was promulgated upon independence in 1958. The Code was prepared by a commission of Ulema (specialists in Islamic jurisprudence and theology) who based the new law on the classical rules of the Maliki *madhhab*. As a result, the Code was often criticised for failing to take into account the circumstances and developments of Moroccan society in the 20th century, and demands for reform grew progressively louder, resulting in a women's movement for reform by the 1980s.[63]

From the perspective of women's rights, the old Moudawana was extremely problematic. Under the old laws, married adult women were placed under the guardianship of their husbands to whom they owed obedience, divorce was extremely difficult, and the courts had no role in a decision by a man to enter into polygamous marriage. El-Hajjami argues that this situation gave rise to instability in the nuclear family and institutionalised violence, and by 1992, the Union for Feminine Action and the National Coordination Committee for Changes to the Moudawana and for the Defence of the Rights of Women, launched a campaign to obtain a million signatures in favour of reform. The campaign led to the late king Hassan II to appoint a commission of Islamic jurists to consider the draft reforms prepared by the women's associations on the condition that Islamic

63 Lecture by Dr Aicha El-Hajjami, 'The New Moroccan Family Code: Its Achievements and the Obstacles which Remain,' May 2008. Presented at the BIICL Conference on 'Shariah, Human Rights and International Law', 5 June 2008.

norms would not be compromised.[64] This resulted in a number of reforms in 1993 which did little to change the actual substance of the *Moudawana* and thus, demands for reform continued.

Following changes to the political scene in Morocco and continuing demands for reform, the King Muhammad VI appointed another reform commission which included Ulema as well as modernists and three women. El-Hajjami argues that the presence of women is significant because it means for the first time, women were involved in the process of *ijtihad*—an activity previously reserved for men alone.

The new *Moudawana* significantly improved women and child rights in Morocco. Among its key reforms include the guarantee that men and women are equal before the law. In his speech to the Moroccan parliament in 2003, King Muhammad VI argued that this right was justified by the *hadith* which stated that 'only an honourable man will honour them (women); and only an ignoble man will humble them'.[65] The abolition of forced guardianship over adult women was also justified by a fresh reading of the Quran's provisions, as were the strict limitations placed on the practice of polygamy.[66] Additionally, women were granted equal rights to divorce with men; the minimum age for both men and women was set at 18; and a number of financial rights were clarified, such as allowing women the right to a share of the family assets acquired in common in the case of the dissolution of marriage. Moreover, the rights of children were also improved 'by making the provisions of the relevant international agreements ratified by Morocco, part of the Family Law'.[67]

King Muhammad VI made sure to emphasise that all these reforms were in conformity with Islamic principles and stated:

> It is necessary to be mindful of the tolerant aims of Islam, which advocates human dignity, equality and harmonious relations, and also to rely on the cohesiveness of the Malikite rite and on Ijtihad, thanks to which Islam is a suitable religion for all times and places. The aim is to draw up a modern Family Law which is consistent with the spirit of our glorious religion.

[64] Lecture by Dr Aicha El-Hajjami, 'The New Moroccan Family Code: Its Achievements and the Obstacles which Remain,' May 2008. Presented at the BIICL Conference on 'Shariah, Human Rights and International Law,' 5 June 2008. El-Hajjami references: Al Alam of 30 September 1992.

[65] King Muhammad VI, October 10, 2003 speech to members of the Moroccan Parliament, Maghreb Arab Presse (Morocco), October 10, 2003 available at: (http://www.map.co.ma/mapeng/speeches/parliament_fall_session.htm).

[66] ibid, King Muhammad VI, October 10, 2003 speech to members of the Moroccan Parliament

[67] ibid, King Muhammad VI, October 10, 2003 speech to members of the Moroccan Parliament.

Indeed, Morocco's new *Moudawana* illustrates the great potential for human rights reform within Sharia where there is a will to undertake such efforts of reform.

B. The use of Islamic tools in the contemporary divorce legislation of Egypt

Contemporary divorce legislation in Egypt shows a very dynamic set of laws which have demonstrated to be innovative within the strict context of Sharia. This section will illustrate the different Islamic tools used in the legislative process of reforming the divorce laws in Egypt. The first of these methods is that of *takhayyur* and *talfiq*, and second is the use by the legislator of the Primary Sources of Sharia and *ijtihad.*

Illustrations of the use of the takhayyur and talfiq

Takhayyur[68] (selecting a favourable interpretation from among the Sunni schools) and *talfiq*[69] (patching together different rules from different schools to create a new rule), have both been popular means of reform in Egypt. Moussa[70] explains that both methods spring from the 'doctrine of supra-madhhab' and Egyptian reformer Muhammad Abduh's arguments that 'the state should not be confined to the rules of one *madhhab* but should be free when appropriate to seek the rules for its purposes in the doctrine of any school of law.'[71] Used effectively, these tools allow for Muslim reformists to apply equally legitimate but more equitable rules in the interests of justice, depending on the circumstances.

The use of *takhayyur* and *talfiq* in the field of family law have enabled the legislature in Egypt to introduce more liberal interpretations of the Maliki school in legislation even though officially, Egypt follows the more restrictive Hanafi School of interpretation. The use of these Islamic tools in reforming the family law in Egypt can be illustrated through the amendment of the law of divorce in Decree-Law No 25 of 1920 and Decree-Law No 25 of 1929.[72]

68 *Takhayyur-* favouring one school's opinion over another within a code of law.

69 *Talf'iq-* "Combining between the positions of the schools so as to produce a hybrid ruling which does not belong to any of them" (Oussama Arabi, ibid 18).

70 Moussa, Jasmine, 'The Reform of Sharia-derived Divorce Legislation in Egypt: International Standards and the Cultural Debate,' *University of Nottingham, Human Rights Law Commentary* Vol. 2, 2006, p. 10.

71 From Moussa, p. 10 quoting: Abu-Odeh, 'Modernising Muslim Family Law: The Case of Egypt', (2004) 37 *Vanderbilt Journal of Transnational Law* 1043 at 1091.

72 Moussa, Jasmine, 'The Reform of Sharia-derived Divorce Legislation in Egypt: International Standards and the Cultural Debate,' *University of Nottingham, Human Rights Law Commentary* Vol. 2, 2006, p. 12.

The law of 1929 departed from the more patriarchal rules of divorce of the Hanafi School, and used substantial provisions from the Maliki School to limit the grounds and methods by which a husband may divorce his wife, thus protecting the interests and status of the wife. Therefore, although Hanafi doctrine accepts the validity of a divorce stated by an intoxicated husband or a husband under duress and acknowledges the validity of conditional divorce[73], the 1929 law selected the interpretations of the Maliki School in order to prohibit a divorce declared by a man who was intoxicated or under duress. The new law also stipulated that conditional divorce was no longer valid and that any declaration of divorce had to conform to the explicit repudiating formula, 'ante taliq'.[74]

The laws of 1920 and 1929 were also effective in increasing the grounds upon which a woman may obtain a judicial divorce, *khul'*. Under classical Hanafi law, the conditions upon which a woman may obtain a divorce by a judge are the most restrictive of all the schools.[75] The new laws incorporated the more liberal position of the Maliki School where a woman can bring forward a claim for dissolution on the grounds of having suffered from harm—*darar*. Articles 4 and 5 of Law No 25 of 1920 included the husband's failure to provide maintenance as sufficient grounds for divorce.[76] Law No 25 of 1929 further increased the scope of *darar* and decision No 432 of the Court of Appeal of 1964 more generously defined *darar* to include 'the husband's systematic maltreatment, either verbal or physical, of the wife in a matter that is not suitable to women of her standing.'[77] Several reforms have occurred since, including Law No 44 of 1979 and arguably, Law No 100 of 1985. However, the most recent and significant reform is the Law Regarding Certain Conditions and Procedures of Litigation in Matters of Personal Status (Law No 1 of 2000), which significantly increased the unhappy wife's right to divorce.

Law No. 1 of 2000 (judicial khul') and the use of ijtihad[78]

Although the Egyptian law of personal status does not meet the standards

[73] Conditional Divorce means that a Muslim husband may stipulate conditions of any particular behaviour on the part of his wife, the breach of which makes divorce effective without immediate declaration.

[74] Moussa, ibid 12.

[75] Lucy Carroll, 'Qu'ran 2:229: "A Charter Granted to the Wife"? Judicial Khul' in Pakistan,' Islamic Law and Society 3.3, 92–93. Requirements include absence for up to 90 years; impotence after one year of trying to have a child; contracted as a minor by one other than the paternal father and grandfather; can prove to the satisfaction of the court that her guardian acted maliciously, negligently or fraudulently in contracting her marriage.

[76] Moussa, 13.

[77] Moussa, 13–16.

[78] For a comprehensive account of the reform of divorce law in Egypt, see: Moussa, Jasmine, 'The Reform of Sharia-derived Divorce Legislation in Egypt: International Standards

provided by CEDAW as to the non-discriminatory norms against women, tremendous progress was made in 2000 in the area of legislation on divorce. The substance of the reform has made a notable difference towards fostering equality between men and women in the matter of divorce in Egypt. However, what is tremendous and promising for further change in this sensitive area of law are the techniques used by the legislator to undertake such change. This reform has been conducted from within the framework of Sharia. In order to conduct this reform, the Egyptian parliament had to undertake to our knowledge for the first time, a direct application of the primary sources of Sharia without referring to any of the interpretive opinions of the Sunni Schools and instead going directly to the Quran and to the Sunnah and engaging in 'neo – *ijtihad*'.[79]

Article 20 of Law No 1 of 2000 introduced a new type of divorce—Judicial *Khul'*—which stipulated that a woman may obtain a divorce from her husband by the courts and without his consent on the condition that she returns her dower to her husband.[80] This differs from the traditional conceptions of *khul* in all four of the schools, as all required the husband's consent.[81] Article 20 states:

> The two spouses may agree between themselves upon *khul'*, but if they do not agree mutually and the wife files a claim requesting it [*khul'*], and ransoms herself and releases herself by *khul' (khala'at zawjaha)* by forfeiting all of her lawful financial rights, and restores to him [her husband] the dower he gave to her [upon marriage], then the court is to divorce her from him.[82]

The new law means that the wife need not prove to the judge's satisfaction any harm (*darar*) she may have endured as required under the previous laws which used the Maliki concept of *khul'* based on the Prophet's precedent in the 'Habiba Case'. The Maliki rule on judicial dissolution differs from the other schools in that when a wife persists in her complaints of suffering *darar* (harm) but could not prove it, arbiters would be appointed to try reconcile the differences between husband and wife. If they decided that

and the Cultural Debate,' *University of Nottingham, Human Rights Law Commentary* Vol. 2, 2006, 8–18 (http://wwwwip.nottingham.ac.uk/shared/shared_hrlcpub/HRLC_Commentary_2005/MOUSSA.pdf).

79 Arabi, 199 (referring to neo-Shafism.)

80 Mashhour, Amira, Islamic Law and Gender Equality—Could There be a Common Ground?: A Study of Divorce and Polygamy in Sharia Law and Contemporary Legislation in Tunisia and Egypt, 27 *Human Rights Quarterly*, 2005, 583.

81 Mashhour, 574–575.

82 Translation taken from Moussa, 16 (Article 20 of Law no. 1 of 2000, Regarding the Promulgation of a Law to Organize Certain Conditions and Procedures in Matters of Personal Status, Official Gazette, Arab Republic of Egypt, No. 4 (29 January 2000).

dissolution of the marriage would be appropriate, they awarded the wife all or part of her *mahr* (dower) depending on her responsibility in causing the breaches in obligations.[83] This type of dissolution itself differs from *khul'* which is present in some form in all the classical schools where a woman may seek to have her marriage dissolved if she 'loathes the man, and does not want to disobey God',[84] on condition that she returns her dower (and sometimes even more) *and* the husband has given his consent.

The new law contains aspects of both of these types of dissolution. Through Judicial *Khul'* the wife may have her marriage dissolved by the judge upon stating that she 'loathes life with her husband, that the marriage cannot continue and she will not be able to live 'within the limits of Allah' if she remains married to him.'[85] Included in the law is the requirement of two arbiters appointed by the court to try and reconcile the parties for at least three months. However, the main feature of the article 20 law is that the husband's consent is not required as it is in *khul'* separation.

The new law gives 'full weight to a wife's desire to separate from her husband, radically (severing) a woman's obtaining separation from her husband's consent to that divorce'.[86] Furthermore, the arbiters appointed have no authority to apportion blame or the amount of compensation due even if the wife claims *darar* but cannot prove it. If she can prove *darar*, the normal *faskh* method of judicial dissolution applies (as previously described), although the procedural difficulties involved in this kind of divorce are considerably responsible for the new law and so if a woman really does have a legitimate grounds for divorce under *faskh*, she may have to forgo her material rights by applying for Judicial *Khul'*.[87] Therefore, as el- Alami asserts, 'the new provision regulating khul' represents progress in as much as it is a recognition of a woman's right of choice, but it does little to rectify the injustice of a system that denies women access to real remedies and just settlement.[88]

[83] Lucy Carroll, *'Qu'ran 2:229: "A Charter Granted to the Wife"? Judicial Khul' in Pakistan,'* Islamic Law and Society 3.3, 99.

[84] Abu Ali Hasan Ibn al- Banna's Commentary on al-Khiraqi's Digest, Kitab al- Muqni fi Sharh Mukhtasar al- Khiraqi, ed. 'Abd al-Aziz al-Bu'aymi, 4 Vols (Riyadh: Maktabat al-Rushd, 1993), 3: 952.

[85] Lynn Welchman, *Beyond the Code: Muslim Family Law and the Shari Judiciary in the Palestinian West Bank* (Kluwer Law International, 2000) 274.

[86] Oussama Arabi, 'The Dawn Of The Third Millennium On Sharia: Egypt's Law No. 1 of 2000, Or Women May Divorce At Will,' *Studies in Modern Islamic Law and Jurisprudence (Arab & Islamic Laws)* (Kluwer Law International, 2001), 171.

[87] Arabi (ibid 13 'brought about by the tragic fate of the greater number of wives suing for divorce under the existing laws.' Also mentioned in Welchman (ibid 11) citing Fahmi (at 15), *Divorcer en Egypte)*.

[88] El- Alami, 'Remedy or Device? The System of Khul and the Effects of its Incorporation into Egyptian Personal Status Law' 6 Yearbook of Islamic and Middle Eastern Law, 1999–2000.

In referring directly to the Quran and the Sunnah to justify the amendment of the law without any reference to juristic interpretations, the legislature of Egypt shifted from its traditional use of the tools of *takhayyur* and *talfiq* alone, and also adopted *ijtihad*—new interpretation of the law based on the primary sources of Sharia.[89] The new legislative amendment was approved by Grand Sheikh of Al Azhar, Egypt's highest Muslim authority and the Islamic Research Academy to be in conformity with Sharia.[90]

Perhaps the most significant aspect of the law of Judicial *Khul'* is that it marks the emergence of a modern *ijtihad* in Egypt. In 1980, Egypt declared a new constitutional policy on Islamic Law stating that 'the principles of Sharia are the main source of legislation.'[91] Interestingly, it was the governing elite and politically oriented that sparked the movement towards 'Sharia-isation'[92] as opposed to the religious establishment. The policy involved 'going back to the revealed sources of Sharia for inspiration in all modern legislation, and to abandon any prior commitment either to the historically established school doctrines of Islamic Law (madhahib) or to culturally sedimented rules of behaviour (urf').'[93] This meant that Egyptian jurists could go beyond the established and dominant rules of the classical laws to which they were previously confined, and on the occasion of the Judicial *Khul'* they did.

The movement towards Sharia-isation in Egypt began with the ideas of reformists such as Muhammad 'Abdhu[94] and his disciple Rashid Rida. They advocated a *Sharia* that would be responsive to a changing reality instead of being 'bound by the shackles of the past.'[95] Abduh argued in favour of reform through *ijtihad*,[96] which would mean returning to the original sources 'in search of the first truths of the faith which were deformed by the accretions of the ages'.[97] In fact, this is the path Egypt has taken for as Tariq al-Bishri[98] declares, 'we are bound ... (for) this is an obligation linked to the faith that we may not obstruct'. The Egyptian courts have responded positively to this movement as well, proclaiming:

89 See Jasmine Moussa, The Reform of Sharia Derived Divorce Legislation in Egypt: International standards and the cultural debate, University of Nottingham, *Human Rights Law Commentary* Vol. 2 (2006), available at: http://www-wip.nottingham.ac.uk/shared/shared_hrlcpub/HRLC_Commentary_2005/MOUSSA.pdf (last accessed 16 April 2008).

90 See Jasmine Moussa (n 22) 18.

91 Oussama Arabi, *Studies in Modern Islamic Law and Jurisprudence* (Kluwer Law International, The Hague, Netherlands, 2001) 197–198.

92 Term used by Arabi, ibid.

93 Oussama Arabi, 'The Dawn Of The Third Millennium On Sharia: Egypt's Law No.1 of 2000, Or Women May Divorce At Will,' Arab Law Quarterly 16/1 2001, 6.

94 Grand Mufti of Egypt, d. 1905.

95 Arabi, 24.

96 ibid, p. 25.

97 ibid, p. 26.

98 An interview with Councilor of State, Taqriq al-Bishri.

> (The) practice of (*ijtihad*) does not confer any sacredness (*qudsiyya*) on the opinion of some jurist or another with regard to the legal matter under consideration, and there is no impediment to revising it, evaluating it, or replacing it by another rule. Interpretive opinions, by themselves, do not possess a binding force on those who do not have the same opinion; one should not, therefore, consider these opinions as a Law of the Sharia that is absolute and incontestable and cannot be contradicted.[99]

The method of reaching reform by use of reasoning and traditional jurisprudential and hermeneutic techniques, illustrates the ability to reform and develop laws within the scope of the Sharia as whole. The reforms in Egypt (and Pakistan which has a similar law) demonstrates a 'dramatic assertion of the right of *ijtihad*'.[100] As noted and translated by Moussa,[101] 'perhaps the most illuminating was the statement made by Fathi Sorour, Chairman of the People's Assembly, immediately following the law's adoption by Parliament.' Sorour emphasised that in drafting Law No. 1 of 2000, the People's Assembly had:

> ... complied with Article 2 of the Egyptian Constitution, which stipulates that the Sharia is the primary source of legislation. In spite of the controversy surrounding the opinions of the jurists, the Assembly has conformed to the Supreme Constitutional court's interpretation of the phrase 'principles of Islamic Sharia' as the clear-cut decrees of the Quran and the Sunnah. *Ijtihad* is limited to issues that are ambiguous and therefore the Assembly has referred to the decrees of the Quran and Sunnah, disregarding specific juristic opinions and *ijtihadat*. The Assembly has selected the interpretations that reinforce the clear-cut decrees [of the Quran and the Sunnah] since the issue at hand does not involve ambiguous provisions. The principles of the Sharia are limited to what was decreed by the Quran and the Sunnah, and the Assembly has respected these sources.[102]

The academics, Nathan Brown and Adel Omar Sherif have found that since the role of the Sharia in the constitution expanded, the Supreme

[99] High Constitutional Court Ruling of March 26, 1994, *Al- Jarida al- Rasmiyya* (The Official Gazette, Arab Republic of Egypt, No. 15, 14/4/1994); French trans., B. Dupret, 'A propos de le constitutionalite de la Shari' a: Presentation et traduction de l'arret du 26 Mars 1994 de la Haute Cour Constitutionelle egyptienne,' *Islamic Law and Society* 4: 1 (1997), 105.

[100] Carroll, 1996: 108.

[101] ibid, 19.

[102] Sorour Fathi, (Chairman of the People's Assembly) Statement before the People's Assembly, 26 January 2000, Minutes of the 29th Parliamentary Session, Official Gazette, 79 (9 March 2000) cited and translated by Jasmine Moussa (n 22), 19.

Constitutional Court of Egypt has 'taken up the task of assisting the peaceful integration of Islamic Sharia principles in the constitutional order and daily life of the Egyptian citizen', though with a significant degree of judicial self-restraint in mind of the political context.[103] However, their role is increasing with the growth of Sharia-related cases which their training in both law and Sharia equip them to handle and according to Brown and Sherif, the SCC have managed to 'strike a balance' between the constitution and Sharia.[104] Furthermore, they also found that the increased role of the Sharia as a legal system in itself, has managed to fulfil the needs and wishes of some of the Muslim populace without compromising the rights and interests of other religious minority groups as the other provisions in the constitution remain as influential as before.[105] This supports the argument made above that reform within the *Sharia* may have a positive effect on changing customs and norms.

C. The use of Islamic tools in the abolition of polygamy in Tunisia

Many Muslim States have tried to limit the injustices caused against women by the institution of polygamous marriage within the Sharia. Generally, the Sharia allows a Muslim male to be married to up to four women at any given time.[106] However, this is on the condition that each wife is treated equally, for as the Quran states:

> Marry such women as seem good to you, two, three, four; but if you fear you will not be equitable, then only one.[107]

The Quran further states:

> You will not be able to be equitable between yours wives, be you ever so eager.[108]

103 Nathan Brown and Adel Omar Sherif, 'Inscribing the Islamic Sharia in Arab Constitutional Law,' in Haddad and Stowasser, *Islamic Law and the Challenges of Modernity*, AltaMira Press, 2004, 73–74

104 Nathan Brown and Adel Omar Sherif, 'Inscribing the Islamic Sharia in Arab Constitutional Law,' in Haddad and Stowasser, *Islamic Law and the Challenges of Modernity*, AltaMira Press, 2004, 74.

105 Nathan Brown and Adel Omar Sherif, 'Inscribing the Islamic Sharia in Arab Constitutional Law,' in Haddad and Stowasser, *Islamic Law and the Challenges of Modernity*, AltaMira Press, 2004, 75.

106 Rehman, Javaid, 'The Sharia, Islamic Family Laws and International Human Rights Law: Examining the Theory and Practice of Polygamy and Talaq,' *International Journal of Law, Policy and the Family* 21, 2007, 114.

107 Qur: IV: 3.

108 Qur: IV: 129.

In light of demands for gender equality and international standards which seek the abolition of polygamy,[109] legislative and administrative reforms have been undertaken by Muslim states in order to mitigate some of the harmful effects of polygamy.

One of the methods through which these reforms have been undertaken is via the legal doctrine of *takhayyur* which 'denotes selection of the most appealing and appropriate doctrine from amongst the existing Islamic schools. Such an approach provides a more equitable solution in circumstances where insistence on the application of the principles derived from any one school would lead to injustice.'[110]

An example of the application of *takhayyur* in this context is in relation to contractual stipulations within the marriage contract. Unlike the other Sunni schools, the Hanbali *madhhab* gave legal value to contractual stipulations added to the marriage contract, including those which sought to prevent or restrict the potential of a polygamous marriage. The Hanbali position on contracts has been adopted in most Middle Eastern countries and South Asian countries.[111] Ottoman Turkey had set a precedent for future States regarding legal reform as early as 1917. Article 61 of the OFLR[112] stated that if contractual stipulations were not abided by, the marriage was irregular, thus releasing the wife from her duty of obedience to the husband.[113]

Recent reforms in this area come from Morocco, where King Muhammad VI[114] enacted changes into the 'Muadawana' family code. Along with making polygamy subject to a judge's authorisation and imposing stringent legal conditions, the new law put the onus on the judge to ensure that there is no presumption of iniquity. Additionally, the woman has a right to stipulate against her husband taking other wives, and the law allows for a public prosecutor to be a party to every legal action involving the enforcement of Family Law stipulations.

[109] General Recommendation 21, Equality in Marriage and Family Relations, UN CEDAWOR, 13th Sess., UN Doc. A/47/38, (1994) para 14: 'Polygamous marriage contravenes a woman's right to equality with men, and can have such serious emotional and financial consequences for her and her dependents that such marriages ought to be discouraged and prohibited. The Committee notes with concern that some States parties, whose constitutions guarantee equal rights, permit polygamous marriage in accordance with personal or customary law. This violates the constitutional rights of women, and breaches the provisions of article 5(a) of the Convention.'

[110] Javaid Rehman, 'The Sharia, Islamic Family Laws and International Human Rights Law: Examining the Theory and Practice of Polygamy and Talaq,' *International Journal of Law, Policy and the Family* 21, 2007, 116.

[111] Doreen Hinchcliffe, 'Polygamy in Traditional and Contemporary Islamic Law', Islam and the Modern Age, 1970, 19.

[112] Ottoman Law of Family Reform.

[113] Lynn Welchman, 'Variations on the theme: Dower Stipulations and Polygynous Unions,' Beyond the Code, 2000, 159.

[114] 10 October 2003.

Another means of reform has been through a 'greater readiness to adopt a contextual and methodological interpretation of the Quranic provisions. This has resulted in significant limitations placed on polygamous marriages for example in Pakistan[115], Syria[116], Iraq[117]or through its outright abolition, as in the case of Tunisia[118,119] Indeed, of these reforms, that in Tunisia has been the most radical to the point that under article 18, polygamy is 'punishable by imprisonment of 1 year or a fine of 240,000 francs or both.'

The prohibition of polygamy in Tunisia and the potential of Ijtihad

Reforms of Tunisian law largely began in 1956 following Tunisia's independence from France and the presidency of the nationalist leader Habib Bourguiba. Bourguiba argued that the unification of the judicial system and the modernizing of the law in the interests of human progress was not only an Islamic obligation, but was an act necessary to establish the sovereignty of success of the newly independent Tunisia.[120]

The project of law reform was undertaken by judges of the civil and religious courts and overseen by the Ministry of Justice. The result was a draft law of 'modern inspiration' which was approved by eminent Muslim jurists and kept to the spirit of Islam despite the innovative reforms.[121] Among the most significant reforms was the abolition of polygamy. Bourguiba is often criticized for this reform on the grounds that it is 'un-Islamic,' but legitimate ijtihad was undertaken to justify the abolition. Indeed, the most renowned jurists and scholars such as Shaykh al-Islam Muhammad Ju'ayt, Shaykh al-Islam and the Shaykh of Zaytuna University approved of the law.[122]

The reasoning behind the prohibition of polygamy was made in light of the Quranic obligation upon the husband to treat all wives equally[123] and the statement that following which claimed that it would be impossible to do so.[124] Bourguiba also argued that polygamy should be prohibited using

115 Muslim Family Law Ordinance (1961).

116 Article 17 Law of Personal Status 1953 (Decree No. 59 of 1953).

117 Article 3, Law of Personal Status 1959.

118 Article 18, Tunisian Code of Personal Status 1956.

119 Rehman, Javaid, 'The Sharia, Islamic Family Laws and International Human Rights Law: Examining the Theory and Practice of Polygamy and Talaq,' 116.

120 Anderson, J.N.D, 'The Tunisian Law of Personal Status,' *The International and Comparative Law Quarterly*, Vol. 7, No. 2, 1958, 263.

121 Anderson, J.N.D, 'The Tunisian Law of Personal Status,' *The International and Comparative Law Quarterly*, Vol. 7, No. 2, 1958, 263.

122 Anderson, J.N.D, 'The Tunisian Law of Personal Status,' *The International and Comparative Law Quarterly*, Vol. 7, No. 2, 1958, 264.

123 Surah 4, 24—Qur'an—'But if you fear you cannot do justice with them, Then take only one wife (or a slave girl) That will be more suitable to prevent you from injustice.'

124 Qur: IV: 129.

the same reasoning used to abolish slavery which was that 'the practice was related to a special context at the time of revelation'.[125]

Bourguiba was not the first to seek the reform or abolition of polygamy. Another early 20th-century Tunisian author and reformist al-Tahi al-Haddad has been recognized as the first to publish a feminist manual on the role of women in Muslim society in the Arab world (Imra tuna fi l-sharia wa l-mujtama).[126] Al-Haddad argued that polygamy 'has no basis in Islam', and that rather, 'it is one of the evils of the pre-Islamic era which Islam has been challenged thorough its gradualistic method'.[127] Al-Haddad argues that if polygamy had not continued following the revelation of these verses that limited the number of wives and imposed the condition of fairness only to state that it was impossible to do so, it 'would have constituted the clearest prohibition'.[128] Bourguiba's contemporary and infamous Egyptian scholar Mohamad Abdhu also held this view. Abdhu reasoned that according to the Quran, monogamous marriage was the Islamic ideal and that its initial allowance was a concession allowed only on the condition of equality.[129] Indeed, this is a common argument which tries to ascertain the ultimate purpose of the Quranic provisions. Khadduri himself argues that 'rather than intending to ratify the practice of polygamy, (Quranic law) sought to reform it to the extent possible at the time', and that:

> ... to abolish polygamy, under the conditions then prevailing in Arabia, would have been an extremely difficult undertaking. By restricting the practice of plural marriage, the ultimate intent of the Prophet was to transform marriage from a polygamous to a monogamous relationship. The ultimate purpose of Quranic marriage law, then, was to legitimate monogamy, rather than endorse polygamy.[130]

Generally, it appears that views on polygamy differ widely among reformers. While some advocate its abolition, others argue that restrictions are necessary on the grounds of the obligation for husbands to be equitable.[131]

125 Mashhour, Amira, Islamic Law and Gender Equality—Could There be a Common Ground?: A Study of Divorce and Polygamy in Sharia Law and Contemporary Legislation in Tunisia and Egypt, *Human Rights Quarterly* 27, 2005, 585.

126 Ronak Husni and Daniel L. Newman, *Muslim Women in Law and Society* (Annotated translation of al-Tahi al-Haddad's *Imra tuna fi l-sharia wa l-mujtama*), Routlege: 2007.

127 Al-Haddad, 63.

128 ibid.

129 Mashhour, Amira, 'Islamic Law and Gender Equality—Could There be a Common Ground?: A Study of Divorce and Polygamy in Sharia Law and Contemporary Legislation in Tunisia and Egypt', 2005 *Human Rights Quarterly* 27, 585.

130 Khadduri, Majid, 'Marriage in Islamic Law: The Modernist Viewpoints', 26 *American Journal of Comparative Law,*1977–1978, 217.

131 Khadduri, Majid, 'Marriage in Islamic Law: The Modernist Viewpoints', 26 *American Journal of Comparative Law,* 1977–1978, 217.

Scholars also differ on many aspects as to how to interpret the verses in the Quran related to polygamy. For example, there are different interpretations as to how to be 'just'/equitable to each of ones wives. Many scholars interpret this as equality in terms of food, clothing and housing among wives—*nafaqa*—or maintenance.[132] Conversely, the dominant view of the Mu'tazille school[133] is that justice/equality must be in terms of love and in light of the second verse on polygamy, it is impossible to be in love with more than one woman at a time. This view was also held by the 19th-century reformer Sayyid Ahmad Khan,[134] and Abdhu too believed that no man would ever be just to more than one wife.[135] Therefore, it is evident from the above that Sharia leaves significant room for reasoning and reform in relation to polygamy thus demonstrating that *ijtihad* can successfully achieve 'a common ground between Islamic law and gender equality'.[136]

D. Legislative Reform within the framework of Shar'a: Pakistan's Rape Law

The Protection of Women (Criminal Laws Amendment) Act 2006 of Pakistan significantly altered the treatment of rape in Pakistani law. The new law provides more protection for women by bringing rape and adultery cases within the scope of the secular criminal laws. Moreover, the stated objective of the Act was also to bring the laws 'in conformity with … the injunctions of Islam'.[137] Previously, rape cases were governed by the Islamic Hudood Ordinances of 1979, more specifically the Zina Ordinance, and these significantly compromised the rights of women and freedoms of women in general, and redress for rape in particular.[138]

The *Zina* Ordinance criminalised all forms of *zina*, defining *zina* as 'wilful sexual intercourse between a man and a woman who are not validly married to each other'. A subcategory of this is *Zina-bil-jabr*—forced *Zina*,

132 Jones, Rachel, 'Polygyny in Islam,' Macalester Islam Journal, Vol. 1 Issue 1, 2006, 64.

133 Mu'tazille school started as an 8th Century religious movement in Basra. It became one of the most important and popular theological schools of Islam. (http://www.muslimphilosophy.com/ei2/mu-tazila.htm).

134 Jones, Rachel, 'Polygyny in Islam', Macalester Islam Journal, Vol. 1 Issue 1, 2006, 65.

135 Khadduri, Majid, Marriage in Islamic Law: The Modernist Viewpoints, 26 *American Journal of Comparative Law*, 1977–1978, 217.

136 Mashhour, Amira, 'Islamic Law and Gender Equality—Could There be a Common Ground?: A Study of Divorce and Polygamy in Sharia Law and Contemporary Legislation in Tunisia and Egypt', 27 *Human Rights Quarterly*, 2005, 595.

137 Preamble of the Protection of Women Act 2006. Please also see 'Statement of Objects and Reasons', http://www.presidentofpakistan.gov.pk/images/women/NewHudoodOrdinance.pdf.

138 Shah, Niaz, *Women, the Koran and International Human Rights Law: The Experience of Pakistan* (Martinus Nijhoff Publishers: Netherlands, 2006) 128; Lau, Martin, 'Human Rights, Natural Justice and Pakistan's Shariat Courts,' in Javaid Rehman and Susan Breau (eds), *Religion, Human Rights and International Law* (Brill, Netherlands, 2007) 359.

ie rape. Both *zina* and rape are punishable by *hadd* (punishments fixed by the Quran and Sunnahh where specific evidentiary requirements apply.) The punishments of *hadd* depend on whether the perpetrator of *zina* or rape is married or unmarried, where if married the punishment is death by stoning and if unmarried the punishment is 100 lashes and possibly in the case of rape, death.[139] What is controversial about this law is that both *zina* and rape are subject to the same stringent evidentiary requirements which are either a confession by the accused, or the testimony of four adult Muslim men of 'good character' who personally witnessed the act of sexual penetration.[140] Furthermore, the victim of the offence may not provide evidence, and expert opinion and forensic evidence are also excluded.[141] These requirements make successful prosecution extremely difficult. Victims who cannot satisfy these standards of proof may also bring claims under the category of *tazir*,[142] where the court has discretion over sentencing (from four to 25 years) and where evidentiary requirements are lower.[143]

Taken as a whole, the laws of the Zina Ordinance were condemned for both preventing effective access to justice and for failing to comply with Sharia in substance[144] as well as spirit.[145] Specific criticisms of the law include the 'self-incrimination' of alleged rape victims of *zina* where rape was not proven and the resulting injustices; inconsistency with the Quran and failure to protect women as obligated;[146] and abuse of the Zina Ordinance where 'according to the National Commission on the Status of Women of Pakistan (2003), 80% of women languishing in jails are there

139 Zina Ordinance, Section 6.

140 Quran (4:15): 'If any of your women are guilty of lewdness, take the evidence of four (Reliable) witnesses from amongst you against them…'

141 Siobhan Mullally, 'As Nearly as May be': Debating Women's Human Rights in Pakistan,' 14 *Social Legal Studies* 2005, 349 See also: Siobhan Mullally, 'Women, Islamisation and Human Rights in Pakistan', in Javaid Rehman and Susan Breau (eds), *Religion, Human Rights and International Law* (Brill, Netherlands, 2007) 391–395.

142 Zina Ordinance, Section 10.

143 Shah, Niaz, *Women, the Koran and International Human Rights Law: The Experience of Pakistan* (Martinus Nijhoff Publishers, Netherlands, 2006) 129.

144 Shah, Niaz, *Women, the Koran and International Human Rights Law: The Experience of Pakistan* (Martinus Nijhoff Publishers, Netherlands, 2006) 127–149; Pakistan (1997) Commission of Inquiry for Women, *Annual Report*; Bubb, Rachel, 'Reform of the Pakistani Rape Law: A Move Backward or Forward?' 11 *Journal of Gender, Race and Justice*, 2007, pp. 71–75; ibid., Mullally, p. 349; Karamah Position Paper, Zina, Rape and Islamic Law: An Islamic Legal Analysis of the Rape Laws of Pakistan (http://www.karamah.org/docs/Zina_article_Final.pdf); The Protection of Women Act 2006. Please also see 'Statement of Objects and Reasons.' http://www.presidentofpakistan.gov.pk/images/women/NewHudoodOrdinance.pdf.

145 Karamah: Citing the Quranic Principle of *adalah* (Justice, Balance and Equity), 15.

146 Rachel Bubb, 'Reform of the Pakistani Rape Law: A Move Backward or Forward?' 11 *Journal of Gender, Race and Justice* 2007, 72.

because of the ambiguous *Zina* Ordinance'.[147] These criticisms will be further elaborated and it will then be possible to analyse how far the new rape laws in the Protection of Women Act improve women's rights while at the same time being further in accordance with Sharia.

Zina as a 'crime against society'

By following the reasoning of the Ordinance, if a woman brought forward a claim of rape under the *Zina* Ordinance and her claim was unproven, her very admission of having been involved in a sexual act would itself constitute admission of *zina* as punishable by *hadd*.[148] Furthermore, a number of cases have been reported where pregnancy resulting from an unproven rape crime has been considered as evidence of *zina*.[149] By removing the crime of rape from the *Zina* Ordinance, the new rape laws mean that such 'self-incrimination' of *zina* and the unjust humiliation and punishment which follow would no longer be possible in theory or practice under the law.[150]

The Zina Ordinance and the Quran

The Zina Ordinance provides two avenues for prosecution: *hadd* and *tazir*. Citing Jehangir and Jillani,[151] Niaz Shah argues that the role of *tazir* which is to punish offences which do not meet *hadd* standards of proof has no basis in the Quran. Rather, where the evidentiary requirements for *zina* are not met, the accused (a woman) should be acquitted and the accuser liable for the offence of *qazf* (false accusation).[152] The relevant verse of the Quran is 24:4 which states:

147 Shah, Niaz, *Women, the Koran and International Human Rights Law: The Experience of Pakistan* (Martinus Nijhoff Publishers, Netherlands, 2006) 137.

148 Karamah Position Paper, Zina, Rape and Islamic Law: An Islamic Legal Analysis of the Rape Laws of Pakistan (http://www.karamah.org/docs/Zina_article_Final.pdf); Bubb, Rachel, 'Reform of the Pakistani Rape Law: A Move Backward or Forward?' 11 *Journal of Gender, Race and Justice* 2007, 72–73.

149 Mullally Siobhan, 'Women, Islamisation and Human Rights in Pakistan,' in Javaid Rehman and Susan Breau (eds), *Religion, Human Rights and International Law* (Brill, Netherlands, 2007) 392 (Mullally cites: *Safia Bibi* NLR 1985 SD 145 and *Shabbir Ahmed* PLD 1983 FSC 110).

150 Rahat Imran, 'Legal Injustices: The Zina Hudood Ordinance of Pakistan and Its Implications for Women', 7 *Journal of International Women's Studies* 2005, 78 and 89; Shah, Niaz, *Women, the Koran and International Human Rights Law: The Experience of Pakistan* (Martinus Nijhoff Publishers, Netherlands, 2006,) 132–136

151 A Jehangir and J Hina (1990) *Hudood Ordinances: A Divine Sanction?* (Rhotas Books, Lahore, 24 1990) 24.

152 Shah, Niaz, *Women, the Koran and International Human Rights Law: The Experience of Pakistan* (Martinus Nijhoff Publishers, Netherlands, 2006) 130.

> And those who launch a charge against chaste women, and produce not four witnesses (to support their allegations),—flog them with eighty stripes; and reject their evidence ever after: for such men are wicked transgressors.

What is important to note is that the verse is directly related to *zina* alone, not rape. Indeed, 'by conflating the crimes of rape and *zina*' the law commit a 'conceptual error' and defies the stances of numerous jurists both past and present.[153] The evidentiary requirement (which does not stipulate the gender or religion of the witness which means exclusion of a woman's testimony 'does not transpire'[154] or rather, is unjustified) may be seen to concern the protection of a woman's honour against fraudulent witnesses. By extending the *hadd* standard of proof to rape, the Ordinance 'seriously jeopardised the women's right to a fair trial' and accorded rapists a form of impunity.[155]

Interestingly, and in direct contrast with the Ordinance, even the most conservative of the eminent classical scholar's in this area, Imam Malik, accepted physical injuries as evidence of rape,[156] while Caliph Omar even accepted the testimony of a single individual who heard the victim call for help.[157] Moreover, the Federal Shariat Court of Pakistan which has the power to invalidate laws which do not conform to Islam[158] has also sought to distinguish the two offences and the corresponding standards of proof. In the case of *Rashida Patel*[159] the Court confirmed the view that rape and *zina* constituted different offences such that different evidentiary requirements were needed, and reduced the number of male witnesses from four to two.

The new rape laws of Pakistan correct these defects in Sharia by:

a) removing *Tazir* offences for *zina* from the Ordinance;
b) removing the evidentiary requirement of four Muslim male witnesses of *zina*. Instead, four adult witnesses will be the standard, and the reform will also affect the Law of Evidence, 1984;

153 Karamah Position Paper, Zina, Rape and Islamic Law: An Islamic Legal Analysis of the Rape Laws of Pakistan, p. 2 and 9. Authors mainly cite: MUWAFFAQ AL-DIN IBN QUDAMAH, AL-MUGHNI (Dar al-Kitab al-'Arabi, n.d Beirut) vol. 10.

154 Shah, Niaz, *Women, the Koran and International Human Rights Law: The Experience of Pakistan* (Martinus Nijhoff Publishers: Netherlands, 2006) 130.

155 ibid, Shah, 130.

156 Karamah Position Paper, MUWAFFAQ AL-DIN IBN QUDAMAH, AL-MUGHNI. (Beirut: Dar al-Kitab al-'Arabi, n.d) vol. 10, 193.

157 Karamah Position Paper, ABU MUHAMMAD ALI IBN SA'ED IBN HAZM, AL-MUHALLA BI AL-ATHAR (Beirut: Dar al-Kutub al-'Ilmiyyah, 1988) vol.12, 259.

158 Lau, Martin, 'Human Rights, Natural Justice and Pakistan's Shariat Courts,' in Javaid Rehman and Susan Breau (eds), *Religion, Human Rights and International Law* (Brill Netherlands, 2007) 359.

159 *Rashida Patel* (PLD 1989 Federal Shariat Court 95).

c) allowing other forms of evidence including indirect and circumstantial evidencc for rape cases under the penal code. Furthermore, in accordance with both the historical Muslim leader Caliph Omar and other Muslim jurists,[160] the new law recognises non-physical coercion such as threats to harm (thus causing fear) as within the scope of the offence of rape;
d) incorporating the offence of *qazf* where the accuser of *zina* has failed to prove their case (thus potentially limiting spiteful cases, such as where a husband seeks to victimise his divorced wife);[161]
e) increasing the powers of the sessions court and decreasing that of the police so preventing abuse of the law.[162]

The new law also abolishes the penalty of death by stoning for those who are married and found guilty of *zina*. This is because the punishment was not mentioned in the Quran.[163] The Federal Shariat Court in *Hazoor Bakhsh*[164] argued this as well, but their judgment was reversed after succumbing to political and religious pressure.[165]

Despite religious conservative opposition to the law, its promulgation succeeded because of the political will of the President, the religious will of Muslim scholars and the bravery of human rights groups.

CONCLUSION

The above examples illustrate the clear potential of Muslim States to reform their laws such that they appeal to both human rights norms whilst remaining within the framework of Sharia. The added affect of these reforms is not only the realisation of human rights norms within the written law, but the actualisation of human rights norms within such religiously conscious societies. Additionally, while it is evident that legislatures and legislation have a role to play in the domestic implementation of human rights, it is also important to consider the role of the judiciary in this regard. Indeed, it is the judiciary who has the responsibility of interpreting the law and ultimately applying it.

160 Karamah Position Paper, Zina, Rape and Islamic Law: An Islamic Legal Analysis of the Rape Laws of Pakistan, p. 10. Authors mainly cite: MUWAFFAQ AL-DIN IBN QUDAMAH, AL-MUGHNI. (Beirut: Dar al-Kitab al-'Arabi, n.d) vol. 10, 159–160.

161 Shah, Niaz, *Women, the Koran and International Human Rights Law: The Experience of Pakistan*, Martinus Nijhoff Publishers: Netherlands, 2006, 138.

162 http://www.gulftimes.com/site/topics/article.asp?cu_no=2&item_no=100412&version=1&template_id=41&parent_id=23-

163 ibid, Shah, 131.

164 PLD 1981 Federal Shariat Court 145.

165 ibid, Shah, 131.

Section Four The Role of the Judiciary in the Application of Human Rights Norms

When it comes to Muslim countries, a lot of attention is focussed on the compliance of laws and government behaviour with human rights. Yet, very little attention is focused on the role of the judiciary in implementing human rights standards. The following section will highlight the importance of the national courts in effecting the implementation of international human rights standards. In order to do so, subsection (1) will provide a brief overview of the judicial systems concerned and thereafter, subsection (2) will provide examples of how the courts have managed to implement human rights through the application of the law.

SUBSECTION ONE: THE JUDICIAL SYSTEMS OF MUSLIM STATES

In addressing the judiciary's role in implementing international human rights standards into domestic practice, it is necessary to begin with an understanding of the nature, structure and constitution of the court system. Thereafter, it will be possible to analyse how international human rights standards influence the courts in their role of developing, interpreting and implementing the law. The following section will provide an overview of the court structure of a selection of Muslim States. This will include an appreciation of the law under which the courts operate—whether Sharia or secular or both and their jurisdiction.

The primary judicial tool of any court system will be the law of the land itself as laid down by the constitution or other legislative provisions. It follows that where—Sharia is in operation, Sharia courts in which judges are trained in Sharia law will normally preside over that system. In previous sections of this study, it has been shown that the employment of Sharia, although a common feature of all Muslim States concerned (except Turkey), varies in its degree of implementation within these States. For example, in Saudi Arabia, it is the Sharia courts which preside over legal affairs and disputes while secular institutions are exceptional and must comply with Islamic principles. Furthermore, the jurisdictional reach of these courts even extend over the non-Muslim litigants resident in these countries. Meanwhile, at the other end of the spectrum, Turkey's legal system incorporates only secular courts, and this is reflective of the fact that Turkey is a constitutionally declared secular State.

Between these two extreme models, other Muslim States maintain court systems in which a degree of both Islamic and secular law is applied, sometimes with corresponding courts which function side by side in reflection of the religious pluralism of the State, and sometimes not. For example, although Tunisia abolished Sharia courts in 1959, the Law of Personal Status and family law is generally influenced by classical Muslim law in the form of Maliki and Hanafi jurisprudence. Incidentally, this law applies to Muslims and non-Muslims alike.[166]

When it comes to having secular and Sharia courts, the two court systems generally tend to work in parallel, maintaining a symbiotic relationship whereby each exercises jurisdiction over a specific and finite area of law, and one does not encroach on the jurisdiction of the other. Traditionally, Sharia courts preside over all matters in relation to family and personal status law—disputes concerning marriage, inheritance, and child custody, while secular courts deal with all other non-family civil matters, as well as criminal and commercial law disputes. However, this traditional demarcation does not necessarily apply in a strictly universal manner as shall be demonstrated further below. In some of these countries, a variety of courts have been established to preside over disputes involving litigants of different religions. In this category, we shall give consideration to the court structures of Lebanon, Egypt, Morocco, Bahrain, and Pakistan.

Bahrain

In Bahrain, the judiciary is divided into two branches, that of the Civil Law Courts and the Sharia (Islamic) Law Courts. The Civil Law Courts have jurisdiction over all commercial, civil and criminal cases, as well as personal status disputes related to non-Muslims. The Sharia Courts deal with personal status matters related to Muslims (whether Bahraini or non-Bahraini.)

The Civil Law Courts are structured in a three-tier system. The Courts of Minor Causes (also called the Lower Courts) and the Court of Execution, have jurisdiction over civil and commercial matters. The Middle Courts have jurisdiction over criminal matters. At the second level is High Court of Appeal, or the Senior Civil Court. Cases at these levels are presided over by a minimum of two judges. The highest court is the Court of Cassation (Mahkamat-al Tamyiz), which was established in 1989. It serves as the final court of appeal for all civil, commercial, and criminal matters, as well as personal status disputes between non-Muslims. There is also a Constitutional Court (established in 2002) which oversees the constitutionality of Bahrain's laws.

The Sharia Courts exercise jurisdiction in relation to Muslim personal status law and family law as well as matters related to inheritance, gifts,

166 http://www.law.emory.edu/ifl/legal/tunisia.htm; An-Na'im, Abdullahi (editor), *Islamic Family Law In a Changing World: A Global Resource Book* (Zed Books, London, 2002) 182.

wills, and charitable donations (waqf). The Courts have two levels, the Senior Sharia Court and the High Sharia Court of Appeal. The Sharia Courts are also divided between cases brought by Sunni Muslims and Jaafari Shi'a Muslims.[167]

The king may issue decrees with the force of law, but they must be referred to both the Consultative Council and the Chamber of Deputies within a month of their promulgation or, if the National Assembly is not in session, within a month of the first new meetings of its respective chambers. If the two chambers do not confirm them, they retroactively cease to have the force of law. International agreements have the force of law once ratified and published in the Official Gazette, as Article 37 of the Constitution clearly provides 'and treaties shall have force of law upon being concluded, ratified and published in the official gazette'.

Egypt

The Egyptian Judiciary has both secular and religious courts. Among the secular courts are those related to administrative and non-administrative divisions, a Supreme Constitutional Court, and penal courts, civil and commercial courts, personal status and family courts, national security courts, labour courts, military courts, and other specialized courts or circuits.

In Egypt, personal status law and family law are governed by Sharia and the judges of the Family Court (formed in 2004), are trained in Sharia. Furthermore, litigants of alternative religions are not required to arbitrate family law matters in the Sharia court system, but instead have recourse to the laws of their own. For example, Coptic Christians marry under Christian law and foreigners marry under the law of their own respective countries of origin. The Courts of First Instance are the first degree courts whose rulings are generally appealed. The next set of courts then are the Courts of Appeal and cover questions of fact as well as law. Judgments from this court may then be appealed to the Court of Cassation on points of law. The court is a secular institution, and it is the final court of adjudication regardless of whether the matter involves Sharia personal law or regular civil law.[168]

The Supreme Constitutional Court of Egypt is empowered by the Constitution to determine matters of constitutionality.[169] The judges of this Court are trained in both secular and Sharia law, and Sharia-related cases may be addressed by the SCC on grounds of constitutionality.

[167] http://www.pogar.org/countries/judiciary.asp?cid=2.
[168] http://www.pogar.org/countries/judiciary.asp?cid=5.
[169] http://www.nyulawglobal.org/globalex/Egypt.htm#_Court_System.

Iran

The Iranian legal system is based on Romano-Germanic law and Islamic law, mainly the Ja'fari school of Shi'a Islam. According to Article 167 of the Constitution, the judge is bound to judge each case on the basis of the codified law. In case of the silence of, the deficiency of or the ambiguity of law, the judges are required to primarily look into credible *Sharia* principles. However, even the codified law must not contradict the spirit of Islam, for:

> [J]udges of courts are obliged to refrain from executing statutes and regulations of the government that are in conflict with the laws and the norms of Islam, or lie outside the competence of the executive power. Everyone has the right to demand the annulment of any such regulation from the Court of Administrative Justice.[170]

Iran has a number of officially recognized minority religions and they include Hanafi Muslims, Zoroastrians, Jews and various Christian denominations. Accordingly, 'a 1933 law relating to the rights of non-Shi'a Iranians, courts are to apply the personal status laws applicable to the litigants belong to officially recognized religions'.[171]

Since the Revolution, the courts are divided as follows: Revolutionary Courts; Public courts; Civil Courts; Special Civil Courts; 1st Class Criminal Courts; 2nd Class Criminal Courts; Courts of Peace; Ordinary Courts of Peace; Independent Courts of Peace; Supreme Court of Cassation.[172]

There are four levels of civil courts which include the Special Civil Courts which have jurisdiction over matters related to family law. There are only two levels of criminal courts, the first level dealing with felony charges and the second involve lighter punitive action.[173] Appeals from these courts may be brought to the Appeal Courts and the Supreme Court. The Supreme Court is the highest court in the country, and may also hear appeals from the Military Courts and the General and Revolutionary Courts. Many aspects of the criminal law are derived from Sharia, and the Supreme Court will hear appeals related to crimes subject to capital punishment, *hadd* punishments and even *diyeh* (compensation paid for taking another's life), among many others. The Supreme Court also supervises the implementation of the laws by the courts in order to ensure uniformity in procedure.[174] The judges of the Supreme Court must be specialists in Islamic law.

170 Article 170 of the Constitution.

171 An-Na'im, Abdullahi (ed), *Islamic Family Law In a Changing World: A Global Resource Book* (Zed Books, London, 2002) 108.

172 An-Na'im, Abdullahi (ed), *Islamic Family Law In a Changing World: A Global Resource Book* (Zed Books, London, 2002) 109.

173 http://www.nyulawglobal.org/globalex/Iran.htm#_The_Court_System.

174 http://www.nyulawglobal.org/globalex/Iran.htm#_The_Court_System.

Aside from these courts, there also exist other judicial institutions such as clerical tribunals and courts which deal with the clergy, and revolutionary tribunals which deal with acts of terrorism and treason. The Court of Administrative Justice handles disputes between the people and the State.[175]

Lebanon

States where the religious courts and secular courts adjudicate in parallel present some of the most interesting cases for examination. In Lebanon, there are religious tribunals for the different faiths present in the country, and regular civilian courts which handle civil and criminal matters. The Christian, Druze, Jewish and Muslim faiths (both Shi'a Ja'fari and Sunni) have their own courts for family law matters.[176] There are approximately 18 officially recognised religious sects in Lebanon, and these also include Ismai'li and Alwai/Nusayri minorities and various Christian denominations.[177]

Religious courts preside over matters with regards to personal status law and their adjudication reflects the religion of the individual litigants involved in each dispute.[178]

For Muslims, there are two levels of Sharia Courts, the Sharia Courts of First Instance and a Supreme Sharia Court in Beirut, and they cater for both Sunni and Ja'fari Shi'a litigants. The separate Druze courts are also divided in the same way.[179]

The secular courts operate on three levels and are sub-divided into civil and criminal. The first courts are the Courts of First Instance whose judgment may then be appealed to the Courts of Appeal. Thereafter, the final court of appeal is the Court of Cassation—Supreme Court. In addition, the Council of State deals with administrative cases, the Constitutional Council[180] was established in 1994 to preside over issues concerning the constitutionality of laws and to arbitrate conflicts that arise from parlia-

[175] http://www.nyulawglobal.org/globalex/Iran.htm#_The_Court_System.

[176] Concerning Inheritance, the non-Muslims follow the national law and the Muslims have their own set of laws implemented in their own courts.

[177] Abdullahi An-Na'im (ed), *Islamic Family Law In a Changing World: A Global Resource Book* (Zed Books, London, 2002) 127.

[178] Abdullahi An-Na'im (ed), *Islamic Family Law In a Changing World: A Global Resource Book* (Zed Books, London, 2002) 127.

[179] Abdullahi An-Na'im (ed), *Islamic Family Law In a Changing World: A Global Resource Book* (Zed Books, London, 2002) 127.

[180] There is no Constitutional Council functioning at the present time in Lebanon. Its functioning has been terminated by the majority in the Parliament in 2005. For more info about the process of deregulation of the highest judicial and political organ in Lebanon : See Nisrine Abiad, 'The Lebanese Institutions: Between Constitutionality and Constitutional Heresies', Yearbook of Islamic and Middle Eastern Law, Volume 12, 2005–2006, 55–56.

mentary and presidential elections, while the Judicial Council adjudicates on threats to national security, all of which are secular.

Morocco

Morocco's predominant Sunni *madhhab* is that of Maliki. The State also has Jewish and Christian minorities.

In Morocco, cases in respect of family and personal status law are presided over by Sharia trained judges of the Sharia division of the Sadad Courts. The 27 Sadad Courts are also divided into a separate Rabbinical division to hear personal status and family disputes between the Jewish community, and finally civil, commercial, administrative and penal divisions.[181] A notable feature of the Moroccan judicial system is that *all* judges, regardless of whether they intend to work with Islamic family law or the secular common law, are trained at the National Institute for Judicial Studies where they undergo three years of study heavily focused on human rights and the rule of law.

Four different court levels operate in Morocco, all under a unified system which is presided over by the Ministry of Justice. The lowest courts are the Communal and District Courts which settle minor offences punishable only by fine. Next are the Sadad Courts which are Courts of First Instance and they hear the full range of civil and criminal disputes. (At equal level are the Trade Courts which hear trade-related disputes.) Decisions made in these courts with penalties exceeding DH300, may be appealed to the Regional Court. The Regional Court also has Sharia sections to hear matters concerning Moroccan Muslims, and their decisions may be appealed to the Courts of Appeal.[182] In certain specified instances, the Supreme Court acts are the final court of appeal.[183]

Four further residual courts, the Special Court of Justice, administrative courts, commercial courts, and military tribunals also exist, but they do not apply any form of Sharia.

Pakistan

The legal system of Pakistan is based on English common law, but all matters of personal status are governed by Sharia as are areas of criminal and commercial law. The dominant *madhhab* is Hanafi, but there is a sizeable minority of Ja'fari and Isma'ili Muslims, as well as Ahmadis which identify themselves as Sunni Muslim but which the State declares as 'non-

181 Abdullahi An-Na'im (ed), *Islamic Family Law In a Changing World: A Global Resource Book* (Zed Books, London, 2002) 179.

182 Abdullahi An-Na'im (ed), *Islamic Family Law In a Changing World: A Global Resource Book* (Zed Books, London, 2002) 179.

183 http://www.pogar.org/countries/judiciary.asp?cid=12; http://www.nyulawglobal.org/globalex/Morocco.htm#_1._Jurisdictions_of_the%201st%20degree.

Muslims.' There are also Christian, Zoroastrian, Hindu, Sikh and Jewish minorities in Pakistan.[184]

The court structure in Pakistan comprises District and Federal courts with a Supreme Court at the apex. District courts occur in every district of each province. The Court of District Judge hears civil claims while the Court of Sessions Judge and Magistrates Court hear matters of criminal law.[185] These courts do not apply the Sharia. Appeals from these courts are heard by the High Court of each province (of which there are four), and the Supreme Court is the final appellate court and resides in Islamabad. It bears exclusive jurisdiction over High Court decisions and legal disputes arising between federal and provincial governments, or between government and individuals or individuals per se.[186]

A Presidential Order of 26 May 1980 established the Federal Shariat Court[187] and this institution exercises exclusive jurisdiction over the determination of whether a law is in conformity with the tenets of Islam.[188] The Court may do this upon petition by a citizen or by its own motion. It is assisted in its tasks by an Islamic advisory council of *ulama* (scholars in Islamic law). Issues pertaining to family law are governed exclusively by courts established specifically for these matters, the Family Courts. The functions and jurisdictions of these courts were established by the West Pakistan Family Courts Act 1964. Appeals from the Family Courts are adjudicated by the High Court. The Federal Shariat Court has exclusive jurisdiction over appeals from the criminal courts under laws relating to Islamic Criminal law of Pakistan, the Hudood Laws, which are laws pertaining to offences to intoxication, theft, Zina (unlawful sexual intercourse) and Qazf (false imputation of Zina).[189]

Saudi Arabia

In Saudi Arabia, the Sharia courts interpret the law in accordance with the Hanbali school of Sunni Islam and their jurisdiction is exercised over both general and residual matters alike. 'Residual' matters refer to any case over which jurisdiction has not been expressly consigned to another specified commission or tribunal. These other 'specialised' tribunals, are those that operate outside the jurisdiction of the Sharia courts and deal with particu-

184 Abdullahi An-Na'im (ed), *Islamic Family Law In a Changing World: A Global Resource Book* (Zed Books, London, 2002) 230.

185 http://www.nyulawglobal.org/globalex/Pakistan.htm#_The_Court_System

186 A full description of the Supreme Court is available at the following address: http://www.supremecourt.gov.pk//intro-0.htm (last accessed 13 March 2008).

187 Article 203 (D) 1—Constitution of Pakistan.

188 For further details on the power an functioning of the Federal Sharia Court, see notably Martin Lau, 'Human Rights, Natural Justice and Pakistan's Sharia Courts', in *Religion, Human Rights and International Law*, edited by Javaid Rehman and Susan C Breau, 359–378.

189 http://www.nyulawglobal.org/globalex/Pakistan.htm#_The_Court_System.

lar areas of law for which the Sharia does not expressly provide, such as certain areas of commercial law, labour law and even administrative law. The very existence of these courts provokes the significant and commonplace observation that the Sharia does not fully address every aspect of modern life that may find itself the subject matter of a legal dispute. Therefore, it has been necessary for even the most religiously observant legal systems, such as those of Saudi Arabia and Iran to adapt their systems to accommodate these pockets of law. It is equally important to note however, that these specialised tribunals, which in Saudi Arabia must be established by royal decree, interpret and apply the relevant laws in strict accordance with Islamic principles. And so, although these courts are not Sharia courts, their underlying principles of adjudication incorporate the values of Sharia.[190]

The Judiciary Act, promulgated by Royal Decree No M/64 dated 14/7/1395H (1975) states in Article 26: 'The Courts (Sharia Courts) shall have jurisdiction over all types of disputes and crimes except those excluded by Law.' Sharia courts have general jurisdiction over all judicial matters such as criminal, civil, property and matrimonial claims, and mainly follow the Hanbali *madhhab* which is the official *madhhab* of the State.[191] The Sharia courts do not decline jurisdiction unless other judicial bodies have been given exclusive jurisdiction. The judicial system is composed of a three-tiered hierarchy of Sharia courts, beginning with the courts of first instance which are divided into five types: general, penal, personal status, commercial and labor. The Court of Appeal (located in Riyadh) sits at the second level and hears appeals from the courts of first instance where applicable. For most matters, it is the final court of appeal.[192] The highest court is the Supreme Court whose task is to ensure that no laws contradict the Sharia and also review judgments passed or approved by the courts of appeal in major cases, particularly murder. Before being referred to the Sharia courts, quarrels of a civil nature may first be subject to a form of dispute resolution in the *amarah;* here, the *amir* will try to steer the disputing parties towards compromise and settlement.[193]

Alongside the Sharia courts are a number of judicial and quasi-judicial institutions of specific jurisdiction, for example, the Chambers of Commerce and Industry or the Commission on Impeachment of Ministers. Decisions made in these institutions may be appealed to the Grievance

190 Abdullahi An-Na'im (ed), *Islamic Family Law In a Changing World: A Global Resource Book* (Zed Books, London, 2002) 137, referring to the constitutional status of Islam.
191 Abdullahi An-Na'im (ed), *Islamic Family Law In a Changing World: A Global Resource Book* (Zed Books, London, 2002) 137.
192 http://www.pogar.org/countries/judiciary.asp?cid=16.
193 Abdullahi An-Na'im (ed), *Islamic Family Law In a Changing World: A Global Resource Book* (Zed Books, London, 2002) 137.

Board which according to Royal Decree of October 2007, is defined as 'an independent administrative judicial body' that reports directly to the King.[194] All the various administrative courts may also appeal to the Grievance Board (and notably, procedures for a fair trial are governed by the Administrative Rules of Procedure of Judicial Bodies.)

With regard to international conventions, they must be promulgated in accordance with Article 70 of the Basic Law of Government, which stipulates as follows: 'International regulations, treaties, conventions and privileges shall be promulgated and amended by Royal Decree.' Once conventions are ratified by royal decree, they form a part of domestic legislation whose provisions can be invoked before the courts and the other judicial and administrative authorities in the Kingdom, thus becoming a part of the Kingdom's domestic legislation.

Tunisia

In contrast to the preceding systems, Tunisia operates only secular courts however, the law related to personal status and family matters is still based on classical Sunni doctrine of the Maliki and Hanafi *madhhab*. Tunisia abolished the use of Sharia Courts in 1956, and this was shortly followed in September 1957 with the dissolution of the Habraic courts that had previously determined disputes between Jewish litigants[195]. These reforms were executed with the aim of encouraging the assimilation of peoples of all faiths in Tunisia.

Tunisia has a single unified judicial structure with separate areas for civil, criminal and administrative law. The civil court and criminal court systems are similar, beginning with 51 District Courts which hear the less problematic and costly cases, eg misdemeanours. At the next level sit the Courts of First Instance which hear appeals from the District Courts. The Court of First Instance can also hear all commercial and civil cases as well as all criminal cases except felonies (which must be heard by a grand jury.) Thereafter sit the Appeals Courts which hear appeals from the Court of First Instance. The final court of appeal is the Supreme Court—Court of Cassation, and it has one criminal division and three civil divisions so may hear disputes of all nature.[196]

Turkey

Turkey maintains secular courts in accordance with the strict secularisation of its constitution and laws. The court system comprises judicial and administrative courts, as well as a military tribunal. The judicial strand

194 http://www.pogar.org/countries/judiciary.asp?cid=16.
195 Jewish Councils were also abolished a year later in July 1958.
196 http://www.pogar.org/countries/judiciary.asp?cid=20.

deals with the majority of Turkey's caseload, presiding over disputes of a civil and criminal nature that involve all citizens. The Constitutional Court and the Court of Appeals are the appellate tribunals, with the latter representing the final court of appeal.

SUBSECTION TWO: THE APPLICATION OF INTERNATIONAL HUMAN RIGHTS NORMS BY NATIONAL COURTS

The view of Justice Abd-el-Rehman Nosseir of the Supreme Constitutional Court of Egypt is that the judiciary is the real bastion of human rights, representing 'the safety valve which balances human rights on the one hand, and public order or the stability of the society on the other'.[197] It is widely acknowledged amongst jurists that the judiciary occupies a unique position with regard to human rights issues.[198] Indeed, the entire gamut of constitutional and legislative guarantees could not reduce human rights violations in a State unless the judiciary gave them real effect. Article 2(3)(b) of ICCPR requires that in addition to legislative measures to enforce human rights, effective remedies must be ensured by competent judicial authorities, as well as administrative and legislative authorities. However, information about the disposition towards human rights of judiciaries in Muslim States is very difficult to ascertain.[199] As Dr Adel Omar Sherif explains, 'protection of human rights depends partly on a robust, fair and independent judiciary willing to hold all political and social actors accountable to legal and constitutional protections'.[200]

It is evident from the above that one of the key elements necessary for the judicial protection of human rights is the real independence of the judiciary. Despite a strong textual and verbal commitment to judicial independence in many Muslim State constitutions, the reality can often be very different. For example, in Saudi Arabia, Article 46 of the Basic Law provides that the judiciary is an independent authority, above which, only the Sharia presides. Meanwhile, the Constitution of Egypt guarantees the independence of the judiciary at different provisions culminating in Article 166 which provides that 'judges are independent. In their performance, they are subject to no authority but that of the law. No authority can interfere

197 Abd-El-Rahman Nosseir, 'The Supreme Constitutional Court of Egypt and the Protection of Human Rights', in Eugene Cotran and Adel Omar Sherif (eds) *The Role of the Judiciary in the Protection of Human Rights* (Brill 1997, in association with CIMEL) 47–59.

198 *Judicial Protection of Human Rights: Myth or Reality* edited by Mark Gibney and Stanislaw Frankowski (Praeger, Westport, Conn, 1999).

199 See Donna E Arzt, 'The application of International Human Rights Law in Islamic States', Human Rights Quarterly 12 (1990) 203–230, 226.

200 Dr Adel Omar Sherif and Dr Nathan J. Brown, 'Judicial Independence in the Arab World', available at http://www.pogar.org/publications/judiciary/sherif/jud-independence.pdf.

in cases or judicial affairs.' Further, Article 82 of the Moroccan constitution says: 'the judicial shall be independent from the legislative and executive branches'. The challenge for these countries is to live up to these norms as political, cultural or economic factors put the reality of judicial independence in question.[201]

This chapter looks at the application of human rights standards by the domestic judicial control. It will provide a survey of decisions given by national secular and Sharia courts selected from within the range of countries within the frame of this study. The adopted structure of the chapter reflects the duality of the judicial system. Section (A) will analyse to what extent the secular courts apply international human rights norms in their jurisprudence. Section (B) will aim to show that the flexibility inherent to the mechanisms of Sharia very often allows the judge to implement human rights standards in the context of each judicial case they are considering.

A. *The application of international human rights norms by the national courts in Muslim states*

One constant task for human rights committees has been to monitor the compliance of State parties with their international obligations, in effect ensuring that laws and practices give effect to the rights provided for as per the usual international human rights instruments. Human rights monitoring bodies have been known to enquire about the implementation of human rights beyond that of abstract national norms. Indeed, they have very precisely and consistently enquired at the occasion of their meetings and correspondence with delegates from different countries about concrete results at the national level, very often putting emphasis on whether provisions of international human rights standards including ICESCR, ICCPR, CEDAW and CRC have been directly invoked before national courts.

Many factors determine the judicial incorporation of international law into domestic practice. Primarily, the use by a State's national courts of international human rights norms would largely depend on the status that these normative standards have in the legal system of the State.[202] To note, we have already discussed perceptions concerning the interrelation between international law and domestic law.[203] Nonetheless, courts would logically be required to use international norms that are regarded as part of the domestic law.

201 See the following section.
202 See Frans Viljoen, 'International Human Rights Law in Africa' (Oxford University Press, 2007) 540.
203 See above, 102.

This section is not meant to be an exhaustive survey on the application of international human right law by the various judiciaries of Muslim countries. The short timeframe devoted for this study and the lack of accessible materials are the determinant factors in excluding them from this work. Rather, this chapter aims to shed some light on the issue of the role of that domestic courts play in implementing international human rights instruments by analysing some interesting examples of jurisprudential practice in Muslim countries. The judicial protection of human rights through the use of international human rights law[204] is a subject of great importance and is relevant to countries all over the world.[205] Such examples, beyond being promising steps towards a better understanding and implementation of international norms in the region, demonstrates a nuanced and pragmatic analysis of the incorporation of international law in domestic practice. This is something that an analysis with a strict focus on notions of 'monism' and 'dualism' in international law are unable to reflect.

The term 'application' has been used for its flexibility as it could refer to 'direct enforcement' of international norms by the courts or their use as 'interpretative guidance'. The term 'application' is also flexible in covering two nuanced judicial approaches towards the use of international law. These are cases in which the courts use international law in their reasoning and cases in which the courts base their decisions directly on the provisions of international law. Interpreting constitutions and laws in the light of international law would deepen national protection of human rights by widening the scope of rights and liberties provided for in national systems.

Egypt

In a meeting of the Committee on the Protection of the Rights of All Migrant workers and Members of their Families (04/06/2007), it was declared that once a treaty had been ratified, it became part of domestic law and acquired an intermediate status between the Constitution and the laws. If treaty provisions conflicted with applicable domestic legislation, the latter would not apply and the treaty would prevail. Moreover, if a law adopted after ratification of an international instrument ran counter to that instrument, the matter should be referred to the Constitutional Court. As an illustration of the principle of the primacy of international law, Mr Wahhab mentioned the case of railway workers who had been prosecuted for going

204 *Judicial Protection of Human Rights: Myth or Reality* edited by Mark Gibney and Stanislaw Frankowski (Praeger, Westport, Conn, 1999).

205 Just to cite one example: the High Court of Australia ruled in 1992 in its decision *Mabo v Queensland*[1992] HCA 23; (1992) 175 CLR 1, that Australian common law should reflect evolving international human rights norms. In this case which concerns the rights of indigenous people, the High Court ruled that the British acquisition of sovereignty over the Australian colonies did not terminate pre-existing rights held by indigenous people in land.

on strike. Their lawyer had argued that since Egypt had ratified the International Covenant of Economic, Social and Cultural Rights which recognised the right to strike, the provisions of the Egyptian Criminal Code which conflicted with the covenant could not be applied. The court had therefore acquitted the workers in conformity with the covenant.[206]

In a significant decision in April 1987,[207] an Egyptian State security tribunal acquitted striking railway workers on the basis of the argument put forward by the defence on the grounds of Egypt's ratification of ICESCR and ICCPR as well as of international labour conventions which recognize the right to strike. The application by other Islamic States of international human rights instruments can be illustrated by the incorporation of the African Charter of Human and People's Rights[208] in the jurisprudence of many domestic African courts.[209]

It is important to note that national courts appear to be more inclined to use regional human rights instruments rather than international ones. Many examples citing African jurisprudence show that national courts in Africa are more disposed to using the African Charter of Human and People's Rights (African charter) compared to the ICCPR and other international instruments which have also been ratified by the concerned African government. For example, the Benin Constitutional Court declared in 1994 that a ministerial decree putting restrictions to the right to free association constituted an unconstitutional action because it encroached upon the domain reserved to the law in terms of the Benin Constitution and Article 10 of the African Charter which provides that 'every individual shall have the right to free association provided that he abides by the law'.[210]

In a spectacular decision of the High Court of Lagos decision in Nigeria, the courts accepted jurisdiction over the case where eleven youths were sentenced to death for robbery by an 'armed robbery tribunal' in 1988, despite the provisions of the 1984 Decree suspending the Constitution. In

[206] UN Committee on the Protection of the Rights of All Migrant workers and Members of their Families 'Summary Record of 50th meeting' CMW/C/SR.50, Palais Wilson, Geneva, 2007, para 23, available at http://www.ohchr.org (last accessed 1 April 2008).

[207] Cited by CH Heyns, F Viljoen, *The Impact of the United Nations Human Rights Treaties on Domestic level* (Kluwer, The Hague, 2002) 234.

[208] The African Charter on Human and Peoples' Rights (also known as the Banjul Charter) is an international human rights instrument that seeks to promote and protect human rights and basic freedoms in the African continent.- For further details see U Oji Umozurike, *The African Charter on Human's and People's Rights* (Martinus Nijhoff Publishers, The Hague/Boston/Leiden, 1997).

[209] See Frans Viljoen, *International Human Rights Law in Africa: National and International Protection* (Oxford University Press, 2007).

[210] This decision is cited by Frans Viljoen, *International Human Rights Law in Africa: National and International Protection* (Oxford University Press, 2007) 543 and is based on his personal perusal of the Court's record in Cotonou, Benin, during April 1995.

deciding that it had jurisdiction, the Court referred to the African Charter:[211]

> The African Charter on Human and Peoples' Rights, of which Nigeria is a signatory is now made into our law by African Charter Act 1983, cited by the learned counsel for the applicants. Even if its aspect in our Constitution is suspended or ousted by any provision of our local law, the international aspect of it cannot unilaterally be abrogated.

As highlighted in Frans Viljoen's work, although this jurisprudence was not regularly followed by all the other courts,[212] it demonstrates the bravery and purposeful attitude of some members of the judiciary to uphold human rights standards and whatever way possible.

Iran

In a report of the Committee on the Elimination of all forms of Racial Discrimination,[213] Mr. Mehrpour (the Iranian representative) stated that the Convention had been approved by the previous Senate and national Congress and in the opinion of the legal experts he had consulted, its provisions could be directly invoked before and by the courts. In a similar vein, a delegate of Iran to the CRC Committee stated that 'Parliament had a legal committee composed of 20 jurists and judges who were fully acquainted with the Convention, which had been translated into Farsi' and that 'the Convention was applied by both parliamentarians and the courts.'[214] As early as 2000, delegates to the CRC Committee have asserted that article 9 of the Iranian Civil Code stipulates that when Iran accedes to an international instrument, its provisions take precedence over domestic legislation and may be invoked directly in the court.[215] Although the delegation provided no details of where the international human rights instruments have been used, several cases in Iranian courts demonstrate that the CRC and the ICCPR have been used in their jurisprudence.

211 *Garba v Lagos State A-G Suit* ID/599M/91 (31 October 1991), cited by Frans Viljoen, *International Human Rights Law in Africa: National and International Protection* (Oxford University Press, 2007) 552.

212 See Frans Viljoen, ibid 552.

213 Report 29/09/2003, para 51, UN Committee on the Elimination of all Forms of Racial Discrimination 'Summary record of the 1597th meeting', CERD/C/SR.1597, Palais des Nations, Geneva, 2003, para 51, available at http://www.ohchr.org (last accessed 1 April 2008).

214 Committee on the Rights of the Child, Summary Record of the 116th meeting, Iran, 28/01/2005, CRC/C/SR.1016, http://www.unhchr.ch/tbs/doc.nsf/(Symbol)/fdb5105af9c5c3bfc1256f9b0050a065?Opendocument.

215 Committee on the Rights of the Child, Summary Record of the 617th meeting, Iran, 14/07/2000, CRC/C/SR.617, http://www.unhchr.ch/tbs/doc.nsf/(Symbol)/202d56b9a0c51cbdc1256921004f775f?Opendocument.

In a 2004 case before Branch One of the General Court of Shushtar[216] where a child brought a claim against another child of eight years of age for intentional bodily harm, the Court issued a verdict of not guilty due to a lack of evidence and the inability to ascertain the offence. While doing so, the Court made reference to a number of Iranian laws as well as Article 40(2) (a) of the Convention on the Rights of the Child.[217] It might be argued that the use of the international instrument in this case was made to show that the Iranian judiciary does use CRC and to avoid further criticism on this front, particularly that in this case the child was not supposed to face capital punishment anyway.

In another 2004 case before Branch One of the General Court of Shushtar,[218] a number of defendants were charged with (a) disobedience, and (b) insulting the Government's officials while on duty. Among the defendants was a student of 18 years of age charged only with disobedience. His father was among the defendants and was found guilty of all charges against him. The 18-year-old was charged with disobedience while two other defendants whilst found guilty of disobedience were not charged with 'insulting government officials' due 'to the lack of jurisprudential and legal evidence and that the charge is not ascertained.' When reaching this judgment, the Court made explicit mention of Article 14(2) of the ICCPR which protects the presumption of innocence.[219] The same article of the ICCPR was invoked by Branch Two of the General Court of Shushtar in 2004[220] related to 'insult and obtrusion,' and several times before Branch One of the General Court of Shushtar in 2004 in cases related to 'theft',[221] 'disturbing the order in court',[222] 'forcible occupation',[223] and the last example, 'bodily harm by bullet'.[224] In the latter case, despite the gravity of the offence, the Court found that there was insufficient evidence and issued a verdict of not guilty. Even before the civil courts of Iran, the ICCPR has been cited as it was in a 2004 case before Branch One of the Civil Court of Shushtar where the court found that in light of several laws of Iran and Article 14(2) of the ICCPR, there was insufficient evidence to hold the defendant accountable for a murder.

[216] Case No: 2629,1,82K, Judgement No: 2603,82, Date of Issue: 14/10/82 (04/01/2004).

[217] CRC Article 40(2)(a): No child shall be alleged as, be accused of, or recognized as having infringed the penal law by reason of acts or omissions that were not prohibited by national or international law at the time they were committed;

[218] Case No: 106,1,83K, Judgement No: 106,83, Date of Issue: 24/1/83 (13/04/2004).

[219] ICCPR, Article 14(2): Everyone charged with a criminal offence shall have the right to be presumed innocent until proved guilty according to law.

[220] Case No:131,2,83K, Judgement No: 127,83, Date of Issue: 10/3/83 (31/05/2004).

[221] Case No:1577,1,83K, Judgement: 1558,83, Date of Issue: 2/6/83 (24/08/2004).

[222] Case No:1454,1,83K, Judgement No: 1485,83, Date of Issue: 15/7/83 (07/10/2004).

[223] Case No:1601,1,83K, Judgement: 1584,83, Date of Issue: 5/9/83 (26/11/2004).

[224] Case No:921,1,83K, Verdicts No: 1266,83, Date of Issue: 10/5/83 (01/08/2004).

The penal courts of Iran have also made use of the ICCPR as evidenced by a case before Branch 102 of the Penal Court of Shushtar in 2004.[225] In this case, several defendants between the ages of 17 and 26 were charged with 'disturbing the order of the Police Station 12, Shushtar by creating tumult and brawl', 'driving geared motorcycle without license', and 'disobeying the Government officials'. While the first and second defendants were found guilty for disturbing order and driving without a license, when it came to the offence of disobedience, the Courts stated that the offence 'is not in a form that can be imagined being committed by the Defendants, therefore in this regard due to non-ascertainment of the offence being committed ... the Court issues and declares the not guilty verdict on the Defendants'. The Court cited Article 14 (2) of the ICCPR protecting the right to be presumed innocent.

Lebanon

In Lebanon, in the case of a conflict between national and international law, the judges are directed to accord priority to international law.[226] Lebanese courts have applied international treaties in their jurisprudences and the Court of Appeal has held that they have an exclusive competency to interpret international treaties in cases involving individual rights and freedoms.[227]

In a judgment given on 12 June 2003 (judgment number 1119/2003),[228] a criminal court judge of Beirut made spectacular use of international human rights norms in both the obiter dicta and ratio of his judgment.

With regard to the facts of the case, the prosecutor of Beirut presented a case against a Sudanese national who illegally entered Lebanese territory, asking the court for a deportation order. The court began by studying the facts and confirmed the violation by the defendant of Article 32 of the 1963 Lebanese Law on the entrance and stay of foreigners which provides for from one month to three years' prison sentences, a fine and deportation for those who enter the country illegally. However, the court then went on to consider the possibility that the deportation of the defendant to his country of origin would expose him to the risk of torture because he belonged to a

225 Case No:74,102,83K, Judgement: 60,83, Date of Issue: 25/5/83 (16/08/2004).

226 Article 2 of the Code of Civil Procedure. However, a Court is not empowered to declare a law invalid on the grounds that it contravenes the Constitution or international conventions. See for references for jurisprudence in this regard, Georges J Assaf, 'The Application of International Human Rights Instruments by the Judiciary in Lebanon', in E Cotran and A Omar Sherif (eds) *The Role of the Judiciary in the Protection of Human Rights* (CIMEL Book Series No. 5, Kluwer Law International, 2007) 86.

227 Georges J Assaf, 'The Application of International Human Rights Instruments by the Judiciary in Lebanon', in E Cotran and A Omar Sherif (eds) *The Role of the Judiciary in the Protection of Human Rights*, (CIMEL Book Series No. 5, Kluwer Law International 2007) 87, 88.

228 Not published.

persecuted ethnic minority. The court noted that Article 3 of the Convention against Torture and Other Cruel, Inhuman or Degrading Treatment or Punishment, as ratified by Lebanon on 5 October 2000, forbids the expulsion, return or expatriation of individuals to another State where there are substantial grounds for believing that the individual could be subjected to torture. The court decided to imprison the defendant for one month for having breached Article 32 and made him pay a fine. However, the court ruled that through the application of the provisions of Article 3 of the convention against torture, expulsion from Lebanon could not have been used as a punishment.

Malaysia

Malaysia is not a party to ICCPR, ICESCR, or CAT, and only acceded to CRC and CEDAW in 1995. Therefore, it is understandable that there is a lack of jurisprudence relating to the application of or reference to these international instruments. However, the following three cases will give a general overview of the application of international treaties (not necessarily human rights treaties) by Malaysian Courts.

In *Smt Maneka Gandhi v Union of India AIR*[229] the Indian Supreme Court set a principle establishing the 'direct effect' of fundamental rights in relation to the UDHR 1948 and the interpretation of the Indian Constitution. The Court held that the UDHR should be used as far as possible in interpreting the Constitution so as to safeguard human rights and apply the standards contained in the international treaty. This principle was approved by the Malaysian Federal Court (Highest Court) in *Dewan Undangan Negeri Kelantan v Nordin bin Salleh*[230] as well as the Court of Appeal in *Tan Tek Seng v Suruhanjaya Perkhidmatan Pendidikan & Anor*;[231] therefore, at least in theory, international human rights treaties may be considered a source of human rights law in Malaysia.

In the case *Public Prosecutor v Orhan Olmez*,[232] the First Secretary of the Embassy of Turkey presented evidence before the magistrate's court in Kuala Lumpur. His attendance was preceded by a diplomatic note from his embassy clearly stating that he would be present during the hearing of the proceeding in his capacity as consul and 'solely for the authentication of legal documents'. However, the Embassy subsequently sent another diplomatic note to the Ministry of Foreign Affairs to say that the First Secretary would no longer be present in court. In response to this, Counsel for the respondent applied to the Court to issue a warrant of arrest to compel the

[229] [1978] SC 597 The actual citation is AIR [1978] SC 597 this is an Indian case and reported in All India Reports(AIR) Supreme Court(SC).

[230] [1992] 1 Malayan Law Journal 697.

[231] [1996] 1 Malayan Law Journal 261.

[232] [1988] 1 Malayan Law Journal 13.

attendance of the First Secretary. The legal question brou
Supreme Court of Malaysia was 'whether or not the State's a
for and allowing the diplomatic agent to give evidence solely fo
cation of the legal documents constitutes a waiver of immunity fr
diction'. Applying Article 32 of the Vienna Convention on Dipl
Relations 1961 which had been transformed into Malaysian law by n
of the Diplomatic Privileges (Vienna Convention) Act 1966, the Supre
Court held that 'a waiver under the Vienna Convention must always be express. The restrictive language in the first diplomatic communication is clear and it cannot be construed as anything like a waiver'.[233]

Another example of the application of international treaties through a statutory instrument is the case of *Regional Centre of Arbitration v Ooi Beng Choo* (No 2). In this case, the court referred to subsidiary legislation known as the Kuala Lumpur Regional Centre for Arbitration (Privileges and Immunities) Regulations 1996 made pursuant to sections 3 and 4 of the International organizations (privileges and Immunities) Act 1992, which was passed by the Malaysian Parliament to implement the Convention on the Privileges and Immunities of the United Nations.[234]

In *MBF Capital Bhd v Dato' Param Cumaraswamy*,[235] the High Court of Malaysia applied the International Organizations (Privileges and Immunities) Act 1992 with reference to the issues of immunity for a Special Rapporteur of the UN Human Rights Commission.

Morocco

On 29 May 2006, the representative of Morocco explained to the committee of ICESCR in Geneva that the Covenant took precedence over domestic law and that several court decisions in Morocco had upheld Covenant rights, including the right to education, the right to work and the right to just and favourable conditions of work.[236] With regard to whether the

233 The Diplomatic Privileges (Vienna Convention) Act 1966 [Act 24 of 1966] has since been revised as the Diplomatic Privileges (Vienna Convention) Act 1966 [Act 636]. See also Schedule to the Act, for the application of Articles of Vienna Convention on Diplomatic Relations (1961) having the force of law in Malaysia.

234 The Court further set the test to be applied in determining whether a statute infringes a particular fundamental right. It was held that the correct test to be applied was as to what is the direct and inevitable consequence or effect of the impugned statute on the fundamental right of the plaintiffs, and if the effect of the statute on the fundamental right is direct or inevitable, then a fortiori the effect must be presumed to have been intended by the statute. Where, therefore, the statute directly affects the fundamental right, or its inevitable effect on the fundamental right is such that it makes the exercise of the right ineffective or illusory, the statute must be held to be unconstitutional, and must be struck down.

235 [1997] 3 MLJ 830.

236 UN Committee on Economic, Social and Cultural rights 'Summary record of the 17th meeting' E/C.12/2006/SR.17, Palais des Nations, Geneva, 2006, para 40 available at: http://www.ohchr.org (last accessed 1 April 2008).

International Covenant's could be invoked in the domestic courts, the representative of Morocco stated that:

> Moroccan legislation did not provide for the application of the Covenant. Parties to a dispute did not have to stipulate which articles of the Covenant had been violated when they brought their case before a court. However, since the Covenant had constitutional status in Morocco, particularly with regard to employment and education, any Moroccan citizen could assert his or her rights under the Covenant.[237]

Pakistan

In the decision of *Humaira Mehmood v State*[238] the Lahore High Court of Pakistan, examining the law surrounding a woman's ability to marry against the wishes of her parents, concluded that a marriage ceremony (*nikah*) performed under coercion was not valid. The High Court explicitly referred to international law in its reasoning where the Court cited Article 16 of the CEDAW and the 1990 Cairo Declaration on Human Rights in Islam which declare women's equal rights to human dignity. As concluded by Mullally who reported on this case, the Court applied an egalitarian approach to Islam, reflecting the High Court's concern in mediating between global and local concerns.[239]

Tunisia

Tunisia presents a very recent example where in March 2008 and in response to a question by the Human Rights Committee to the Tunisian delegation as to whether the provisions of the Covenant had been invoked directly before Tunisian courts and administrative bodies, a member of the delegation replied that it was important not only to accede to the Convention but also to implement it in everyday life. He added that Tunisian courts at all levels had to take such treaties into account and that there had also been several instances in which courts had held in favour of litigants by citing international human rights instruments such as the Universal Declaration of Human Rights and the Convention on the Rights of the Child. For example, in one such case which had involved establishing a child's paternity after DNA tests, the Court of First Instance had found that 'filiation is a child's right'—a first in Tunisia —and stressed that

[237] Committee on Economic, Social and Cultural rights, 'Summary record of the 17th meeting', E/C.12/2006/SR.17, Palais des Nations, Geneva, 29 May 2006, at para. 40 available at: http://www.ohchr.org (last accessed 1 April 2008).

[238] *Humaira Mehmood v State* (PLD , Lahore, 1999) 494.

[239] Siobhan Mullally, 'Women, Islamisation and Human Rights in Pakistan' in Javaid Rehman and Susan C Breau (eds), *Religion, Human Rights and International Law* (Koninklijke Brill NV, Netherlands, 2007) 403.

filiation, as defined in the Personal Status Code, must be interpreted broadly and in accordance with the relevant articles of the Convention on the Rights of the Child which protects against all forms of discrimination or penalty based on the status of a child's parents.[240]

Similarly, in another DNA paternity test case aiming to establishing the filiation of a child, the Tribunal of first instance of La Manoba in Tunisia passed a judgment on 2 December 2003[241] explicitly interpreting national law in accordance with the stipulations of the Convention on the Rights of the Child, ratified by Tunisia in 1991. The Tribunal noted:

> Filiation is the right of a child and cannot be limited or restricted by any kind of agreed relations between the parents. Filiation as defined in Article 68 of the Code of Personal Status should be interpreted in a broad way in accordance with Article 2 parag. 2 of the Convention on the Rights of the Child ratified on 29 November 1991 by a legislative Act, which provides for protection of the child against all forms of discrimination or punishment on the basis of the legal status of the parents. The deprivation of the right of filiation for a child so justified by the fact that the parents are not legally married constitutes a sanction imposed on the child and a violation of his or her fundamental rights.[242]

In its judgment of 27 June 2000,[243] another tribunal in Tunisia has refused to give effect on Tunisian territory to a repudiation of marriage in Egypt, invoking two main arguments. The Court cited the incompatibility of the institution of repudiation with the principle of the equality between spouses as entrenched in Articles 1,2,7 and 16 (1) and (2) of the Universal Declaration of Human Rights, and the provisions of Articles 1,2 and 16(c) of the 1979 Women's Convention. This reasoning has been used again by the same tribunal in an un-published decision of 2003[244] preventing a repudiation undertaken in Morocco having a legal effect in Tunisia.

240 General Assembly, Department of Public Information, HR/CT/693, 'Human Rights Committee Report: Tunisia', 2008, available at : http://www.un.org/News/Press/docs/2008/hrct693.doc.htm (last accessed 1 April 2008).

241 Case number 53/16189 of 2 December 2003, cited in the report containing the responses of Tunisia to the list of questions addressed by the UN Human Rights Committee, CCPR/C/TUN/Q/5/add.1 on the 25 February 2008, available at: http://www.ohchr.org (last accessed 1 April 2008).

242 Translated by the author of this book.

243 Case number 34179 of 27 June 2000 cited in the written answers to the Human Rights Committee by the Government of Tunisia, CCPR/C/TUN/Q/5/Add.1, 2008, available at: http://www2.ohchr.org/english/bodies/hrc/docs/AdvanceDocs/CCPR.C.TUN.Q.5Add1.doc, 2, (last accessed 1 April 2008), and commented by Ben Jemia in *Revue tunisienne de droit*, 2000, 429.

244 Cited by S Ben Achour, 'L'ordre juridique Tunisien Face a la Repudiation Islamique', in *Polygamie et repudiations dans les relations internationals, Tunis,* Faculte des Sciences juridiques, politiques et socials, Colloque du 16 Avril 2004 (Sous Presse) 35.

In a decision delivered on 6 January 2004, the Appeal Court of Tunisia heard an appeal brought by the Tunisian heirs of a Tunisian woman married in Switzerland to a Belgian citizen. The appealed against judgment of the Court of First Instance granted the Belgian's application to have his wife's death certificate cancelled on the grounds that his name was not included among the heirs. The Appeal Court rejected the appeal and upheld the first court's judgment, dismissing the appellants' arguments that the marriage contracted in Switzerland was null and void owing to the impediment constituted by the prohibition on Muslim women marrying non-Muslim men and that consequently the husband could not be included among the list of legitimate heirs to the deceased's estate.

In the reasons it gives for its decision to reject the appeal, the Court argues in substance that:

> [T]he assertion that the difference in religion constitutes an impediment to marriage and therefore to inheritance is a violation of article 6 of the Constitution, which guarantees the principle of the equality of all before the law and introduces a difference in treatment between men, who are apparently free to marry non-Muslims, and women, who are apparently not, as well as a difference in treatment in matters of inheritance, contrary to the freedom of conscience and religion also guaranteed by the Constitution and by the international instruments ratified by Tunisia.[245]

In a judgment of 1994,[246] the Administrative Tribunal based its reasoning on Article 19 of the Universal Declaration of Human Rights and on Article 18 of the Constitution of Tunisia to rule that a public authority is not allowed to mention the political, philosophical or religious beliefs of a civil servant nor judge him for his own ideas, as long as he behaves during the exercise of his service in a way appropriate to the undertaking of his work.

On 21 May 1996, the same Administrative Tribunal reiterated the use of international law in its judgment against the decision taken by the Minister of Interior Affairs to declassify the Tunisian League for the protection of human rights as a human rights association, instead classifying it as a general association. The court argued that the decision constituted a violation of Article 22 of the International Covenant on Civil and Political Rights and should on that basis be quashed.

[245] Case number 120 of 6 January 2004 cited in the report containing the responses of Tunisia to the list of questions addressed by the UN Human Rights Committee, CCPR/C/TUN/Q/5/add.1 on the 25 February 2008, available at: http://www.ohchr.org (last accessed 22 April 2008).

[246] Case number 2193 of 1 June 1994, cited in report containing the responses of Tunisia to the list of questions addressed by the UN Human Rights Committee, CCPR/C/TUN/Q/5/add.1 on the 25 February 2008, available at http://www.ohchr.org (last accessed 1 April 2008).

The very recent report of the State of Tunisia to the Human Rights Committee on the CRC also produces many illustrations of the use of international human rights norms by the constitutional council in Tunisia. Under the Constitutional Acts of 27 October 1997 and 1 June 2002, the Council is instructed to ascertain the conformity and compatibility of all draft laws with the Constitution and in particular with its provisions concerning human rights. Accordingly, on the controversial issue of the right of access of grandparents to their grandchildren, the Constitutional Council noted in its opinion[247] that 'the United Nations Convention on the Rights of the Child of 20 November 1989, which has been ratified by the Tunisian Republic, gives precedence to the child's best interests and the child's right to preserve their family ties and lays down rights and obligations not only of parents, but also, where applicable, of members of the extended family' and that 'the fact of granting grandparents the right of access after the death of one of the parents, taking account of the best interests of the child, is likely to strengthen family ties and thus represents one aspect of family protection as provided by the Constitution and the principles accepted by the Tunisian Republic, and embodied in the United Nations Convention on the Rights of the Child'. Following this reasoning the Council had decided that Article 66 of the Personal status code was in conformity with the provisions of the Tunisian Constitution.

Turkey

Danistay, the Highest Administrative Court in Turkey held in 1991 that international agreements are hierarchically superior to the Turkish legal code and have binding effect on administrative and judicial bodies.[248] Thus, international agreements duly put into effect carry the force of law and no appeal to the Constitutional Court can be made on the basis of the unconstitutionality of these agreements.[249] The provisions of international human rights treaties ratified by Turkey may therefore be directly invoked before Turkish courts.

On July 27, 2006, the Istanbul Primary Criminal Court No 2 dealt with the case of a Turkish journalist regarding freedom of speech.[250] The Office of the Chief of General Staff initiated the prosecution brought against journalist Perihan Ma?den who was charged under article 318 for an article she

247 See opinion No 02-2006 cited in the report containing the responses of Tunisia to the list of questions addressed by the UN Human Rights Committee, CCPR/C/TUN/Q/5/add.1 on the 25 February 2008, available at: http://www.ohchr.org (last accessed 22 April 2008).

248 Danistay 5. Chamber, No. 1991/933, cited in Mehves Bingöllü and Sezgin Tanrikulu *Turkey—A Comparison of the EU Directive & Protocol 12 with Anti-Discrimination Legislation* , European Roma Rights Migration Policy Group, Brussels (2002).

249 Article 90 of the Constitution of Turkey.

250 Case Number 2006/140 Istambul second Criminal Court of First Instance cited at http://www.antenna-tr.org/ctl/index.asp?lgg=en (last accessed 1 April 2008).

wrote entitled 'Conscientious Objection is a Human Right' in the weekly journal Yeni Aktüel in December 2005. In that article Perihan Ma?den stated that 'service to the fatherland does not necessarily mean picking up a weapon. This service could be done by cleaning in a creche, driving an ambulance or teaching English in a children's home.' The public prosecutor charged her with 'prompting, encouraging or spreading propaganda to deter people from accomplishing military service'. In disagreement with the prosecutor, the court found in favour of Perihan Ma?den on the grounds that the expression of her views were protected by Article 26 of the Turkish Constitution and Article 10 of the European Convention on Human Rights. This provided for the freedom of expression for all, which included the freedom to hold opinions and to receive and impart information and ideas, regardless of frontiers and free from interference by public authorities.

B. The implementation of human rights standards through the use of Islamic jurisprudence

This section seeks to provide examples from the defined selection of Muslim States which aim at demonstrating that the Sharia has a built-in capacity to meet the needs of all eventualities, irrespective of changes in time, place, environment and conditions.[251] Indeed, as noted by Shaheen Sardar Ali, Sharia is not a monolithic concept and so, it is susceptible to varying interpretations. Its holds many juristic concepts including *ijtihad*, *takhayuir* and *talfiq* that if used would mirror the tolerant and democratic nature of the Islamic legal tradition. The proper use of the Islamic instruments would set some ground rules for a non-discriminatory polity.[252] Ali presents these mechanisms as milestones of Muslim history with the potential to empower women and to advance a non-discriminatory Islam.[253]

A greater implementation of international human rights norms may be achieved through supporting an extended and more open role for Sharia courts in Muslim States. With respect to this, it is important to note that Sharia Courts are constitutionally endowed with a progressive mandate to change its own jurisprudence. There are no rules of precedent, *stare decisis* in Sharia and judges cannot even follow their own precedent jurisprudence. Their actions are to be dictated by adopting the most pleasing solution to

[251] See Moulavi M.H. Babu Sahib, 'Justice and the Sharia' in *Administration of the Sharia Court system, papers and proceedings of the conference Administration of the Sharia Court system, 7–13 August 1983, Manila Philippines* (University of the Philippines, Quezon City, 1985) 127.

[252] See Shaheen Sardar Ali, 'Reclaiming our histories: A Reflection on Women, Islam and Human Rights in contemporary Muslim Communities', *Paper for Human Rights Day*, 10 December 2003, Islamabad, available at: http://sachet.org.pk/home/gender_columns/webcolumn_26.asp (last accessed 1 April 2008).

[253] ibid.

God and to the truth. Moreover, despite the fact that each Muslim country's jurisprudence normally feel obliged to follow the general path of one particular school of *fiqh*, Sharia judges in their application of the law retain a broad ambit of choice in this area. Indeed, Islamic jurisprudence encompasses different methodologies which would reflect its flexibility in this respect. Firstly, different interpretations often occur within a school and the judge may choose his favoured interpretation among them. Secondly, the judge can apply the Sharia principle '*taghayyur al-ayyam yaqtadi taghayyur al-ahkam*' (change in time calls for a change in rules). Finally, the judge is empowered to use the principle of *ijtihad* which allows a judge to make a legal decision by the independent interpretation of legal sources, (ie the Quran and the Sunnah). As we will see below in a plethora of different decisions, the use of *ijtihad* by Sharia judges has demonstrated itself to be an effective tool towards a harmonization of Islam and international human rights law.

The jurisprudential flexibility described above applies even in the most orthodox Islamic legal system—that of Saudi Arabia. This is evidenced by the statement of Shaykh Salih bin Muhammad al-Lahaydan, president of the permanent board of the Supreme Judicial Council and member of the Board of Senior 'Ulama:

> The Qadi of Saudi Arabia is not obliged or compelled to restrict himself to the school of Ahmad [Ibn Hanbal], but rather has the right to judge in the case in accordance with that to witch his ijtihad leads, even if that is not the Hanbali school ... It is not said to him, perform ijtihad within the school or without it; rather, he is requested to judge by that which he believes to be the truth.[254]

Frank E Vogel also provides an interesting and useful insight into Saudi case law where he states that:

> [C]ase-law is not published, indeed is not even public. This is true at both the trial and appellate levels; in fact, appeals decisions are the more difficult to obtain, with proceedings before the Boards of Review even being called secret. Appellate procedure is conducted wholly on the written trial record prepared by the trial judge, including a memorandum of appeal submitted by the appellant and usually involves no meetings with the parties. I repeatedly requested—supported from a letter from the Minister of Justice himself—to be allowed to read some appellate case,

254 Shaykh Salih bin Muhammad al-Lahaydan, president of the permanent Board of the Supreme Judicial Council and a member of the Board of Senior 'Ulama', written responses, 13 Jan 1985 cited by Frank E Vogel, *Islamic Law and Legal System, Studies of Saudi Arabia* (Brill NV, Leiden, 2000) 83.

> even purged of identifying matter. The appellate judges politely denied these requests. Instead what I present here was a glint by dint of paying innumerable visits to the Supreme Judicial Council over a period of eighteen months. The great majority of these visits produced only glasses of tea with court staff; a prized few of them led to quarter-hour oral or written exchanges of questions and answers.[255]

Also demonstrating that Sharia in Saudi Arabia is flexible rather than rigid, Vogel goes on to explain that:

> Saudi Qadis are not formally bound by taqlid to the Hanbali School, much less to its standard or preferred opinion. So, in theory qadis are free to apply any of the broad variety of views typically offered in the Hanbali School (which often incorporate all the major views available even from other schools). Some deviations from standard views occur commonly enough among the Saudi judges to have become well known minority positions, such as a holding that triple divorce counts as single.[256]

The absence of codification has positive aspects with regard to flexibility and high adaptations skills, but it also has many drawbacks, particularly if we think about the virtues of codification in harmonising the application of law, promoting certainty and reducing the likelihood of contradictory judgments as a result.

Bahrain

A review of the judgments of the Constitutional Court of Bahrain[257] demonstrates the potential of the Court to implement the human rights standards enshrined in Bahrain's constitution which states that 'Islamic Sharia is the main source of legislation.'[258] The Constitution also provides for various rights and duties, as well as the Constitutional Court's role in overseeing the constitutionality of laws and statutes and ensuring their conformity with such rights and duties, and may do so even retrospectively.[259]

Finally, Article 106 of the Constitution states:

[255] Frank E Vogel, *Islamic Law and Legal System, Studies of Saudi Arabia* (Brill NV, Leiden, 2000) 98.
[256] Frank E Vogel, *Islamic Law and Legal System, Studies of Saudi Arabia* (Brill NV, Leiden, 20000 126.
[257] For an overview of human rights developments in Bahrain's constitution: http://www.pogar.org/countries/humanrights.asp?cid=2.
[258] Constitution of the Kingdom of Bahrain (2002), Article 2
[259] Legislative Decree No. 27/2002 established the Constitutional Court (Article 18).

> A judgment by the Court that a text in a law or a regulation is unconstitutional shall have a direct effect unless the Court specifies a subsequent date for the purpose. Thus if the Court's adjudication on unconstitutionality is related to a text in the penal code then the convictions made on the basis of such a text are deemed null and void.

Bahrain's constitutional court website provides access to eight judgements from 2003 to 2005 in English (10 in Arabic until 2008). Of these judgments, the court's sixth ruling[260] provides an example of the potential of the court to improve human rights standards in Bahrain. The court found that Section 157 of the Penal Code (Legislative Decrees No. 15/1976 and amended 9/1982) related to what constitutes 'criminal conspiracy' was unconstitutional because it contravened Articles 4, 18, 19, 20(a) and (c) and 31 of the Constitution, most of with were related to human rights norms.

The concerned law punished any party to an agreement to commit any of the offences defined in sections 147 to 155 of the penal code with anything from temporary incarceration to life imprisonment. The Court notes that 'the text under objection went beyond the bounds of criminalising only acts and omissions' as it 'imposed punishment on a party to the aforementioned agreement who neither committed a physical act forbidden by the legislature nor unlawfully omitted to do any act which he was bound to do; i.e. the physical ingredient which is vital to the very existence of the offence is absent; hence there can be no offence.'[261]

The court concluded that the law was not in accordance with Article 20(a) of the Constitution which states: 'there shall be no crime and no punishment except under a law'. The law would have had to define a punishable offence which had a physical ingredient in order to be valid under Article 20. To reach this conclusion, the court argued that:

> [P]enal enactments are greatly restrictive and have far reaching effect on individual freedom. They are liable to be used by the legislature as a means of doing away with the substance of the freedom. To avert this eventuality the Constitution circumscribed such enactments with severe strictures and explicit guidelines. Most notable among these guidelines is the requirement for the highest and most manifest standard of certitude in penal enactments.

The court further stated that:

260 Constitutional Court Ruling No.C/S/3/04 and C/S/4/04, Judicial Year (2). (http://www.constitutional-court.org.bh/CCB/en/Judgments/Sixth_Judgement.aspx) (last accessed 14 August 2008).

261 Constitutional Court Ruling No.C/S/3/04 and C/S/4/04, Judicial Year (2) (http://www.constitutional-court.org.bh/CCB/en/Judgments/Sixth_Judgement.aspx).

> [T]he text overstepped the boundaries of legislative discretion in that it ignored the presumption of innocence and contradicted the principle of legitimacy of crimes and punishments, thereby forfeiting justification for its existence and constituting unwarranted strictures against individual freedom.

The other article upon which the law was found to be unconstitutional directly relate to matters of justice, freedom and equality (article 4);[262] human dignity (article 18);[263] personal freedom, rule of law and due process (article 19); no crime and no punishment except under a law and due process (article 20 (a) and (c)),[264] and rule of law and the essence of personal rights and freedoms (article 31).[265] The reasoning of the Bahraini Constitutional Court provides a source of optimism and demonstrates the potential of courts in implementing *certain* human rights standards even in the face of political opposition (a matter the court addressed in this case as well, for the laws concerned crimes related to the internal security of the State).

Egypt

With respect to Egypt, it is important to cite a decision of the Supreme Constitutional Court of Egypt of 26 March 1994[266] in which the judges based their decision on the flexibility of Islamic law and on the necessity incumbent on political authorities to apply *ijtihad* in order to make sure that their norms are in harmony with society.

With regard to the facts of this case, a father challenged the constitutionality of an Egyptian Law (Article 18b of Law No 100 of 1985 on the father's maintenance obligation toward his child) on the basis that this law contradicted the predominant opinion of the Hanafi school of thought. Upon application of the law of 1985, the plaintiff has been condemned by the court of appeal to pay the maintenance for his 21-year-old daughter

262 Article 4: Justice is the basis of government. Cooperation and mutual respect provide a firm bond between citizens. Freedom, equality, security, trust, knowledge, social solidarity and equality of opportunity for citizens are pillars of society guaranteed by the State.

263 Article 18: People are equal in human dignity, and citizens are equal before the law in public rights and duties. There shall be no discrimination among them on the basis of sex, origin, language, religion or creed.

264 Article 20: a. There shall be no crime and no punishment except under a law, and punishment only for acts committed subsequent to the effective date of the law providing for the same.
c. An accused person is innocent until proved guilty in a legal trial in which he is assured of the necessary guarantees to exercise the right of defence at all stages of the investigation and trial in accordance with the law.

265 Article 31: The public rights and freedoms stated in this Constitution may only be regulated or limited by or in accordance with the law, and such regulation or limitation may not prejudice the essence of the right or freedom.

266 SCC, 26 March 1994, Mahkama (1996, 6: 23–60).

retroactively for 20 years, whereas upon application of the Hanafi doctrine, the father's obligation cannot last longer than the time for which the maintenance is needed (ie rendering retroactive effect a moot point). As argued by Baber Johansen and other Islamic scholars, 'since the twelfth century, and perhaps before that, the Hanafi jurists have held that even a qadi's judgment obligating the father to pay a certain amount of maintenance is extinguished once the time unit fixed for the maintenance payment passes.'[267]

The 1994 decision of the court as analysed by Johansen stated that:

> [T]here are no eternal and unchanging rules that forbid the retroactive effect of judicial decisions imposing maintenance obligations on a father, and the legal reasoning of past generations of Muslim jurists produces only changing and modifiable rules that bind neither the jurists nor the political authorities or the legislature of the twentieth century. The norms promulgated by the modern legislator in the field, says the court, enjoy precedence over all norm suggested by Muslim jurists in the past which, in the final instance, are also based on individual legal reasoning only.[268]

The court further stated that:

> [T]he change of time calls for abandoning this type (Hanafi doctrine) of legal reasoning in order to keep operational the flexibility that Islamic law encompasses in its practical norms. These are open for development, mindful of the law's ties to the interest of the people and their renewed needs and their changing practices, so long as these do not conflict with a definite revealed rule. This flexibility contradicts [the idea] that the political authorities are fettered by specific legal opinions an not allowed to deviate from them or that their efforts to engage with legal reasoning should stop at a moment in time already left behind by those interests which have to be taken into consideration by the law. This Islamic Law, in its roots and sources, develops by necessity, and rejects all deadlock and stagnation and the efforts of individual reasoning are not restricted by anything—in the areas in which no revealed texts settle the questions—except by the general rules [of Islamic normativity] and by considerations that do not paralyse the theology of the sacred law. Within this it is a rational duty, a requirement of religious ethics, and it

267 See Baber Johansen, 'The Constitution and the Principles of Islamic Normativity against the Rules of fiqh. A judgement of the Supreme Constitutional Court of Egypt', Muhammad Khalid Masud, Rudolph Peters and David S. Powers (eds) *Dispensing Justice in Islam, Qadis and their judgments* (Brill, Leiden–Boston, 2006) 169–193, 186.

268 ibid, Johansen.

serves the realization of considerable interests to abandon the assumption defended by the Hanafis and their followers.[269]

This tension between different trends within the Islamic legal spheres, which is from one side a tendency to implement a conservative Islamic order and from the other side, a more progressive and reformist mainstream which tries to interpret Islamic principles through the prism of modern human right norms, is sometimes reflected in the jurisprudence of Sharia courts themselves. Certain cases heard by Islamic courts in Muslim countries display this friction. In fact, this challenge is particularly noticeable when the divergence of interpretations and views concern the same case as interpreted by two different courts, for example an Islamic court of First Degree and an Islamic Court of Appeal, or on occasion a Court of Appeal and a Supreme Court.

The *Safiyyatu Hussaini* case in Sokoto State in Northern Nigeria raised the subject of an alleged extra-marital sexual intercourse that led to the birth of a child. The analysis attested to the judicial dichotomy between the Sharia lower court and the Sharia Court of Appeal with regard to the enforcement of more severe Quranic penalties. In this case, and as asserted by Rudulph Peters' paper,[270] the Upper Sharia court seemed to be quite willing to pronounce a sentence of death by stoning on the basis of what, even according to classical Islamic standard are rather thin grounds, by superficially referring to some textual arguments from the Maliki school.[271] Conversely, the Sharia Court of Appeal seemed to adopt an opposing attitude trying to prevent the application of the *hadd* punishment for unlawful intercourse insofar as it was possible. Peters shows in his article how the Sharia Appeal Court used all possible arguments and stretched the classical doctrine to its utmost in order to quash the trial court judgment on as many grounds as possible.[272]

The Upper Court has extended its classic role in enlarging the scope of Islamic norms by restricting the enforcement of stoning to death by deciding not to apply the Maliki doctrine that states that pregnancy of unmarried woman is by itself an evidence for adultery. For this purpose, the court

[269] I am reproducing this paragraph of the decision as cited and translated by Baber Johansen in his paper; 'The Constitution and the Principles of Islamic Normativity against the Rules of fiqh. A judgement of the Supreme Constitutional Court of Egypt', Muhammad Khalid Masud, Rudolph Peters and David S. Powers (eds) *Dispensing Justice in Islam, Qadis and their judgments*, (Brill, Leiden–Boston, 2006) 191.

[270] See Rudolph Peters, 'The Re-islamisation of criminal law in Northern Nigeria and the Judiciary: The Safiyyatu Hussaini Case', Muhammad Khalid Masud, Rudolph Peters and David S. Power (eds) *Dispensing Justice in Islam, Qadis and their judgments* (Brill, 2006) 219–241.

[271] ibid, 240

[272] ibid, 240

has undeniably used *ijtihad* to affirm a new rule providing that the investigation of *zina* cases on the basis of mere suspicion (eg the pregnancy of an unmarried woman) is unlawful. In its attempts to prevent the woman from being stoned to death, the Appeal Court went further in applying a rule which is by itself scientifically questionable. The rule states that women may rebut allegations of adultery because during the five years following the dissolution of her last marriage, her claim that the child with which she is pregnant was fathered by her former husband creates a situation of uncertainty or doubt about the unlawfulness if the proven act. This is known as *shubha* in Islamic law. This situation averted the application of the punishment by stoning the lady to death.[273]

Iran

Present divorce laws in Iran allow for women to apply for divorce on several grounds which include: mental illness of the husband; physical defects making the husband unable to perform sexually; where the husband lacks qualifications stipulated expressly in the marriage contract; where the wife has obtained agency from the husband to divorce herself; where the husband fails to provide maintenance and cannot be forced to do so; and where the marriage causes hardship and difficulty for the wife.[274] It is up to the woman to prove her case such that the judge orders the husband to divorce his wife or dissolves the marriage himself. In many cases, it is argued that the husband usually only agrees to divorce if the wife returns the dower (*mahr*) granted to her at marriage. Thus, it remains controversial as to whether or not a husband must consent to *khul'* or *mubarat* divorce. As a result of these difficulties in proof and ambiguities in the law, the Iranian courts have an important role in determining the standards of evidence required, filling the gaps in the law, and interpreting certain concepts contained in the law.

A recent case demonstrates the positive role the courts have played in clarifying certain ambiguities in the law, particularly the requirement of a husband's consent when it comes to *khul'*. The case involved the Court of First Instance of Isfahan concerning a woman seeking divorce on the grounds of hardship and distress due to mistreatment by her husband just after a few months of their marriage in 2005, and suspicion that he had remarried.[275] The husband opposed the divorce and argued that (a) he liked her, and (b) she was not obedient. The Court of First Instance decided against the wife, arguing that according to hadith, divorce was in the hands

[273] ibid, 241

[274] Lecture given by Dr. Mohammad Habibi Mojandeh, 'Divorce in the Triangle of International Human Rights, Islamic Jurisprudence, and the Iranian Legal System,' presented at the BIICL Conference on 5 June 2008.

[275] Case 23/h84-495.

of men alone. The woman then appealed and the first ruling was overturned. The Appeal Court of Isfahan found that the woman had grounds for divorce on the basis of hardship and distress, and took into account the lapse of more than five years from marriage; the inability of the spouses to found a family which is considered part of the husband's duty; and the wife's willingness to give up most of her *mahr* which demonstrates the weak nature of the relationship. The husband was ordered to divorce his wife irrevocably. In 2006, the Supreme Court Chamber upheld the Appeal Court's ruling.

The Supreme Court's decision ended up filling an important gap in the law relating *khul'* and the role of the husband's consent. When deciding the case, the Court referred to a fatwa (advisory opinion) of a grand Ayatollah to the effect that if it is proved that continuing marriage caused great hardship for the woman, the judge could commence with a *khul'* divorce regardless of the husband's consent.

Lebanon

In a decision of 16 February 2000 given by the High Sunni Court of Beirut presided over by Sheikh Moufid Chalak,[276] the court refused to give effect to a well-known principle in Islamic jurisprudence (*fiqh*), explicitly basing its choice of law on the implementation of the principle of *takhayyur*. The court stated that even if there is in the *fiqh* an explicit text allowing the husband to accommodate his wife in a flat that is 'borrowed' and not legally rented or owned by him, there is on the other hand an underlying principle in the *fiqh* providing that judgments may change in line with a change of circumstances. Thus, as today's circumstances are very different from those of in ancient history in which people were supposedly more pure, reliable and could be trusted, this change in the circumstances would justify the refusal of the courts in accepting the *fiqhi* principle in these particular circumstances.

With regard to custody, Sharia courts in Lebanon seem more inclined to adopt[277] the 'best interest of the child' approach as the main criterion in deciding with who the child should be placed. In many decisions, judges meticulously examine the specific circumstances of each case instead of automatically applying the Islamic rules. These rules provide that in case of divorce the woman's custody of a boy terminates when he is seven years' old, whereas the custody of a girl terminates when she reaches puberty (some schools of thoughts say at the age of nine; other schools say that girls

[276] See Ali Nadim Homsani, Majmouaat al mabadi' wal kawai'd al chari'ya wal kanouniyya, Manchourat el Halabi el houkoukiyya, 2003, 21–23.

[277] Interview conducted by the author in May 2007 at Dar el Fatwa, Beirut with Judge Mohammad Nokhary.

should remain with their mothers until they get married) and that a boy or a girl having passed the period of *hizanah*, must necessarily remain in the charge of the father.

A decision of 4 February 1987 given by the Highest Assembly of the Islamic Sunni courts implemented the criterion of 'the best interests of the child' by adopting an extensive and progressive interpretation of the principle invoked by the father in this case. The father argued that the absence of the woman from home during the day was a determining factor in the woman losing her right to custody of the child. However, the Court looked at the specific context of the case and provided that even if the woman is working all day outside the home, the child's grandmother and aunt could take care of her when she finished school and the mother would be available thereafter. It is evident from the above case that the courts can put the interests of the child first, should they choose to.

Pakistan

The Federal Shariat Court is empowered by the Constitution to examine and adjudicate upon questions as to whether or not any law or provision of law is repugnant to the injunctions of Islam, as laid down in the Quran and Sunnah. Some scholars believe that this means that the Federal Shariat Court is constitutionally empowered to undertake *ijtihad*[278] and that by doing so, an 'Islamic review of legislation could incorporate a constitutionally guaranteed fundamental right (for example the right to equality in Article 14 of the 1973 constitution) without any conceptual difficulty'.[279] Thus, whilst an Islamic court tasked with examining the validity of the laws on the basis of Islam could cause unease in light of its potential to have a negative impact on the process of democratization and implementation of better human rights standards within the State,[280] at times, this direct appeal to the primary sources of the Sharia has allowed Pakistan's judiciary to improve the situation of women in Pakistan.[281]

In his study of the Pakistani courts, Dr Martin Lau has found that by using *ijtihad*, the courts have helped entrench some fundamental rights

278 See Niaz Shah, *Women, the Koran and International Human Rights Law, the Experience of Pakistan* (Martinus Nijhoff Publishers, 2006) 84.

279 Martin Lau, Human Rights 'Natural Justice and Pakistan's Sharia Courts', Javaid Rehman and Susan Breau (eds) *Religion, Human Rights and International Law— A Critical Examination of Islamic States* (Martinus Nijhoff 2007) 364.

280 See Ann E. Mayer, *Islam and Human Rights* (Westview Press, Boulder, 1995), AA An-Naim, *'Civil Rights in the Islamic constitutional tradition: shared ideals and divergent regimes'* (The John Marshall Law Review 1992) 267–293.

281 See Javaid Rehman, The Sharia, 'Islamic Family Laws and International Human Rights Law: Examining the Theory and Practice of Polygamy and Talaq', International Journal of Law and the Family, volume 108, April 2007, L Carroll (1996) 'Quran 2:229: 'A charter granted for life?': *Judicial Khul in Pakistan*', 3 Islamic Law and Society 1, 91–126.

within Pakistan's set of norms and cites several cases to this effect.[282] Moreover, the use of *ijtihad* as a means of incorporation of human rights standards is not confined to Islamic courts and may be seen in the jurisprudence of others courts such as the Lahore High Court and the Supreme Court.[283] More recently, Dr. Aisha Shahid carried out a review of family law cases heard by the superior courts of Pakistan and some provide evidence of the application of Islamic jurisprudence in a manner which protects the rights of women.[284]

In a 2006 case on *khul'* (judicial dissolution), the husband challenged a decision which granted his wife a divorce without her having to repay the dower.[285] In response to this, the court argued that 'restitution of dower is not an indispensable condition for grant of *khula'* and after referring to a verse of the Quran further stated that 'if the contention of the petitioner (husband) is accepted then a destitute wife who is found otherwise entitled to *khula*, will stand deprived of the right simply because of her incapacity to return the benefits, which will be highly unfair and against the spirit of law and justice.' In another case which may arguably seen as protecting the right to marry, the courts held in *Fazli Subhan v Mst Sabreen,*[286] that a woman would remarry her former husband after a *khula'* divorce without having to have an intermediary marriage (*halala*). In support of this decision, the court looked at the purpose of the *halala* requirement itself, which was supposed to act as a means of preventing husbands from abusing unilateral divorces.

Finally, in an important case of custody and guardianship, the courts found against a husband's claims for custody over his children following the second marriage of their mother, his former wife.[287] Here, the court argued that based on the Prophet's Sunnah, it was clear that the Prophet believed that the best person to take care of the child was the mother herself. The

[282] Martin Lau, Human Rights 'Natural Justice and Pakistan's Sharia Courts', Javaid Rehman and Susan Breau (eds) *Religion, Human rights and international law, critical examination of Islamic states* (Martinus Nijhoff, 2007) 359–378 (See: *Pakistan v Public at Large* PLD 1986 SC 304; *Iftikharuddin v Federal Government* (1992) PLD FSC 188) See also: Niaz Shah, *Women, the Koran and International Human Rights Law, the Experience of Pakistan* (Martinus Nijhoff, 2006) who gives the example of *Hazoor Bakhash v Federation of Pakistan* (1980) PLD FSC 145.

[283] See Javaid Rehman, *The Sharia, 'Islamic Family Laws and International Human Rights Law: Examining the theory and practice of polygamy and Talaq'*, International Journal of Law and the Family, volume 108, April 2007, L Carroll (1996) 'Quran 2:229: 'A charter granted for life?': *Judicial Khul in Pakistan*', 3 Islamic Law and Society 1, 91–126; see also: *Khurshid Bibi v Muhammad Amin* (1967) PLD SC 97.

[284] Based on a lecture by Dr. Ayesha Shahid, 'Sharia and Implementation of Human Rights norms of Equality and Non-Discrimination in the Family: A Case Study of Family Law in Pakistan,' presented at the BIICL Conference 'Islam, the Application of Sharia and Human Rights,' on 5 June 2008.

[285] *Aurangzeb v Mst Gulnaz* PLD 2006 Kar 568.

[286] PLD 2007 Kar.

[287] *Rukhsana Malik v Abdul Aziz* PLD 2004 Lah 801.

court went on to reaffirm a previous judgment which held that 'the overriding and paramount consideration always is the welfare of the minor.' Dr Shahid argues that the courts decision to uphold the 'best interest of the child' as being of paramount importance, also serves as an indirect acknowledgment of the UN Convention on the Rights of the Child. In light of the above, it is evident that where courts choose to do so, principles of Islamic jurisprudence and be interpreted and applied in a manner which protects certain human rights, particularly in relation to women and family.

CONCLUSION

Few generalizations can be made about the impact of Sharia on the ratification and implementation of international human rights conventions by Muslim States. To begin with, the possible impact of Sharia on a Muslim State's engagement with international human rights conventions may to some degree depend on the normative status of Sharia within the hierarchy of norms within the State. Even then there are circumstances which illustrate that the role of Sharia is relatively inconsequential.

Having examined the cross-section of diverse Muslim States and their various declarations, reservations and arguments regarding limitations placed on their ratification and implementation of international human rights treaties, it appears that many limitations are justified by using Sharia. However, whilst religious considerations clearly have some impact, in the majority of the reservations examined, the justifications used were largely artificial and ambiguous.

This is clearly evident when considering the incoherent practices of Muslim States when lodging reservations grounded in Sharia. An analysis of the rationale and reasoning behind some of these very sweeping reservations made in the name of Islam illustrates the use of Sharia as a means of hiding political or other considerations. As a result, the practices of Muslim States become confusingly paradoxical. For example, on the one hand, a State formulates a reservation against a specific article in the name of Sharia and, on the other hand, it fully accepts an article of a similar or same effect in another human rights treaty. This was clearly seen with regard to Egypt where Sharia was used to justify limitations to CEDAW, but it accepted those very principles within the framework of the ICCPR. These actions, among many other factors articulated in this study, appear to support the suspicion that Muslim States avoid certain provisions in order to enlarge their margin of power or maintain their popular legitimacy under the 'legitimate' cover of 'sacred' Islamic considerations.

While some Muslim States do not appear to be as conflicted in their engagements with human rights treaties, others provide examples of legislative amendments at the internal level which not only apply human rights norms but which also remain within the very framework of Sharia. The nature of Sharia and its susceptibility to reform, as demonstrated by Egypt's reforms to divorce law and Morocco's new laws of personal status, prove that laws and norms derived from Sharia can be compatible with human rights. An analysis of some of these legislative and Sharia-compliant reforms, as well as the positive jurisprudence of the secular and Sharia courts, demonstrate the great potential for improving human rights practices in Muslim States.

Even in the context of the Islamic Republic of Iran, the theocratic regime cannot enact unchangeable and permanent laws set out in accordance with fixed principles of the Sharia or frozen human rights policies. This is evident not only from the reinstatement of elements of the Family Protection Law of 1967 through amendments in 1992 to Divorce Regulations which had been previously denounced as incompatible with Sharia following the Revolution, but also more recently, from statements made by the Iranian delegation to the Committee of the CRC in 2005 with reference to reforming the minimum age of marriage. The Iranian delegate stated that 'relevant Shariah provisions were currently being reconsidered in the light of the need for children to have attained a certain level of maturity before entering into marriage. The Government was considering the preparation of legal provisions to formalize the reforms.'[288] Evidently, activating the inherent mechanisms of Sharia and interpreting Sharia in order to reform the law is a possible path even where the constitutional framework privileges Sharia.

Other interesting examples are provided by Egypt with regard to Law No. 1 of 2000 concerning the woman's right to divorce in which the legislature has referred directly to the Qu'ran and the Sunna to justify the amendment of the law without any reference to juristic interpretations adopting the new interpretation of the law based on the primary sources of the Sharia. Other example could be given by Pakistan with regard to the reform of rape law through the Protection of Women (Criminal Laws Amendment) Act 2006 and by the Moroccan Family Code (Moudawana) of February 2004 which has used basis Islamic principles in order to advance women and children rights.

Examples on the role of the Islamic courts in using ijtihad aimed at fostering the implementation of better human rights norms are numerous. For example, in a decision of 16 February 2000 given by the High Sunni Court of Beirut presided over by Sheikh Moufid Chalak, the Court refused to give effect to a well known principle in Islamic jurisprudence (fiqh), explicitly basing its choice of law on the implementation of the principle of

[288] Committee on the Rights of the Child: Consideration of Reports, 2005 (Iran), ¶ 68, U.N. Doc. CRC/C/SR.1016 (28 Jan 2005).

takhayyur. The Court stated that even if there is in the fiqh an explicit text allowing the husband to accommodate his wife in a flat that is 'borrowed' and not legally rented or owned by him, there is an underlying principle in the fiqh providing that judgments may change in line with a change of circumstances. Thus, as today's circumstances are very different from those of the past, this change in the circumstances would justify the refusal of the courts in accepting the fiqhi principle in these particular circumstances. Also note that in multi-confessional Lebanon in which the State has totally delegated the field of family law to the different 18 communities recognised on Lebanese territory has meant that Lebanon is unable to reform the family law in accordance with its obligations resulting from the State's international engagements.

Indeed, the Sharia could form a 'tool in establishing widespread compliance' of international legal norms.[289] Legal tools such as ijtihad and thakhayyur which exist within the jurisprudential framework of Sharia have allowed for great reform in Muslim States. This research has shown that it is not Sharia which is preventing the implementation of human rights or justifying their violation in Muslim States. Rather, it is a lack of political will among the governing establishment of Muslim States that are largely responsible for the poor human rights records. Thus, in light of the incongruities in State practices when it comes to both the ratification of international human rights conventions and the implementation of human rights norms, particularly within the framework of Sharia, the use of Sharia as a reason by governments to limit the State's engagement with international human rights norms is no longer convincing in law. It is evident that despite claims made by Muslim States, the Sharia has little to do with their decisions to abstain from ratifying international treaties or to limit the treaties by use of general or broad reservations. The very nature of Sharia, demonstrates the potential of reform in the interests of human rights. Indeed, the widespread debate surrounding human rights and Islam, the inconsistencies in the use of reservations by Muslim States; the creation of Muslim human rights instruments such as the Cairo Declaration on Human Rights and the Covenant on the Rights of Child in Islam; attempts to reform the laws in domestic legal systems; and the extended role of the judiciary in applying human rights norms, may all be seen as a consequence of internal tensions within the purported interpretations of the Sharia and a genuine will for a change.

This study reaches the conclusion that the use of Sharia could lead to a harmonization of international standards of human rights with those in

289 Ahmad E. Nassar, 'The International Criminal Court and the Applicability of International Jurisdiction under Islamic Law', 4 Chi J Int'l L. 587 (2003) 591.

application in Muslim States. Some comparative aspects of amendments to legislative texts in the Muslim world show that the reconciliation of this legislation with the international human rights standards do not necessarily imply a secular legal framework and could be carried out within the framework of Sharia. In fact, the inherent flexibility of Sharia encompassing different legal tools creates room for interpretation and adaptation to changes of context and circumstance.[290] Adopting Sharia derived national laws, such as those in Egypt, Morocco and Tunisia, can constitute a decisive step towards harmonising national legislation with international human rights standards. This is because leaving important areas of legislation impervious to State control and under the sole influence of religious authorities (in the form of religious courts who develop and apply these laws under a minimal State control as seen in Lebanon and Bahrain), prevents the reform of these laws in accordance with international human rights treaties.

Consequently, this study finds that the process of reforming Islamic law (mainly in matters of personal status) is a two-stage process. First, it would require the nationalisation of these sets of laws such that the State enacts the legislation defining and structuring the laws as interpreted by Sharia. Second, the State would have to undertake a reform of these laws in accordance with the principles of Sharia. Although the adoption of Sharia law is sometimes seen by some scholars to be a traditional and retrograde approach, it has been proven that this step has allowed the State to ensure that the laws and norms of Sharia develop in conformity with human rights norms. For example, during the 1950s and 1960s, the nationalisation of Islamic family law became a major trend among different Muslim States with Egypt and Tunisia going as far as abolishing Sharia courts. Scholars have argued that the adoption of national codes as happened in Egypt, Tunisia and Morrocco, represented by that time the first examples in history of a codification of principles derived from the Shari'a but enacted as law by a human legislature.[291]

An examination of a cross-section of Muslim States with varied political structures reveals that not only do the same types of human rights violations occur across the board despite doctrinal, ideological, and religious differences but also that, upon closer examination, it is evident that Sharia is not the root cause of human rights violations. Rather, the human rights violations within these States are most closely associated with the inherent nature of military or authoritarian government. Such violations follow from the tendency of such regimes to be intolerant of any political opposition,

[290] See Abdullahi An-Naim, Toward an Islamic Reformation: Civil Liberties, Human Rights and International Law (Syracuse NY, Syracuse University Press, 1990).

[291] J Anderson, 'Modern Trends in Islam: Legal Reform and Modernisation in the Middle East' [1971] 20 ICLQ 1–21.

preoccupied with their own security and survival, and determined to pursue harsh policies, regardless of the consequences to the general population.[292] Moreover, other political, sociological and structural factors contribute to causing human rights violations in Muslim States, notably the Israeli-Palestinian conflict in the Middle East; the occupation of Lebanon by Syria for more than 17 years; and the Kurdish rebellion in Turkey.

Therefore the role of Sharia does not sufficiently account for the range of limitations against international human rights conventions and violations of human rights in practice. Despite the differences in the implementation of Sharia or even the non-implementation of Sharia, all these Muslim States share similarly poor records for their observation of civil and political rights, strongly suggesting that, although the implementation of Sharia may be a common denominator among the States, it is not the definitive factor preventing them from complying with the international law to which they are bound.

292 A An-Na'im, 'The application of Sharia (Islamic Law) and Human Rights violations in the Sudan, in *Islamic Law Reform and Human Rights Challenges and Rejoinders* (Tore Lindholm and Kari Vogt (eds), Nordic Human Rights Publications, 1993) 136.

APPENDIX

EGYPT

Convention	Signature (date)	Ratification/ Accession (date)	Articles where RUDs apply	State objections to some or all aspects of the reservations/declarations		
				'declaration amounts to a reservation'	'contrary'/ 'raises doubt' to 'object and purpose	Other
ICERD	28/09/1966	01/05/1967	–	–	–	–
ICCPR	04/08/1967	14/01/1982	Treaty Generally Declaration: ... Taking into consideration the provisions of the Islamic Sharia and the fact that they do not conflict with the text annexed to the instrument, we accept, support and ratify it	–	–	–
ICESCR	04/08/1967	14/01/1982	Treaty Generally *Declaration:* ... Taking into consideration the provisions of the Islamic Sharia and the fact that they do not conflict with the text annexed to the instrument, we accept, support and ratify it	–	–	–
CEDAW	16/07/1980	18/09/1981	**Art. 2, 9(2) [withdrawn on 04/01 2008], 16, 29** *upon signature and confirmed upon ratification:* <u>In respect of article 16</u>: Reservation to the text of article 16 concerning the equality of men and women in all matters relating	**Germany, Mexico, The Netherlands Sweden**	**Germany, The Netherlands Sweden**	**Germany:** 'In relation to the Federal Republic of Germany, they may not be invoked in support of a legal practice which does not pay due regard to the legal status afforded to women and children in the Federal

EGYPT *(continued)*

Convention	Signature (date)	Ratification/ Accession (date)	Articles where RUDs apply	State objections to some or all aspects of the reservations/declarations		
				'declaration amounts to a reservation'	'contrary'/ 'raises doubt' to 'object and purpose	Other
			to marriage and family relations during the marriage and upon its dissolution, without prejudice to the Islamic *Sharia's* provisions whereby women are accorded rights equivalent to those of their spouses so as to ensure a just balance between them. This is out of respect for the sacrosanct nature of the firm religious beliefs which govern marital relations in Egypt and which may not be called in question and in view of the fact that one of the most important bases of these relations is an equivalency of rights and duties so as to ensure complementary which guarantees true equality between the spouses. The provisions of the *Sharia* lay down that the husband shall pay bridal money to the wife and maintain her fully and shall also make a payment to her upon divorce, whereas the wife retains full rights over her property and is not obliged to spend anything on her keep. The *Sharia* therefore restricts the wife's rights to divorce by making it contingent on a judge's ruling, whereas no			Republic of Germany in conformity with the above-mentioned articles of the Convention.' **Mexico:** 'reservations, if implemented, would inevitably result in discrimination against women on the basis of sex, which is contrary to all the articles of the Convention. The principles of equal rights of men and women and non-discrimination on the basis of sex, which are embodied in the second preambular paragraph and Article 1, paragraph 3, of the Charter of the United Nations, to which Egypt is a signatory, and in articles 2 and 16 of the Universal Declaration of Human Rights of 1948, were previously accepted by the Government of Egypt when it acceded, ..., to the International Covenant on Civil and Political Rights and the International

			such restriction is laid down in the case of the husband. In respect of article 29: The Egyptian delegation also maintains the reservation contained in article 29, paragraph 2, concerning the right of a State signatory to the Convention to declare that it does not consider itself bound by paragraph 1 of that article concerning the submission to an arbitral body of any dispute which may arise between States concerning the interpretation or application of the Convention. This is in order to avoid being bound by the system of arbitration in this field. Reservation made upon ratification: General reservation on article 2: The Arab Republic of Egypt is willing to comply with the content of this article, provided that such compliance does not run counter to the Islamic *Sharia*.			Covenant on Economic, Social and Cultural Rights. The above principles were stated in article 2, paragraph 1, and article 3 of the former Covenant and in article 2, paragraph 2, and article 3 of the latter. Consequently, it is inconsistent with these contractual obligations previously assumed by Egypt for its Government now to claim that it has reservations, on the same subject, about the 1979 Convention.'
CAT	–	25/06/1986	–	–	–	–
CRC	05/02/1990	06/07/1990	**Art. 20** [**withdrawn on 31/07/2003**], **Art. 21** [**withdrawn on 31/07/2003**]	–	–	–

IRAN (ISLAMIC REPUBLIC OF)

Convention	Signature (date)	Ratification/ Accession (date)	Articles where RUDs apply	State objections to some or all aspects of the reservations/declarations		
				'declaration amounts to a reservation'	'contrary'/ 'raises doubt' to 'object and purpose	Other
IICERD	08/03/1967	29/08/1968	–	–	–	–
ICCPR	04/04/1968	24/06/1975	–	–	–	–
ICESCR	04/04/1968	24/06/1975	–	–	–	–
CEDAW	–	–	–	–	–	–
CAT	–	–	–	–	–	–
CRC	05/09/1991	13/07/1994	Treaty Generally Upon signature: Reservation: 'The Islamic Republic of Iran is making reservation to the articles and provisions which may be contrary to the Islamic Shariah, and preserves the right to make such particular declaration, upon its ratification'. Upon ratification: Reservation: 'The Government of the Islamic Republic of Iran reserves the right not to apply any provisions or articles of the Convention that are incompatible with Islamic Laws and the international legislation in effect.'	**Denmark, Finland, Germany, Ireland, Italy, The Netherlands, Norway, Portugal, Sweden**	**Netherlands Norway, Portugal, Sweden**	**Italy:** 'This reservation, owing to its unlimited scope and undefined character, is inadmissible under international law' **Germany:** 'This reservation, owing to its indefinite nature, does not meet the requirements of international law'

Convention	Signature (date)	Ratification/ Accession (date)	Articles where RUDs apply	State objections to some or all aspects of the reservations/declarations		
				'declaration amounts to a reservation'	'contrary'/ 'raises doubt' to 'object and purpose	Other
CERD	18/02/1969	14/01/1970	**Treaty Generally, Art. 22** Upon signature: 'The Ministry for Foreign Affairs of the Republic of Iraq hereby declares that signature for and on behalf of the Republic of Iraq of the Convention on the Elimination of All Forms of Racial Discrimination, which was adopted by the General Assembly of the United Nations on 21 December 1965, as well as approval by the Arab States of the said Convention and entry into it by their respective governments, shall in no way signify recognition of Israel or lead to entry by the Arab States into such dealings with Israel as may be regulated by the said Convention. 'Furthermore, the Government of the Republic of Iraq does not consider itself bound by the provisions of article twenty-two of the Convention aforementioned and affirms its reservation that it does not accept the compulsory jurisdiction of the International Court of Justice provided for in the said article.'	**Israel**		**Isreal:** In a communication received by the Secretary-General on 10 July 1969, the Government of Israel declared: '[Israel] has noted the political character of the declaration made by the Government of Iraq on signing the above Convention. In the view of the Government of Israel, the Convention is not the proper place for making such political pronouncements. The Government of Israel will, in so far as concerns the substance of the matter, adopt towards the Government of Iraq an attitude of complete reciprocity. Moreover, it is the view of the Government of Israel that no legal relevance can be attached to those Iraqi statements which purport to represent the views of the other States'.

IRAQ *(continued)*

Convention	Signature (date)	Ratification/ Accession (date)	Articles where RUDs apply	State objections to some or all aspects of the reservations/declarations		
				'declaration amounts to a reservation'	'contrary'/ 'raises doubt' to 'object and purpose	Other
			Upon ratification: 1. The acceptance and ratification of the Convention by Iraq shall in no way signify recognition of Israel or be conducive to entry by Iraq into such dealings with Israel as are regulated by the Convention; 2. Iraq does not accept the provisions of article 22 of the Convention, concerning the compulsory jurisdiction of the International Court of Justice. The Republic of Iraq does not consider itself to be bound by the provisions of article 22 of the Convention and deems it necessary that in all cases the approval of all parties to the dispute be secured before the case is referred to the International Court of Justice.			
ICCPR	**18/02/1969**	**25/01/1971**	**Treaty Generally** Upon signature and confirmed upon ratification: 'The entry of the Republic of Iraq as a	**Israel**	–	

			party to the International Covenant on Economic, Social and Cultural Rights and the International Covenant on Civil and Political Rights shall in no way signify recognition of Israel nor shall it entail any obligation towards Israel under the said two Covenants.' 'The entry of the Republic of Iraq as a party to the above two Covenants shall not constitute entry by it as a party to the Optional Protocol to the International Covenant on Civil and Political Rights.' Upon ratification: 'Ratification by Iraq ... shall in no way signify recognition of Israel nor shall it be conducive to entry with her into such dealings as are regulated by the said [Covenant].'			
ICESCR	18/02/1969	25/01/1971	**Treaty Generally** Upon signature and confirmed upon ratification: 'The entry of the Republic of Iraq as a party to the International Covenant on Economic, Social and Cultural Rights and the International Covenant on Civil and Political Rights shall in no way signify recognition of Israel nor shall it entail any obligation towards Israel under the said two Covenants.' 'The entry of the Republic of Iraq as a party to the above two Covenants shall not constitute entry by it as a party to the Optional Protocol to the International Covenant on Civil and Political Rights.'	**Israel**	–	**Isreal:** In two communications received by the Secretary-General on 10 July 1969 and 23 March 1971 respectively, the Government of Israel declared that it 'has noted the political character of the declaration made by the Government of Iraq on signing and ratifying the above Covenants. In the view of the Government of Israel, these two Covenants are not the proper place for making such political pronouncements. The Government of Israel will, in so far as concerns the substance

Convention	Signature (date)	Ratification/ Accession (date)	Articles where RUDs apply	State objections to some or all aspects of the reservations/declarations		
				'declaration amounts to a reservation'	'contrary'/ 'raises doubt' to 'object and purpose	Other
			Upon ratification: 'Ratification by Iraq ... shall in no way signify recognition of Israel nor shall it be conducive to entry with her into such dealings as are regulated by the said [Covenant].'			of the matter, adopt towards the Government of Iraq an attitude of complete reciprocity.
CEDAW	–	13/08/1986	**Treaty Generally, Art. 2(f) & (g), 9(1) & (2), 16, 29(1)** Reservations: 1. Approval of and accession to this Convention shall not mean that the Republic of Iraq is bound by the provisions of article 2, paragraphs (f) and (g), of article 9, paragraphs 1 and 2, nor of article 16 of the Convention. The reservation to this last-mentioned article shall be without prejudice to the provisions of the Islamic Shariah according women rights equivalent to the rights of their spouses so as to ensure a just balance between them. Iraq also enters a reservation to article 29, paragraph 1, of this Convention with regard to the principle of international arbitration in connection with	**Germany, Mexico, The Netherlands, Sweden and Israel**	**The Netherlands, Sweden, Israel**	**Isreal**: *'The Government of the State of Israel will, in so far as concerns the substance of the matter, adopt towards Iraq an attitude of complete reciprocity'*

			the interpretation or application of this Convention. 2. This approval in no way implies recognition of or entry into any relations with Israel .		
CAT	–	–	–	–	
CRC	–	15/06/1994	**Art. 14(1)** Reservation: The Government of Iraq has seen fit to accept [the Convention] ... subject to a reservation in respect to article 14, paragraph 1, concerning the child's freedom of religion, as allowing a child to change his or her religion runs counter to the provisions of the *Islamic Shariah*.	–	–

MALAYSIA

Convention	Signature (date)	Ratification/ Accession (date)	Articles where RUDs apply	State objections to some or all aspects of the reservations/declarations		
				'declaration amounts to a reservation'	'contrary'/ 'raises doubt' to 'object and purpose	Other
ICERD	–	–	–	–	–	–
ICCPR	–	–	–	–	–	–
ICESCR	–	–	–	–	–	–
CEDAW	–	05/07/1995	**Treaty Generally, Art. 2(f) [withdrawn on 6 February 1998], 5(a), 7(b), 9(1) [withdrawn on 6 February 1998], 9(2), 11, 16(1)(a), 16(1)(b) [withdrawn on 6 February 1998], 16(1)(d) [withdrawn on 6 February 1998], 16(1)(e) [withdrawn on 6 February 1998], 16(1)(h) [withdrawn on 6 February 1998], 16(2),** The Government of Malaysia declares hat Malaysia's accession is subject to the understanding that the provisions of the Convention do not conflict with the provisions of the Islamic Sharia' law and the Federal Constitution of Malaysia. With regards thereto, further, the Government of Malaysia does not consider itself bound by the provisions of articles 2 (f), 5 (a), 7 (b), 9 and 16 of	**Denmark, Finland, France, Germany, The Netherlands, Norway, Sweden**	**Denmark, Finland, Germany, The Netherlands, Norway, Sweden**	**Finland:** 'The reservations made by Malaysia, consisting of a general reference to religious and national law without specifying the contents thereof and without stating unequivocally the provisions the legal effect of which may be excluded or modified, do not clearly define to the other Parties of the Convention the extent to which the reserving State commits itself to the Convention' **France (20 July 1998:)** France considers that the reservation made by Malaysia, as expressed in the partial with-drawal and modifications made

the aforesaid Convention.
In relation to article 11, Malaysia interprets the provisions of this article as a reference to the prohibition of discrimination on the basis of equality between men and women only.
<u>Modification - 6 February 1998:</u>
With respect to article 5 (a) of the Convention, ... Malaysia declares that the provision is subject to the Syariah law on the division of inherited property.
With respect to article 7 (b) of the Convention... Malaysia declares that the application of said article 7 (b) shall not affect appointment to certain public offices like the Mufti Syariah Court Judges, and the Imam which is in accordance with the provisions of the Islamic Shariah law.
With respect to article 9, paragraph 2 of the Convention, ...Malaysia declares that its reservation will be reviewed if the Government amends the relevant law.
With respect to article 16.1 (a) and paragraph 2, ... Malaysia declares that under the Syariah law and the laws of Malaysia the age limit for marriage for women is sixteen and men is eighteen.'

by Malaysia on 6 February 1998, is incompatible with the object and purpose of the Convention. France therefore objects to the [reservation].

This objection shall not otherwise affect the entry into force of the Convention between France and Malaysia.

Netherlands (21 July 1998): '... Netherlands has examined the modfication of the reservations made by Malaysia to article 5(a) and 16.1. (a) and paragraph 2 of the [Convention].

...Netherlands acknowledges that Malaysia has specified these reservations, made at the time of its accession to the Convention. Nevertheless the... Netherlands wishes to declare that it assumes that Malaysia will ensure implementation of the rights enshrined in the above articles and will strive to bring its relevant national legislation into conformity with the obligations imposed by the Convention. ...Consequently, the modification in question is not accepted, the Government of France having objected thereto.

Convention	Signature (date)	Ratification/ Accession (date)	Articles where RUDs apply	State objections to some or all aspects of the reservations/declarations		
				'declaration amounts to a reservation'	'contrary'/ 'raises doubt' to 'object and purpose	Other
ICAT	–	–	–	–	–	–
CRC	-	17/02/1995	**Art. 1, 2, 7, 13, 14, 15, 22 [withdrawn], 28(1)(a), 28(1)(b) [withdrawn], 28(1)(c) [withdrawn], 28(1)(d) [withdrawn], 28(1)(e) [withdrawn], 28(2) [withdrawn], 28(3) [withdrawn], 40(3) [withdrawn], 40(4) [withdrawn], 44 [withdrawn], 45 [withdrawn], 37** Reservation: 'The Government of Malaysia accepts the provisions of the Convention on the Rights of the Child but expresses reservations with respect to articles 1, 2, 7, 13, 14, 15, [...], 28, [paragraph 1 (a)] 37, [...] of the Convention and declares that the said provisions shall be applicable only if they are in conformity with the Constitution, national laws and national policies of the Government of Malaysia.' 23 March 1999 Declaration: With respect to article 28 paragraph 1 (a),	**Austria, Belgium, Denmark, Finland, Germany, Ireland, The Netherlands, Norway, Portugal, Sweden**	**Finland, Germany, Ireland, The Netherlands, Norway, Portugal, Sweden**	**Austria:** 'Austria considers these reservations as not affecting any provision the implementation of which is essential to fulfilling the object and purpose of the [Convention]. Austria, however, objects to the admissibility of the reservations in question if the application of this reservation negatively affects the compliance of Malaysia with its obligations under the [Convention] essential for the fulfilment of its object and purpose' **Finland:** 'reservation is subject to the general principle of the observance of the treaties according to which a party may not invoke its internal law, much less its national policies, as

the Government of Malaysia wishes to declare that in Malaysia, even though primary education is not compulsory and available free to all, primary education is available to everybody and Malaysia has achieved a high rate of enrolment for primary education i.e. at the rate of 98 per cent enrolment/.

justification for its failure to perform its treaty obligations...The Government of Finland further notes that the reservation made by the Government of Malaysia is devoid of legal effect.'

Regarding the withdrawals:

Belgium (1 July 1996):
believes that this reservation is ncompatible with the object and purpose of the Convention and that, consequently, in accordance with article 51, paragraph 2, of the Convention, it is not permitted.

Denmark (2 July 1996):
'The reservation is covering multiple provisions, including central provisions of the Convention. Furthermore, it is a general principle of international law that internal law may not be invoked as justification for failure to perform treaty obligations. Consequently, ...Denmark considers the said reservation as being incompatible with the object and purpose of the Convention and accordingly inadmissible and without effect under international law. The Convention remains in force in its entirety between Malaysia and Denmark.

MOROCCO

Convention	Signature (date)	Ratification/ Accession (date)	Articles where RUDs apply	State objections to some or all aspects of the reservations/declarations		
				'declaration amounts to a reservation'	'contrary'/ 'raises doubt' to 'object and purpose	Other
ICERD	18/09/1967	18/12/1970	**Art. 22** The Kingdom of Morocco does not consider itself bound by the provisions of article 22 of the Convention, under which any dispute between two or more States Parties with respect to the interpretation or application of the Convention is, at the request of any of the parties to the dispute, to be referred to the International Court of Justice for decision. The Kingdom of Morocco states that, in each individual case, the consent of all parties to such a dispute is necessary for referring the dispute to the International Court of Justice.	–	–	–
ICCPR	19/01/1977	03/05/1979	–	–	–	–
ICESCR	19/01/1977	03/05/1979	–	–	–	–
CEDAW	–	21/06/1993	**Art. 2, 9(2), 15(4), 16, 29(1)** <u>Declarations:</u> 1. With regard to article 2: The Government of the Kingdom of Morocco express its readiness to apply the provisions of this article provided that:	The Netherlands	The Netherlands	

– They are without prejudice to the constitutional requirement that regulate the rules of succession to the throne of the Kingdom of Morocco ;

- They do not conflict with the provisions of the Islamic Shariah. It should be noted that certain of the provisions contained in the Moroccan Code of Personal Status according women rights that differ from the rights conferred on men may not be infringed upon or abrogated because they derive primarily from the Islamic Shariah, which strives, among its other objectives, to strike a balance between the spouses in order to preserve the coherence of family life.

2. With regard to article 15, paragraph 4: Morocco declares that it can only be bound by the provisions of this paragraph, in particular those relating to the right of women to choose their residence and domicile, to the extent that they are not incompatible with articles 34 and 36 of the Moroccan Code of Personal Status.

<u>Reservation:</u>

1. With regard to article 9, paragraph 2: The Government of the Kingdom of Morocco makes a reservation with regard to this article in view of the fact that the Law of Moroccan Nationality permits a child to bear the nationality of its mother only in the cases where it is born to an unknown father, regardless of place of birth, or to a stateless father, when born in Morocco, and it does so in order to guarantee to

MOROCCO *(continued)*

Convention	Signature (date)	Ratification/ Accession (date)	Articles where RUDs apply	State objections to some or all aspects of the reservations/declarations		
				'declaration amounts to a reservation'	'contrary'/ 'raises doubt' to 'object and purpose	Other
			each child its right to a nationality. Further, a child born in Morocco of a Moroccan mother and a foreign father may acquire the nationality of its mother by declaring, within two years of reaching the age of majority, its desire to acquire that nationality, provided that, on making such declaration, its customary and regular residence is in Morocco . 1. With regard to article 16: The Government of the Kingdom of Morocco makes a reservation with regard to the provisions of this article, particularly those relating to the equality of men and women, in respect of rights and responsibilities on entry into and at dissolution of marriage. Equality of this kind is considered incompatible with the Islamic Shariah, which guarantees to each of the spouses rights and responsibilities within a framework of equilibrium and complementary in order to preserve the sacred bond of matrimony. The provisions of the Islamic Shariah oblige			

			the husband to provide a nuptial gift upon marriage and to support his family, while the wife is not required by law to support the family. Further, at dissolution of marriage, the husband is obliged to pay maintenance. In contrast, the wife enjoys complete freedom of disposition of her property during the marriage and upon its dissolution without supervision by the husband, the husband having no jurisdiction over his wife's property. For these reasons, the Islamic Shariah confers the right of divorce on a woman only by decision of a Shariah judge. 1. With regard to article 29: The Government of the Kingdom of Morocco does not consider itself bound by the first paragraph of this article, which provides that `Any dispute between two or more States Parties concerning the interpretation or application of the present Convention which is not settled by negotiation shall, at the request of one of them, be submitted to arbitration. The Government of the Kingdom of Morocco is of the view that any dispute of this kind can only be referred to arbitration by agreement of all the parties to the dispute.	
CAT	08/01/1986	21/06/1993	**Art. 21 [withdrawn on 19/10/2006]**, 30(1)	–
CRC	26/01/1990	21/06/1993	**Art. 14 [withdrawn 19/10/2006]**	

PAKISTAN

Convention	Signature (date)	Ratification/ Accession (date)	Articles where RUDs apply	State objections to some or all aspects of the reservations/declarations		
				'declaration amounts to a reservation'	'contrary'/ 'raises doubt' to 'object and purpose	Other
ICERD	19/09/1966	21/09/1966	–	–	–	–
ICCPR	17/04/2008	–	–	–	–	–
ICESCR	03/11/2004	17/04/2008	**Treaty Generally** Declaration: 'While the Government of Islamic Republic of Pakistan accepts the provisions embodied in the International Covenant on Economic, Social and Cultural Rights, it will implement the said provisions in a progressive manner, in keeping with the existing economic conditions and the development plans of the country. The provisions of the Covenant shall, however, be subject to the provisions of the constitution of the Islamic Republic of Pakistan.'	**Austria, Denmark, Finland, France, Germany, Latvia, The Netherlands, Norway, Spain, Sweden, The United Kingdom**	**Austria, Denmark, France, Germany, Norway, Spain, Sweden**	**Spain:** 'A reservation that includes a general reference to national law without specifying its contents does not make it possible to determine clearly the extent to which the Islamic Republic of Pakistan has accepted the obligations of the Covenant ...' **UK:** '[it is a] reservation which seeks to limit the scope of the Covenant on a unilateral basis'
CEDAW	–	12/03/1996	**Treaty Generally, Art. 29(1)** Declaration: 'The accession by [the] Government of the Islamic Republic of Pakistan to the [said Convention] is subject to the provisions of the Constitution of the	**Austria, Denmark, Finland, Germany, The Netherlands,**	**Austria, Denmark, Finland, Sweden, The Netherlands,**	**Finland:** 'A reservation which consists of a general reference to religious law without specifying its contents does not clearly define to the other Parties of the Convention the extent to which

			Islamic Republic of Pakistan.' Reservation: 'The Government of the Islamic Republic of Pakistan declares that it does not consider itself bound by paragraph 1 of article 29 of the Convention.'	**Norway, Portugal, Sweden**	**Norway**	the reserving State commits itself to the Convention'
CAT	–	–	–	–	–	–
CRC	20/09/1990	12/11/1990	Treaty Generally [withdrawn on 23/07/1997]	**Denmark, Finland, Ireland, The Netherlands, Norway, Portugal, Sweden**	**Denmark, Ireland, The Netherlands, Norway, Portugal, Sweden**	–

SAUDI ARABIA

Convention	Signature (date)	Ratification/ Accession (date)	Articles where RUDs apply	State objections to some or all aspects of the reservations/declarations		
				'declaration amounts to a reservation'	'contrary'/ 'raises doubt' to 'object and purpose	Other
ICERD	–	23/09/1997	**Treaty Generally, Art. 22** [The Government of Saudi Arabia declares that it will] implement the provisions [of the above Convention], providing these do not conflict with the precepts of the Islamic *Shariah*.	**Austria, Finland, Germany, The Netherlands, Norway, Spain, Sweden**	**Austria, Finland, Germany, The Netherlands, Norway, Spain, Sweden**	**Sweden:** 'general reservations of the kind made by … Saudi Arabia, which do not clearly specify the provisions of the Convention to which they apply and the extent of the derogation therefrom, contribute to undermining the basis of international treaty law'
ICCPR	–	–	–	–	–	–
ICESCR	–	–	–	–	–	–
CEDAW	07/09/2000	07/09/2000	**Treaty Generally, Art. 9(2), 29(1)** '1. In case of contradiction between any term of the Convention and the norms of islamic law, the Kingdom is not under obligation to observe the contradictory terms of the Convention. *2. The Kingdom does not consider itself bound by paragraph 2 of article 9 of the Convention and paragraph 1 of article 29 of the Convention.'*	**Austria, Denmark, Finland, France, Germany, Ireland, The Netherlands, Norway, Portugal, Spain,**	**Austria, Denmark, Finland, Germany, Ireland, The Netherlands, Norway, Portugal, Spain, Sweden**	**Denmark:** 'the general reservation with reference to the provisions of Islamic law are of unlimited scope and undefined character' **Finland:** 'A reservation which consists of a general reference to religious law and national law without specifying its contents… does not clearly define to

				Sweden, The United Kingdom		other Parties to the Convention the extent to which the reserving State commits itself to the Convention…' (also **Ireland, Norway Portugal, Spain, Sweden, UK**)
CAT	–	23/09/1997	Art. 20, 30(1) The Kingdom of Saudi Arabia does not recognize the jurisdiction of the Committee as provided for in article 20 of this Convention. The Kingdom of Saudi Arabia shall not be bound by the provisions of paragraph (1) of article 30 of this Convention.	–	–	–
CRC	–	26/01/1996	**Treaty Generally** [The Government of Saudi Arabia enters] reservations with respect to all such articles as are in conflict with the provisions of Islamic law.	**Austria, Denmark, Finland, Germany, Ireland, The Netherlands, Norway, Portugal, Sweden**	**Austria, Denmark**	–

TUNISIA

Convention	Signature (date)	Ratification/ Accession (date)	Articles where RUDs apply	State objections to some or all aspects of the reservations/declarations		
				'declaration amounts to a reservation'	'contrary'/ 'raises doubt' to 'object and purpose	Other
ICERD	12/04/1966	13/01/1967	–	–	–	–
ICCPR	30/04/1968	18/03/1969	On 24 June 1993, Tunisia mad a Declaration, under Article 41 of the Covenant, recognizing the competence of the Human Rights Committee The Government of the Republic of Tunisia declares that it recognizes the competence of the Human Rights Committee established under article 28 of the [said Covenant] ..., to receive and consider communications to the effect that a State Party claims that the Republic of Tunisia is not fulfilling its obligations under the Covenant. The State Party submitting such communications to the Committee must have made a declaration recognizing in regard to itself the competence of the Committee under article 41 of the [said Covenant].	–	–	–
ICESCR	30/04/1968	18/03/1969	–	–	–	–

CEDAW	24/07/1980	20/09/1985	**Treaty Generally, Art. 9(2), 15(4), 16(1), (c), (d), (f), (g) & (h), 29(1)** 1. General declaration: The Tunisian Government declares that it shall not take any organizational or legislative decision in conformity with the requirements of this Convention where such a decision would conflict with the provisions of chapter I of the Tunisian Constitution. 2. Reservation concerning article 9, paragraph 2: The Tunisian Government expresses its reservation with regard to the provisions in article 9, paragraph 2 of the Convention, which must not conflict with the provisions of chapter VI of the Tunisian Nationality Code. 3. Reservation concerning article 16, paragraphs (c), (d), (f), (g) and (h): The Tunisian Government considers itself not bound by article 16, paragraphs (c), (d) and (f) of the Convention and declares that paragraphs (g) and (h) of that article must not conflict with the provisions of the Personal Status Code concerning the granting of family names to children and the acquisition of property through inheritance. 4. Reservation concerning article 29, paragraph 1: The Tunisian Government declares, in conformity with the requirements of article 29, paragraph 2 of the Convention, that it shall not be bound by the provisions of paragraph 1 of that article which	**Germany, The Netherlands Sweden**

Convention	Signature (date)	Ratification/ Accession (date)	Articles where RUDs apply	State objections to some or all aspects of the reservations/declarations		
				'declaration amounts to a reservation'	'contrary'/ 'raises doubt' to 'object and purpose	Other
			specify that any dispute between two or more States Parties concerning the interpretation or application of the present Convention which is not settled by negotiation shall be referred to the International Court of Justice at the request of any one of those parties. The Tunisian Government considers that such disputes should be submitted for arbitration or consideration by the International Court of Justice only with the consent of all parties to the dispute. 5. Declaration concerning article 15, paragraph 4: In accordance with the provisions of the Vienna Convention on the Law of Treaties, dated 23 May 1969, the Tunisian Government emphasizes that the requirements of article 15, paragraph 4, of the Convention on the Elimination of All forms of Discrimination against Women, and particularly that part relating to the right of women to choose their residence and domicile, must not be interpreted in a			

			manner which conflicts with the provisions of the Personal Status Code on this subject, as set forth in chapters 23 and 61 of the Code.		–	–
CAT	26/08/1987	23/09/1988	**Art. 20 [withdrawn on 23/09/1988], 21 [withdrawn on 23/09/1988]**		–	–
CRC	26/02/1990	30/01/1992	**Treaty Generally, Art. 2, 6, 7, 40(2) (b) (v) [withdrawn on 01/03/2002]** Declarations: 1. The Government of the Republic of Tunisia declares that it shall not, in implementation of this Convention, adopt any legislative or statutory decision that conflicts with the Tunisian Constitution. ... 3. The Government of the Republic of Tunisia declares that the Preamble to and the provisions of the Convention, in particular article 6, shall not be interpreted in such a way as to impede the application of Tunisian legislation concerning voluntary termination of pregnancy. Reservations: 1. The Government of the Republic of Tunisia enters a reservation with regard to the provisions of article 2 of the convention, which may not impede implementation of the provisions of its national legislation concerning personal status, particularly in relation to marriage and inheritance rights. ...	**Germany, Ireland**	**Ireland**	

TUNISIA *(continued)*

Convention	Signature (date)	Ratification/ Accession (date)	Articles where RUDs apply	State objections to some or all aspects of the reservations/declarations		
				'declaration amounts to a reservation'	'contrary'/ 'raises doubt' to 'object and purpose	Other
			3. The Government of the Republic of Tunisia considers that article 7 of the Convention cannot be interpreted as prohibiting implementation of the provisions of national legislation relating to nationality and, in particular, to cases in which it is forfeited.			

TURKEY

Convention	Signature (date)	Ratification/ Accession (date)	Articles where RUDs apply	State objections to some or all aspects of the reservations/declarations		
				'declaration amounts to a reservation'	'contrary'/ 'raises doubt' to 'object and purpose	Other
ICERD	13/10/1972	16/09/2002	**Treaty Generally, Art. 22** The Republic of Turkey declares that it will implement the provisions of this Convention only to the States Parties with which it has diplomatic relations. The Republic of Turkey declares that this Convention is ratified exclusively with regard to the national territory where the Constitution and the legal and administrative order of the Republic of Turkey are applied. The Republic of Turkey does not consider itself bound by Article 22 of this Convention. The explicit consent of the Republic of Turkey is necessary in each individual case before any dispute to which the Republic of Turkey is party concerning the interpretation or application of this Convention may be referred to the International Court of Justice.'	**Cyprus** **Sweden** **United Kingdom**	**Sweden**	–

Convention	Signature (date)	Ratification/ Accession (date)	Articles where RUDs apply	State objections to some or all aspects of the reservations/declarations		
				'declaration amounts to a reservation'	'contrary'/ 'raises doubt' to 'object and purpose	Other
ICCPR	15/08/2000	23/09/2003	**Treaty Generally, Art. 27** The Republic of Turkey declares that; it will implement its obligations under the Covenant in accordance to the obligations under the Charter of the United Nations (especially Article 1 and 2 thereof). The Republic of Turkey declares that it will implement the provisions of this Covenant only to the States with which it has diplomatic relations. The Republic of Turkey declares that this Convention is ratified exclusively with regard to the national territory where the Constitution and the legal and administrative order of the Republic of Turkey are applied. The Republic of Turkey reserves the right to interpret and apply the provisions of Article 27 of the International Covenant on Civil and Political Rights in accordance with the related provisions and rules of the Constitution of the Republic of Turkey and the Treaty of Lausanne of 24 July 1923 and its Appendixes.	**Cyprus** **Finland** **Germany** **Greece** **Portugal** **Sweden**	**Greece** **Portugal** **Sweden**	**Finland:** 'assumes that … Turkey will ensure the implementation of the rights of minorities recognised in the Covenant and will do its utmost to bring its national legislation into compliance with the obligations under the Covenant with a view to withdrawing the reservation'

ICESCR	15/08/2000	23/09/2003	**Treaty Generally, Art. 13 (3) & (4)** The Republic of Turkey declares that; it will implement its obligations under the Covenant in accordance to the obligations under the Charter of the United Nations (especially Article 1 and 2 thereof). The Republic of Turkey declares that it will implement the provisions of this Covenant only to the States with which it has diplomatic relations. The Republic of Turkey declares that this Convention is ratified exclusively with regard to the national territory where the Constitution and the legal and administrative order of the Republic of Turkey are applied. The Republic of Turkey reserves the right to interpret and apply the provisions of the paragraph (3) and (4) of the Article 13 of the Covenant on Economic, Social and Cultural Rights in accordance to the provisions under the Article 3, 14 and 42 of the Constitution of the Republic of Turkey.'	Cyprus Finland Germany Greece Portugal Sweden	Cyprus Greece Sweden	–	
CEDAW	–	20/09/1985	**Art. 29(1), 15(2) [withdrawn on 20/09/1999], 15(4) [withdrawn on 20/09/1999], Art. 16(1)© [withdrawn on 20/09/1999], 16(1)(d) [withdrawn on 20/09/1999], 16(1)(f) [withdrawn on 20/09/1999], 16(1)(g) [withdrawn on 20/09/1999]**	Germany Mexico Netherlands		–	–

TURKEY *(continued)*

Convention	Signature (date)	Ratification/ Accession (date)	Articles where RUDs apply	State objections to some or all aspects of the reservations/declarations		
				'declaration amounts to a reservation'	'contrary'/ 'raises doubt' to 'object and purpose	Other
CAT	25/01/1988	02/08/1988	**Art. 30(1)** The Government of Turkey declares in accordance with article 30, paragraph 2, of the Convention, that it does not consider itself bound by the provisions of paragraph 1 of this article.	–	–	–
CRC	14/09/1990	04/04/1995	**Arts. 17, 29, 30** The Republic of Turkey reserves the right to interpret and apply the provisions of articles 17, 29 and 30 of the United Nations Convention on the Rights of the Child according to the letter and the spirit of the Constitution of the Republic of Turkey and those of the Treaty of Lausanne of 24 July 1923.	**Ireland** **Netherlands** **Portugal**	**Ireland** **Netherlands** **Portugal**	–

Bibliography

ABDO, GENEIVE, *No God, But God: Egypt and the Triumph of Islam* (Oxford: Oxford University Press, 2000).

AL-FARUQI, L., *Women, Muslim Societies and Islam* (Indianapolis: Amer Trust Publications, 1988).

ALI, M. C., *The Proposed Political, Legal, and Social Reforms in the Ottoman Empire and Other Mohammadan States: Reforms Under Moslem Rule*, (Bombay: Education Society Press, 1883).

ALI, S. S., 'Development of the International Norm of Non-Discrimination on the Basis of Sex: An Evaluation of Women's Human Rights in International Law' in Ali, S.S., *Gender and Human Rights in Islam and International Law: Equal Before Allah, Unequal Before Man?* (Kluwer Law International, The Hague, 2000).

AN-NA'IM, ABDULLAHI, *'Islamic Family Law In a Changing World: A Global Resource Book'*, (London: Zed Books, 2002)

An-NA'Im Abdullahi, *Toward an Islamic Reformation : Civil Liberties, Human Rights and International Law* (Syracuse NY, Syracuse University Press), 1990

ANTOINE, NASRI, *Inventaire des droits fondamentaux en matière de procédure civile au liban*, (Brussels: Bruylant, 2005).

BADERIN, MASHOOD A., *International Human Rights and Islamic Law* (Oxford: Oxford University Press, 2005).

BAMBALE, YAHAYA YUNUSA, *Crimes and Punishments under Islamic Law* (Oxford: Malthouse, 2003).

BARBER, BENJAMIN, *Jihad vs. McWorld: How Globalism and Tribalism are Reshaping the World* (New York: Ballantine Books, 1995).

BARNES, HUGH and BIGHAM, ALEX, *Understanding Iran: People Politics and Power* (London: Foreign Policy Centre, 2006).

BECHERT, HEINZ, KÜNG, HANS, VAN ESS, JOSEF, and VON STIETENCRON, HEINRICH, *Christianity and the World Religions, Paths of Dialogue with Islam, Hinduism and Buddhism* (Glasgow: Collins, 1985).

BOTIVEAU, BERNARD, *Loi Islamique et Droit dan les Societes Arabes* (Karthala: Iremam, 1993).

BROHI, A.K., *Fundamental Law of Pakistan*, (Karachi: Din Muhammadi Press, 1958).

CASSESE, ANTONIO, *International Law* (Oxford: Oxford University Press, 2005).

CHARLESWORTH, H., and CHINKIN, C., *The Boundaries of International Law: A Feminist Analysis* (Manchester: Manchester University Press, 2000).

CHENG, BIN, *General Principles of Law as Applied by International Courts and Tribunals*, (London: Stevens & Sons Limited, 1953).

CHOUDHURY, G.W., *Constitutional Development in Pakistan* (Longman, 1969).

CONFORTI, B., and FRANCIONI, F., *Enforcing International Human Rights in Domestic Courts*, (The Hague: Kluwer Law International, 1997).

DECOCQ, A., *Une certaine idée du droit,* (Litec, 2004).

DIXON, M., and MCCORQUODALE, R., *Cases and Materials on International Law* (4th ed.) (Oxford: Oxford University Press, 2003).

DOI, A.R., *Women in Sharia* (London: Taha Publishers, 1989).

DONOHUE, J.J., and ESPOSITO, J.L. (*eds*), *Islam in Transition: Muslim Perspectives* (Oxford: Oxford University Press, 1982).

DRAGO, G., *Contentieux Constitutionnel Français* (Paris: PUF, Themis, 1999).

EBADI, SHIRIN, *Iran Awakening: A Memoir of Revolution and Hope* (Rider & Co., 2006).

EL-AWA, MOHAMED S., *Punishment in Islamic Law: A Comparative Study* (Indianapolis: American Trust Publications, 1982).

EL-BAHNASSAWI, S., *Women between Islam and World Legislations* (Kuwait: Dar Al-Oalam, 1985).

EL FADL, K.A., *Islam and the Challenge of Democracy* (Princeton: Princeton University Press, 2004).

EPHROZ, K.N., *Women and Law: Muslim Personal Law Perspective* (Jaipur: Rawat Publications, 2003).

ESPOSITO, JL., with DELONG-BAS, N.J., *Women in Muslim Family Law* (2nd ed.) (New York: Syracuse University Press, 2001).

FALK, RICHARD A., *The Role of Domestic Courts in the International Legal Order* (New York: Syracuse University Press, 1964).

FATIMA, SHAHEED, *Using International Law in Domestic Courts* (Portland: Hart Publishing, 2005).

FITZMAURICE, G., *The Law and Procedure of the International Court of Justice* (Cambridge: Grotius Publications, 1986).

GANJI, M., *International Protection of Human Rights* (Geneva, 1962).

GANNAGE, P., *L'application du principe de proximité dans le systèmes inter-personnels – l'exemple des droits proche-orientaux* (Litec, 2004).

GIBNEY, M., and FRANKOWSKI, S., *Judicial Protection of Human Rights: Myth or Reality?* (Westport: Praeger, 1999).

GLEDHILL, ALAN, *Pakistan – The Development of its Laws and Constitution* (London: Stevens & Sons, 1967)

GLENDON, MARY ANNE, *A World Made New: Eleanor Roosevelt and the Universal Declaration of Human Rights,* (Random House, 2001)

GUSTAFSON, C., and JUVILER, P. (eds) *Religion and Human Rights: Competing Claims?* (M.E. Sharpe, 1999).

HALLAQ, WAEL, *The Origins and Evolution of Islamic Law* (Cambridge: Cambridge University Press, 2005).

HENKEN, LOUIS, *The Age of Rights* (New York: Colombia University Press, 1990).

HEYNS, CHRISTOF, and VILJOEN, FRANS, *The Impact of the United Nations Human Rights Treaties on the Domestic Level* (The Hague: Kluwer Law International, 2002).

HODGSON, M.G.S., *The Venture of Islam: Conscience and History in a World Civilization, Vol 1: The Classical Age of Islam* (Chicago: University of Chicago Press 1974).

HOMSANI, A. N., Majmouaat al mabadi' wal kawai'd al chari'ya wal kanouniyya, (Manchourat el Halabi el houkoukiyya, Lebanon, 2003.

INTERNATIONAL COMMISSION OF JURISTS, KUWAIT UNIVERSITY, and UNION OF ARAB LAWYERS, *Human Rights in Islam: Report of a Seminar Held in Kuwait, December 1980* (International Commission of Jurists, 1982).

JAYAWICKRAMA, NIHAL, *The Judicial Application of Human Rights Law: National, Regional and International Jurisprudence* (Cambridge: Cambridge University Press, 2002).

KHOMEINI, *Islam and Revolution* (Berkeley 1981, translated by H. Algar).

LAUREN, PAUL GORDON, *The Evolution of International Human Rights: Visions Seen* (Pennsylvania: University of Pennsylvania Press, 2003).

LEV, DANIEL, *Islamic Courts in Indonesia* (California: University of California Press, 1973).

LEVY, REUBEN, *An Introduction to the Sociology of Islam, Volume I* (London: Williams and Norgate Limited, 1957).

LEVY, REUBEN, *The Social Structure of Islam* (Cambridge: Cambridge University Press, UK, 1957)

LICHTENSTADTER, ILSE, *Women in the Aiyam Al-'Arab: A Study of Female Life During Warfare in Pre-Islamic Arabia* (London: Royal Asiatic Society, 1935).

LIJNZAAD, LIESBETH, '*Reservations to Un-Human Rights Treaties: Ratify or Ruin?*' (Dordrecht: Martinus Nijhoff Publishers, 1995).

LIPPMAN, M., MCCONVILLE, S. and YERUSHALMI, M., *Islamic Criminal Law and Procedure: An Introduction* (New York: Praeger, 1988).

MAHMOOD, T.,*Statuses of Personal Law in Islamic Countries, History Texts and Analysis* (2nd ed.) (Delhi: India and Islamic Research Council, 1995).

MALLAT, CHIBLI, *The Renewal of Islamic Law, Muhammad Baqer as Sadr, Najaf and the Shi'i International* (Cambridge: Cambridge University Press, 1993).

MAUDUDI, SAYYID ABUL A'LA, *The Islamic law and constitution* (4th ed.) (Lahore: Islamic Publications Ltd, 1969).

MAYER, ANNE ELIZABETH, *Islam and Human Rights: Tradition and Politics* (Colorado: Westview Press, 1995).

MEHDI, RUBYA, *The Islamization of the Law in Pakistan* (Richmond: Curzon Press, 1994).

MIR-HOSSEINI, ZIBA, *Islam and Gender* (Princeton: I.B. Tauris, 2000).

MUNIR, MUHAMMAD, *Constitution of the Islamic Republic of Pakistan* (Law Publishing Company, 1976).

NASHAT, G., AND TUCKER, J., *Women in the Middle East and North Africa: Restoring Women to History* (Indianapolis: Indiana University Press, 1999).

NASIR, JAMAL, *The Islamic Law of Personal Status* (3rd ed.) (The Hague: Kluwer Law International, 2002).

NASIR, J.J., *The Status of Women Under Islamic Law and Under Modern Islamic Legislation* (2nd ed.) (London: Graham & Trotman, 1994).

NEUMAYER, ERIC, 'Qualified Ratifications: Explaining Reservations to International Human Rights Treaties', *Journal of Legal Studies*, 36 (2) (2007) 397–430.

NOWAK, MANFRED, *Human Rights Handbook for Parliamentarians, N° 8.* (France: SADAG, 2005).

NOYON, JENNIFER 'Islam, Politics and Pluralism: Theory and Practice in Turkey, Jordan, Tunisia and Algeria' *Royal Institute of International Affairs* (London: 2003)

OJI UMOZURIKE, U, *The African Charter on Human's and People's Rights* (The Hague/Boston/Leiden, Martinus Nijhoff Publishers 1997)

PEARL, DAVID AND MENSKI, WERNER, *Muslim Family Law* (London: Sweet and Maxwell, 3rd ed, 1998)

PETERS, R., *Crime and Punishment in Islamic Law: Theory and Practices form the Sixteenth to the Twenty-first Century* (Cambridge: Cambridge University Press, 2005).

POWERS, DAVID, *Studies in Quran and Hadith: The Formation of the Islamic Law of Inheritance* (Berkeley: University of California Press, 1986).

RAHIM, ABDUR, *The Principles of Islamic Jurisprudence: According to the Hanafi, Maliki, Shafi'I and Hanbali Schools* (New Delhi: Kitab Bhavan, 1994).

REHMAN, J., *International Human Rights Law* (Longman, London and New York, 2008) 1120.

REHMAN, J., BREAU, S (eds) *Religion, Human Rights and International Law: A Critical Examination of Islamic State Practices* (Martinus Nijhoff Publishers, The Hague, 2007) 640_(http://www.brill.nl/default.aspx?partid=10&pid=25136).

RIZVI, S.S.R., *Constitution of the Islamic Republic of Pakistan* (Lahore: Nadeem Law Book House, 1992).

SCHIRAZI, ASGHAR, *The Constitution of Iran, Politics and the State in the Islamic Republic* (London: I.B. Tauris, 1997).

SEN, AMARTYA, *Poverty and Famines: An Essay on Entitlements and Deprivation* (Oxford: Clarendon Press, 1982).

SHAH, NIAZ, Women, *the Koran and International Human Rights Law, the Experience of Pakistan* (Leiden: Martinus Nijhoff Publishers, 2006).

SHAW, MALCOLM N., *International Law* (4th ed.) (Cambridge: Cambridge University Press, 1997).

STAHNKE, TAD, and BLITT, ROBERT C., 'The religion-state relationship and the right to freedom of religion or belief: A comparative textual analysis of the Constitutions of Predominantly Muslim countries' [2005] 36 Georgetown Journal of International Law.

SUDRE, F., *Droit International et Europeen des Droits de l'Homme Numero 134* (8eme ed.) (France: Presses Universitaires de France, 2006).

SYED, M.A., *The Position of Women in Islam: A Progressive View* (Albany, NY: SUNY Press, 2004).

VERDOODT, ALBERT, *Naissance et signification de la Declaration Universelle des droits de l'homme*, (Louvain-Paris: Editions Nauwelaerts, 1963).

VILJOEN, FRANS, *International Human Rights Law in Africa*, (Oxford: Oxford University Press, 2007).

VOGEL, F.E., *Islamic Law and Legal Systems: Studies of Saudi Arabia* (Leiden: Brill, 2000).

WATT, M., *Islam and the Integration of Society* (London: Routledge & Keagan Paul Ltd, 1961).

WATT, MONTGOMERY W., *Muhammad at Mecca* (Oxford: Clarendon Press 1953).

WILSON, PETER W., and GRAHAM, DOUGLAS F., *Saudi Arabia: The Coming Storm* (New York: M.E. Sharpe, 1994).

YILMAZ, IHSAN, *Muslim Laws, Politics and Society in Modern Nation States: Dynamic Legal Pluralisms in England, Turkey, and Pakistan* (Aldershot: Ashgate, 2005).

ZOLLER, E., *Bonne foi en droit international public* (Paris : Pedone, 1977).

ZUHUR, SHERIFA, *Gender, Sexuality and the Criminal Laws in the Middle East and North Africa: A Comparative Study* (Istanbul: Women for Women's Human Rights, 2005).

ARTICLES IN BOOKS

ABDEL HALEEM, MOHAMMAD, 'Human Rights in Islam and the United Nations Instruments', in Cotran, E., and Sherif, A., (eds), *Democracy, the Rule of Law, and Islam* (Kluwer Law International, 1999) 435.

ABD-EL-RAHMAN NOSSEIR, 'The Supreme Constitutional Court of Egypt and the Protection of Human Rights', in Eugene Cotran and Adel Omar Sherif (eds), *The Role of the Judiciary in the Protection of Human Rights* (Brill 1997, in association with CIMEL)

AKHAVAN, PAYAM, 'Implications of Twelver Shi'ih Mihdism on Religious Tolerance: The Case of the Baha'i Minority in the Islamic Republic of Iran', in Lindholm, T., and Vogt, K. (eds) *Islamic Law Reform and Human Rights—Challenges and Rejoinders* (Copenhagen: Nordic Human Rights Publications, 1993) 197.

AL-'AWAA, M S., 'The Basis of Islamic Penal Legislation', in Bassiouni, MC.

(ed.), *The Islamic Criminal Justice System* (New York: Oceana Publications Inc, 1982).

AL-HIBRI, A., 'A Study of Islamic Herstory: Or How Did we Ever Get into This Mess?', in Al-Hibri, A (ed) *Women and Islam* (Oxford: Pergamon Press, 1982).

ALI, S. S., 'The Twain Doth Meet! A Preliminary Exploration of the Theory and Practice of as-Siyar and International Law in the Contemporary World', in Rehman, J., Breau, S. (eds), *Religion, Human Rights and International Law: A Critical Examination of Islamic State Practices* (Martinus Nijhoff, Leiden, 2007).

ALI, S. S., 'A Comparative Perspective of the United Nations Convention on the Rights of the Child and the Principles of Islamic Law: Law Reform and Children's Rights in Muslim Jurisdictions', in Goonasekere, S. (ed.), *Protecting the World's Children: Impact of the UN convention on the Rights of the Child in Diverse Legal Systems* (Cambridge University Press, 2007).

ALI, S. S., 'Religious Pluralism, Human Rights and Citizenship in Europe: Some Preliminary Reflections on an evolving Methodology for Consensus', in Leonon, T., Goldschmidt, J. (eds), *Religious Pluralism and Human Rights in Europe* (Intersentia, Utrecht, 2007).

AN-NA'IM, A.A., 'The Application of Shari'a (Islamic Law) and Human Rights Violations in the Sudan', in Lindholm, T., and Vogt, K. (eds) *Islamic Law Reform and Human Rights—Challenges and Rejoinders* (Copenhagen: Nordic Human Rights Publications, 1993) 135.

ARKOUN, MOHAMMED, 'The Concept of Islamic Reformation', in Lindholm, Tore and Vogt, Kari (eds), *Islamic Law Reform and Human Rights, Challenges and Rejoinders* (Oslo: Nordic Human Rights Publication, 1992).

ASSAF, GEORGES J., 'The Application of International Human Rights Instruments by the Judiciary in Lebanon', in Eugene Cotran and Adel Omar Sherif (eds), *The Role of the Judiciary in the Protection of Human Rights*, CIMEL Book Series No. 5 (Kluwer Law International, 1997) 86–92.

BADERIN, M.A., 'Islam, Human Rights and Development in Muslim States' in Rehman, J. and Breau, S. (eds), *Religion, Human Rights and International Law* (Martinus Nijhoff, The Hague, 2007).

BASSIOUNI, C., 'Sources of Islamic Law and the Protection of Human Rights in the Islamic Criminal Justice System', in M.C. Bassiouni (ed.), *The Islamic Criminal Justice System* (New York: Oceana Publications Inc, 1982) 38.

BAYEFESKY, ANNE F., 'General approaches to the domestic application of women's international human rights law', in Cook (ed.), *Human Rights of Human,* (Philadelphia: University of Pennsylvania Press, 1994) 360.

BEDGGOOD, MARGARET, and WHI, LEAH, 'Women, Religion, and the Law in New Zealand: the Complexity of Accommodating Different Value Systems in Law', in Evans, C., and Whitings, A., (eds) *Mixed Blessings: Laws, Religions, and Women's Rights in the Asia-Pacific Region* (Leiden: Martinus Nijhoff Publishers, 2006) 129.

BEIGZADEH, EBRAHIM, 'Intégration des norms internationales en droit iranien', in Delmas- Marty, Mireille, (ed.) *Criminalité économique et Atteintes à la Dignité de la Personne, Vol.VI, Europe- Pays d 'Islam* (Paris : MSH, 1999) 286.

BEN ACHOUR, YADH, 'Le livre, la balance et le glaive: La symbolique du droit et de la politique dans le coran' in Les droits fondamentaux : Inventaire et théorie générale, éditions Bruylan-Bruxelles, USJ-CEDROMA, Beyrouth, 2003.

BEN HALIMA, SASSI, 'Religion et statut personnel en Tunisie', in Droit et Religion, Editions Bruylant-Bruxelles, USJ-CEDROMA, Beyrouth 2003.

BLACK, ANN, 'Islamization, Modernity, and the Re-positioning of Women in Brunei', in Evans, Carolyn and Whitings, Amanda, (eds) *Mixed Blessings: Laws, Religions, and Women's Rights in the Asia-Pacific Region* (Martinus Nijhoff Publishers, 2006).

BROWN, NATHAN J., 'Islamic Constitutionalism in Theory and Practice', in Cotran, E., Sherif, A., (eds.) *Democracy, the Rule of Law, and Islam* (Kluwer Law International, 1999) 491–505.

BUTEGWA, FLORENCE, 'International Human Rights Law and Practice: Implications for Women', in *From Basic Needs to Basic Rights: Women's claim to Human Rights*, Margaret Shuler (ed) (Washington, D.C.: Women, Law and Development International, 1995).

CHIBLI, MALLAT, 'A Comparative Note on the Judicial Protection of Basic Rights: Some Theoretical and Practical Issues', *The Role of the Judiciary in the Protection of Human Rights,* Cotran, E., Sherif, A.O., (eds), CIMEL Book Series No. 5 (Kluwer Law International, 1997) 393–399.

DENZA, EILEEN, 'The Relationship Between International and National Law', in Evans, Malcolm D., (ed.), *International Law* (2nd ed.), (Oxford: Oxford University Press, 2006) 423–448.

DIAB, NASRI, 'Inventaire des Droits Fondamentaux en Matière de Procédure Civile au Liban', in *Les Droits Fondamentaux : Inventaire et Théorie Générale : Colloque de Beyrouth, 6 et 7 Novembre 2003* (Bruylant, Bruxelles, 2005).

EL-AWA, M.S., 'Confession and Other Methods of Evidence in Islamic Procedural Jurisprudence' in Haleem, M A., Sherif, AO., and Daniels, K., (eds) *Criminal Justice in Islam: Judicial Procedure in the Shari'a* (London: I.B. Tauris 2003) 17–34.

EL-DIN, MAHMOUD S.G., 'Democracy and Human Rights in Kuwait; The Role of the Constitution', in Cotran, E. and Yamani, M., (eds), *The Rule of Law in the Middle East and the Islamic World; Human Rights and the Judicial Process*, (New York: I.B. Taurus, 2000) 86.

EL-GINDY, GAMIL M., 'The Shura and Human Rights in Islamic Law – The Relevance of Democracy', in *The Rule of Law in the Middle East and the Islamic World: Human Rights and the Judicial Process,* Cotran, E., Yamani, M., (eds), (New York: I.B. Taurus, 2000) 164–180.

EL-MOLLA, MOHAMMED, and MURRAY, JOHN, 'Islamic *Shari'a* and Constitutional Interpretation in Egypt', in Cotran, E., Sherif, A., (eds) *Democracy, the Rule of Law, and Islam* (The Hague: Kluwer Law International, 1999) 507.

ELTAYEB, MOHAMED S. M., 'A Human Rights Framework for Defining and Understanding Intra-Religious Persecution in Muslim Countries', in Ghanea, N. (ed.), *The Challenge of Religious Discrimination at the Dawn of the New Millenium* (Boston: Martinus Nijhoff Publishers, 2003) 83–105.

EVANS, C., and WHITING, A., 'Situating the Issues, Framing the Analysis', in Evans, C., and Whitings, A., (eds.) *Mixed Blessings: Laws, Religions, and Women's Rights in the Asia-Pacific Region* (Leiden: Martinus Nijhoff Publishers, 2006) 1.

GABR, HATEM A. L., 'Recent Judgments of the Supreme Constitutional Court of the Arabic Republic of Egypt Upholding Human Rights', *The Role of the Judiciary in the Protection of Human Rights,* Cotran, E., Sherif, A.O., (eds.), CIMEL Book Series No. 5. (Kluwer Law International, 1997) 61–76.

GANNAGE, P., 'Le Principe d'égalité et le Pluralisme des Statuts Personnels dans les Etats Multicommunautaires', in *L'avenir du Droit : Mélanges en Hommage à François Terré* (Paris: Presses Universitaires de France, 1999) 431.

GHANEA, NAZILA, 'Faith in Human Rights, Human Rights in Faith', in Ghanea, N. (ed.) *The Challenge of Religious Discrimination at the Dawn of the New Millenium* (Boston: Martinus Nijhoff Publishers, 2003) 107.

HENKIN, LOUIS, 'International Human Rights as Rights,' in *Human Rights: NOMOS XX111*, Pennock, J. R., and Chapman J. W. (eds) (New York: New York University Press, 1981) 258.

IBRAHIM, SAEED, and MEHEMEED, NASIR, 'Basic Principles of Criminal Procedure under Islamic Shari'a' in Haleem, M A., Sherif, AO., and Daniels, K., (eds.), *Criminal Justice in Islam: Judicial Procedure in the Shari'a* (London: I.B. Tauris, 2003) 17–34.

IQBAL, J., 'The Concept of State in Islam' in Ahmad, M., (ed.), *State, Politics and Islam* (Indianapolis: American Trust Publications, 1986) 37.

JAHEL, SELIM, 'Chari'a et convention européenne des droits de l'homme', in *Une certaine idée du droit, mélanges André Decocq* (Litec, 2004) 335–368.

JOHANSEN, BABER, 'The constitution and the principles of Islamic normativity against the rules of fiqh. A judgement of the Supreme Constitutional Court of Egypt', in Masud, M.K.; Peters, R. and Powers, D.S., *Dispensing Justice in Islam, Qadis and their Judgments*, (Leiden: Brill, 2006) 169–193.

KELSAY, JOHN, 'Saudi Arabia, Pakistan, and the Universal Declaration of Human Rights', in Little, David, Kelsay, John, and Sachedina, Abdulaziz, (eds), *Human Rights and the Conflict of Cultures: Western and Islamic Perspectives on Religious liberty* (Columbia: University of South California Press, 1988).

KLEIN, ECKART, 'Reflections on Article 5 of the International Covenant on Civil and Political Rights', in Ando, Nisuke (ed.) *Towards Implementing Universal Human Rights* (The Hague: Martinus Nijhoff Publishers, 2004) 127.

LAU, MARTIN, 'The Islamization of Laws in Pakistan—Impact on the Independence of the Judiciary', in Cotran, E., Yamani, M., (eds), *The Rule of Law in the Middle East and the Islamic World: Human Rights and the Judicial Process* (New York: I.B. Taurus, 2000) 150–163.

LAU, MARTIN, 'Human Rights, Natural Justice and Pakistan's Shariah Courts', in Rehman, J., and Breau, S., (eds), *Religion, Human rights and International law: A critical examination of Islamic states*, (Martinus Nijhoff Publishers, 2007) 359–378.

MAHMASANI, SUBHI, 'Adaptation of Islamic Jurisprudence to Modern Social Needs', in Donohue, J.J. and Esposito, J.L. (eds), *Islam in Transition: Muslim Perspectives* (Oxford: Oxford University Press, 1982) 181.

MAYER, A. E., 'Protection for religious freedom: The grim legacy of Zaheeruddin v. State', in Cotran, E., and Sherif, A., (eds.) *Democracy, the Rule of Law, and Islam* (The Hague: Kluwer Law International, 1999) 545–567.

MIR-HOSSEINI, ZIBA, 'Islam and Gender Justice', in Cornell, V.J., and Safi, O. (eds), *Voices of Islam*, (Westport: Praeger, 2007).

MULLALLY, SIOBHAN, 'Women, Islamisation and Human Rights in Pakistan', in Rehman. J., and Breau, S. C., (eds), *Religion, Human Rights and International Law*, (Koninklijke Brill NV, 2007) 378–408.

MURRAY, JOHN, and EL-MOLLAH, MOHAMMAD, 'Islamic Sharia and constitutional interpretation in Egypt', in Cotran, Eugene and Sherif, Adel O. (eds), *Democracy, the rule of law and Islam* (The Hague: Kluwer Law International, 1999) 507–524.

NOSSEIR, ABD-EL-RAHMAN, 'The supreme constitutional court of Egypt and the protection of human rights', in Cotran, Eugene and Sherif, Adel O., (eds), *The Role of the Judiciary in the Protection of Human Rights*, CIMEL Book Series No. 5 (The Hague: Kluwer Law International, 1997) 47–59.

PETERS, RUDOLPH, 'The Re-Islamisation of Criminal Law in Northern

Nigeria and the Judiciary: The Safiyyatu Hussaini Case', in Masud, M.K.; Peters, R. and Powers, D.S., *Dispensing Justice in Islam, Qadis and their Judgments*, (Leiden: Brill, 2006) 219–241.

PISCATORI, JAMES, 'Human Rights in Islamic Political Culture', in Thompson, K. (ed.), *The Moral Imperatives of Human Rights* (Washington, D.C.: University Press of America, 1980) 139.

REHMAN, J., 'Rights of Religious Minorities: Accommodating Religious Identities in an Islamic State: International law, Freedom of Religion and the Rights of Religious Minorities' in Mashood Baderin (ed.), *International Law and Islamic Law* (Ashgate, London, 2008) 571–598.

REHMAN, J., BREAU, S., 'Introductory Reflections' in Rehman and Breau (eds) *Religion, Human Rights and International Law: A Critical Examination of Islamic Law and Practices* (Martinus Nijhoff Publishers, The Hague, 2007) 3–22.

ROBINSON, KATHRYN, 'Muslim Women's Political Struggle for Marriage Law Reform in Contemporary Indonesia', in Evans, C., and Whitings, A., (eds) *Mixed Blessings: Laws, Religions, and Women's Rights in the Asia-Pacific Region* (Leiden: Martinus Nijhoff Publishers, 2006) 183.

SALAMA, M.M., 'General Principles of Criminal Evidence in Islamic Jurisprudence Confession and other methods of evidence in Islamic procedural jurisprudence', in MC Bassiouni (ed.) *The Islamic Criminal Justice System* (New York: Oceana Publications Inc, 1982) 109–122.

SHERIF, ADEL OMAR, 'Generalities on Criminal Procedure under Islamic Shari'a', in Haleem, M A., Sherif, AO., and Daniels, K., (eds), *Criminal Justice in Islam: Judicial Procedure in the Shari'a* (London: I.B. Tauris 2003) 3–16.

SHERIF, ADEL OMAR, 'Unshakable tendency in the protection of human rights: Adherence to international instruments on human rights by the supreme constitutional court of Egypt', in Cotran, E., and Sherif, A.O., (eds), *the Role of the Judiciary in the Protection of Human Rights*, CIMEL Book Series No. 5 (The Hague: Kluwer Law International,1997) 35–45.

SHERIF, ADEL OMAR, 'The Rule of Law in Egypt from a Judicial Perspective—A Digest of the Landmark Decisions of the Supreme Constitutional Court', in Cotran, E., Yamani, M., (eds.), *The Rule of Law in the Middle East and the Islamic World: Human Rights and the Judicial Process*, (New York: I.B. Taurus, 2000) 1–34.

SLYZ, GEORGE, 'International Law in National Courts', in Franck, T., Fox, G., (eds.), *International Law Decisions in National Courts*, (Transnational Publishers, 1996) 71–106.

TIBI, BASSAM, 'Islamic Law/Shari'a and Human Rights: International Law and International Relations', in Lindholm, T., and Vogt, K. (eds.) *Islamic Law Reform and Human Rights—Challenges and Rejoinders* (Copenhagen: Nordic Human Rights Publications, 1993) 75.

VOGEL, FRANK E., 'Conformity with Islamic *Shari'a* and Constitutionality Under Article 2: Some Issues of Theory, Practice, and Comparison', in Cotran, E., and Sherif, A., (eds.) *Democracy, the Rule of Law, and Islam* (The Hague: Kluwer Law International, 1999) 525–544.

VOGEL, FRANK E., 'The Rule of Law in Saudi Arabia', in Cotran, E., and Yamani, M., (eds), *The Rule of Law in the Middle East and the Islamic World: Human Rights and the Judicial Process* (New York: I.B. Taurus, 2000) 128–136.

WENDI, ABD A-N A., WAZANI, R., AND HALASA, A., 'The Rule of Law and Human Rights in Jordan' in Cotran, E., and Yamani, M., (eds.),*The Rule of Law in the Middle East and the Islamic World: Human Rights and the Judicial Process* (New York: I.B. Taurus, 2000) 81–90.

YAMANI, MAI, 'Muslim Women and Human Rights in Saudi Arabia', Cotran, E., and Yamani, M., (eds.), *The Rule of Law in the Middle East and the Islamic World: Human Rights and the Judicial Process* (New York: I. B. Taurus, 2000) 137–143.

LAW REVIEW/PERIODICALS

ABA-NAMAY, RASHED, 'The Recent Constitutional Reforms in Saudi Arabia' *International and Comparative Law Quarterly*, Vol. 42 (1993) 298

ABBOT, FREELAND, 'Pakistan's New Marriage Law: A Reflection of Qur'Anic Interpretation', *Asian Survey,* Vol. 1, No. 11 (Jan. 1962) 26–32.

ABTAHI, HIRAD, 'The Islamic Republic of Iran and the ICC', *Journal of International Criminal Justice* 3 (2005) 635–648.

AFSHARI, REZA, 'On Historiography of Human Rights Reflections on Paul Gorden Lauren's "The Evolution of International Human Rights: Visions Seen"', *Human Rights Quarterly* Vol. 29, No. 1 (2007): 1–67.

AHMAD, SALBIAH, 'Islam in Malaysia: Constitutional and Human Rights Perspectives', *Muslim World Journal of Human Rights*, Vol. 2, Issue 1, Article 7 (2005).

AHMED, LEILA, 'Western Ethnocentrism and Perceptions of the Harem', *Feminist Studies*, Vol. 8, No. 3, (Autumn 1982) 521–534.

AHMED, LEILA, 'Women and the Advent of Islam', *Signs*, Vol. 11, No. 4 (Summer 1986) 665–691.

ALAM, SHAH M., 'Enforcement of International Human Rights Law by Domestic Courts: A Theoretical and Practical Study', *Netherlands International Law Review*, LIII (2006) 399–438.

AL-HARGAN, ABDULHAMID, A., 'Saudi Arabia and the International Covenant on Civil and Political rights 1966: A stalemate Situation' The International Journal of Human Rights Vol. 9, No.4 (2005) 491–505

AL-SAYYID, MUSTAPHA K., 'Theoretical issues in the Arab human rights movement', *Arab Studies Quarterly,* (Winter 1997).

ALI, SHAHEEN S. and REHMAN, JAVAID, 'The Concept of Jihad in Islamic International Law', *Journal of Conflict & Security Law*, (Winter 2005).

ALI, S. S., REHMAN, J. 'Right to Freedom of Religion versus Right to Equality in International Human Rights law: Conflicting Norms or Hierarchical Human Rights? A case study of Pakistan' (2003) 21 *Nordic Journal for Human Rights* 404–429.

AMIEN, WAHEEDA, 'Overcoming the Conflict between the Right to Freedom of Religion and Women's Rights to Equality: A South African Case Study of Muslim Marriages', *Human Rights Quarterly*, Vol. 28, No. 3 (August 2006) 729–754.

ANDERSON, J N D, 'Modern Trends in Islam: legal Reform and Modernisation in the Middle East' *International and Comparative law Quarterly*, Vol.20, No.1 (1971) 1–21

ANDERSON, J N D, 'The Tunisian Law of Personal Status' *International and Comparative Law Quarterly*, Vol.7, No.2 (1958) 262–279

AN-NA'IM, ABDULLAHI A., 'Religious Minorities under Islamic Law and the limits of Cultural relativism', *Human Rights Quarterly*, Vol. 9 (1987) 1–18.

AN-NA'IM, ABDULLAHI A., 'Human Rights in the Arab world: A Regional Perspective' *Human Rights Quarterly*, Vol. 23 (2001) 701–732.

AN-NA'IM, ABDULLAHI A., 'Civil Rights in the Islamic constitutional tradition: shared ideals and divergent regimes', *The John Marshall Law Review*, 25 (1992) 267–293.

ANSARI, NAZISH, 'Malaysia: Limitations of the Human Rights Discourse and the Deployment of Rights in a Religious Identity Debate', *Muslim World Journal of Human Rights*, Vol. 1, Issue 1, Article 3 (2004).

ARABI, OUSSAMA, 'The Dawning of the Third Millenium on Sharia: Egypt's Law No.1 of 2000' *Arab Law Quarterly* 16:1 (2001) 2–21

ARJOMAND, S.A., 'Islamic Constitutionalism', *Annual Review of Law & Social Sciences*, Vol. 3 (December 2007) 115–140.

ARZT, DONNA E., 'The Application of International Human Rights Law in Islamic States', *Human Rights Quarterly* 12 (1990) 203–230.

AZARIAN, MOHAMMAD K., KENDALL, JERRY D., and WIECHMAN, DENIS J., 'Islamic Law: Myths and Realities' *Criminal Justice International* (2006). Available at: http://muslim-canada.org/Islam_myths.htm.

BADERIN, MASHOOD A., 'A Macroscopic Analysis of the Practice of Muslim State Parties to International Human Rights Treaties: Conflict or Congruence?' *Human Rights Law Review,* Volume 1, Number 2, 2001

BADERIN, MASHOOD A., 'Effective Legal Representation in "Shari'ah" Courts as a Means of Addressing Human Rights Concerns in the Islamic Criminal Justice System of Muslim States', *Yearbook of Islamic and Middle Eastern Law*, 11.2004–2005 (2006) 135–167.

BADERIN, MASHOOD A., 'Islam and the Realization of Human Rights in the

Muslim World: A Reflection on Two Essential Approaches and Two Divergent Perspectives,' *Muslim World Journal of Human Rights*, Vol. 4, Issue1, Article 5 (2007). Available at: http://www.bepress.com/mwjhr/vol4/iss1/art5

BADERIN, M.A., 'Islam and the Realization of Human Rights in the Muslim World: A Reflection on Two Essential Approaches and Two Divergent Perspectives', Muslim World Journal of Human Rights 4.1 (2007).

BAKHT, NATASHA, 'Family Arbitration Using Sharia Law: Examining Ontario's Arbitration Act and its Impact on Women', *Muslim World Journal of Human Rights*, Vol. 1, Issue 1, Article 7 (2004).

BÄLZ, KILIAN, 'Human Rights, the Rule of Law and the Construction of Tradition: The Egyptian Supreme Administrative Court and Female Circumcision', *Egypte/Monde Arabe* 34 (1998) 141–153.

BANKS, DAVID J., 'Islam and Inheritance in Malaya: Culture Conflict or Islamic Revolution?', *American Ethnologist*, Vol.3, No. 4. (November 1976) 573–586.

BEHROUZ, A.N., 'Transforming Islamic Family Law: State Responsibility and the Role of Internal Initiative', *Columbia Law Review*, Vol. 109 (June 2003) 1136–1162.

BEN ACHOUR, YADH, 'La civilisation islamique et le droit international', Revue Générale de Droit International Public, Vol. 110, No. 1, 19–38.

BEN JEMIA, MONIA, « L'EXEQUATUR DES DÉCISIONS ÉTRANGÈRES EN MATIÈRE DE STATUT PERSONNEL », REVUE TUNISIENNE DE DROIT, 2000, 139–157.

BERWEEN, MOHAMED, 'The Fundamental Human Rights: An Islamic Perspective', *The International Journal of Human Rights*, Vol.6, No.1 (Spring 2002) 61–78.

BIELEFELDT, HEINER, '"Western" versus "Islamic" Human Rights Conceptions?: A Critique of Cultural Essentialism in the Discussion on Human Rights', *Political Theory*, Vol.28, No. 1 (February 2000) 90–121.

BIANCHI, ANDREA, 'International Law and US Courts : The Myth of Lohengrin Revisited', *European Journal of International Law* Vol. 15, No. 4 (2004) 751–781.

BILANI, BÉCHIR, 'Les principes généraux de la chari'a et les droits de la faemme', in *Les droits fondamentaux inventaire et théorie générale* (Bruylant, Bruxelles, 2005).

BOWETT, DEREK W., 'Reservations to non-restricted Multilateral treaties', 48th *British Yearbook of International Law* (1976–1977) 67–92.

BOYLE-LEWICKI, E., 'Need World's Collide: The Hudad Crimes of Islamic Law and International Human Rights', 13 *New York International Law Review* 43 (2000).

BREMS, EVA, 'Reconciling Universality and Diversity in International Human

Rights: A Theoretical and Methodological Framework and Its application in the Context of Islam', *Human Rights Review* (April–June 2004).

BUSKEN, LEON, 'Recent Debates on Family Law Reform in Morocco: Islamic Law as Politics in an Emerging Public Sphere', 10 *Islamic Law and Society*, No. 1 (2003) 69–131.

CARROLL L., 'Quran 2:229: "A Charter Granted for Life?": Judicial Khul in Pakistan', 3 *Islamic Law and Society* No.1 (1996) 91–126.

CAVANAUGH, KATHLEEN, 'Islam and the European Project', *Muslim World Journal of Human Rights*, Vol. 4, Issue 1, Article 6 (2007).

CHASE, A.T., and ALAUG, A.K., 'Health, Human Rights, and Islam: A Focus on Yemen', *International Journal of Health and Human Rights,* Vol.8, No.1 (2005).

CHASE, A.T., 'Liberal Islam and "Islam and Human Rights": A Sceptic's View', *Religion and Human Rights,* Vol. 1 (2006) 145.

CHASE, A.T., 'The Transnational Muslim World, the Foundations and Origins of Human Rights, and their Ongoing Intersections', *Muslim World Journal of Human Rights,* Vol. 4, Issue 1, Article 1 (2007).

CHAUDHRY, Z., 'The Myth of Misogyny: A Reanalysis of Women's Inheritance in Islamic Law', 61 *Albany Law Review* (1997) 511–536.

CHEKIR, HAFIDHA, 'Women, the law, and the family in Tunisia', *Gender and Development*, Vol 4, No. 2 (June 1996) 43–46.

CLARK, BELINDA, 'The Vienna Convention Reservations Regime and the Convention on Discrimination Against Women' 85 *American Journal of International Law* (1991): 281–321.

COGGINS, W., 'Succession in Traditional Islamic Law' 60 *Journal of the Missouri Bar* (2004) 180.

COLLIER, J. G., 'Is International Law Really Part of the Law of England?' *International and Comparative Law Quarterly*, Vol.38 (October 1989) 924–935.

CONNORS, JANES, 'The Women's Convention in the Muslim World', in *Human Rights as General Norms and a State's Right to Opt Out: Reservations and Objections to Human Rights Conventions* (BIICL, 1997) 85–103.

COOK, REBECCA, 'Reservations to the Convention on the Elimination of All Forms of Discrimination Against Women' 30 Virginia Journal of International Law (1990): 643–716.

DAGI, IHSAN D., 'Rethinking Human Rights, Democracy, and the West: Post-Islamist Intellectuals in Turkey', *Critique: Critical Middle Eastern Studies,* 13(2), (Summer 2004) 135–151.

DESPHANDE, P., 'The Role of Women in Two Islamic Fundamentalist Countries: Afghanistan and Saudi Arabia' (2001) 22 *Women's Rights Law Reporter* 193.

DRENIK, SIMONA, 'Human Rights of Women and Their Acceptance in Muslim Societies', *Human Security Perspectives*, Vol. 1, Issue 1 (2004).

EDWARDS JR., RICHARD W., 'Reservations to Treaties', *Michigan Journal of International Law*, 10 Mich. J. Int'l L. 362, (Spring 1989).

EL-DIN, GAMAL ESSAM, and HOWEIDY, AMIRA, 'Mixed Reaction to Hesba Law', *Al-Ahram* (Cairo) 354–355.

FALK, RICHARD, 'False Universalism and the Geopolitics of Exclusion: The Case of Islam', *Third World Quarterly*, Vol. 18, No. 1 (1997) 7–23.

FATEMI, S.M.G.S., 'Autonomy and Equal Right to Divorce with Specific Reference to Shi'I *Fiqh* and the Iranian Legal System', *Islam and Christian-Muslim Relations*, Vol.17, No.3 (July 2006) 281–294.

FATEMI, S.M.G.S., 'Who is a Refugee? Comparison of a Misconstrued Concept in International Human Rights, *Shi'I Fiqh* and the Iranian Legal System', *International Journal of Human Rights*, Vol. 9, No. 2 (June 2005) 183–223.

FERJANI, MOHAMED-CHERIF, 'Islam and Politics: The Terms of the Debate', *History and Anthropology*, Vol 16, No. 1 (March 2005) 75–83.

FREAMON, BERNARD K., 'Slavery, Freedom, and the Doctrine of Consensus in Islamic Jurisprudence', 11 Harv. Hum. Rts. J. 1.

FULCHIRON, HUGUES, 'Ne Répudiez point....: Pour une interprétation raisonnée des arrêts du 17 février 2004', *R.I.D.C.* (1-2006) 7–26.

GANNAGÉ, L., 'Le Relativisme des Droites de l'Homme dans l'Espace Méditerranéen—Regards du Proche-Orient sur la Reconnaissance en France de Répudiations de Droit Musulman', R.I.D.C. (1-2006) 102–116.

GAWLIKOWSKI, KRZYSZTOF, 'From False "Western Universalism" Towards True "Universal Universalism"', *Dialogue and Universalism*, No. 10-12/2004.

General Comment No. 24 of the Human Rights Committee of the ICCPR, 15 Human Rights Law Journal (1994) 464.

GHARI, S. MOHAMMAD, and FATEMI, S., 'Autonomy and Equal Right to Divorce with specific reference to Shi'I Fiqh and the Iranian legal system', in *Islam and Christian—Muslim Relations*, Vol. 17, No. 3 (July 2006) 286.

GILLES, BLANCHI, and RYCX, JEAN-FRANCOIS, 'Références à l'Islam dans le droit public positif en pays arabes', *Revue Française d'Etudes Constitutionnelles et Politiques Paris* n°12 (1980) 57–70.

GOODMAN, RYAN, 'Human Rights Treaties, Invalid Reservations, and State Consent', *The American Journal of International Law*, Vol. 96 (1999) 531.

HALPER, LOUISE, 'Negotiations of Law and Gender: Living Shari'a in Iran', *Washington & Lee Public Law* Paper No. 2003-18, October 2003.

HALPER, LOUISE, 'Law, Authority and Gender in Post-Revolutionary Iran'. *Washington & Lee Legal Studies Research paper Series*, No. 2006-09.

HAJJAR, LISA, 'Religion, State Power, and Domestic Violence in Muslim

Societies: A Framework for Comparative Analysis' 29 *Law and Social Inquiry* (2004) 1.

HARLAND, CHRISTOPHER, 'The Status of the International Covenant on Civil and Political Rights (ICCPR) in the Domestic Law of State Parties: An Initial Global Survey through UN Human Rights Committee Documents' *Human Rights* Quarterly, Vol. 22, No. 1, (February 2000) 225.

HASHEMI, KAMRAN, 'Religious Legal Traditions, Muslim States and the Convention on the Rights of the Child: An Essay on the Relevant Documentation' *Human Rights Quarterly*, 29 (2007) 194–227

HASSAN, RIFFAT, 'On Human Rights and the Qur'anic Perspective', *Journal of Ecumenical Studies,* Vol. 19, No. 3 (Summer 1982) 51–65.

HATHAWAY, OONA A., 'Do Human Rights Treaties Make a Difference?' 111 *Yale Law Journal* 1870 (2002).

HERMAN, EDWARD, 'The United States versus Human Rights in the Third World', 4 *Harvard Human Rights Journal* (1991) 85.

HILLE, ROLF, 'Human Rights and Islam—Is the "Clash of Civilisations" already pre-programmed?', *ERT* 30:4 (2006) 352–361.

HOVEYDA, FEREYDOUN, 'Democracy and Islam', *American Foreign Policy Interests,* 26.3 (2004) 229–233.

IBRAHIM, MAHMOOD, 'Social and Economic Conditions in Pre-Islamic Mecca', *International Journal of Middle East Studies,* Vol. 14, No. 3 (August 1982) 343–358.

IGNATIEFF, MICHAEL, 'The Attack on Human Rights', *Foreign Affairs*, Vol. 8, No. 6 (November/December 2001) 102–116.

JANSEN, YAKARE-OULE, 'Muslim Brides and the Ghost of the Shari'a: Have the Recent Law Reforms in Egypt, Tunisia and Morocco Improved Women's Position in Marriage and Divorce, and can Religious Moderates Bring Reform and Make It Stick?', *Northwestern University Journal of International Human Rights,* Vol. 5, 2, 181(2007)

JORDAN, DAVID A., 'The Dark Ages of Islam: Ijtihad, Apostasy and Human Rights in Contemporary Islamic Jurisprudence', 9 *Wash. & Lee Race & Ethnic Anc. L.J.* 55.

KAR, MEHRANGIZ, 'The Transnational Muslim World, Human Rights and the Rights of Women and Sexual Minorities: Iranian Law and Women's Rights', *Muslim World Journal of Human Rights* Vol. 4, Issue 1, Article 9 (2007).

KHAN, ALI, 'The Reopening of the Islamic Code: The Second Era of Ijtihad', 1 *U. St. Thomas L.J.* 341 (2003).

KIRGIS, FREDERIC L., 'Reservations to Treaties and United States Practice', *ASIL Insights*, (May 2003). Available at: http://www.asil.org/insights/insigh105.htm

KORKELIA, KONSTANTIN, 'New Challenges to the Regime of Reservations Under the International Covenant on Civil and Political Rights', *European Journal of International Law* (April 2002).

KOUDE, ROGER M.K., 'Peut-on, à bon droit parler d'une conception africaine des droits de l'homme?' *Rev. trim. dr. h.* (65/2005).

KUPER, JENNY, 'Reservations, declarations and objections to the 1989 convention on the rights of the child', in *Human rights as general norms and a state's right to opt out: reservations and objections to human rights conventions, BIICL* (1997) 104–113.

LEBLANC, LAWRENCE J., 'Reservations to the Convention on the Rights of the Child: A Macroscopic View of State Practice', *The International Journal of Children's Rights* 4 (1996) 357–381.

LÉCUYER, YANNICK, 'L'islam, la turquie et la cour européenne des droites de l'homme', *Rev. trim. dr. h.* (67/2006) 735–759.

LINDHOLM, TORE, 'Response to Reza Afshari on Islamic Cultural Relativism in Human Rights Discourse' *Human Rights Quarterly*, Vol.16, No.4 (1994) 791–794

LOMBARDINI, MICHELE, 'The International Islamic Court of Justice: Towards an International Islamic Legal System?', 14 *Leiden Journal of International Law* (2001) 665–680.

MAHIEDDIN, NAHAS M., 'La dissolution du mariage par la volonté unilatérale de l'un des époux en droit musulman et en droit algérien', *R.I.D.C.* (1-2006) 73–100.

MARTIN, J.P., 'The Three Monotheistic World Religions and International Human Rights', *Journal of Social Issues,* Vol.61, No. 4 (2005) 827–845.

MAYER, ANN ELIZABETH, 'The Universality of Human Rights: Lessons From the Islamic Republic of Iran' *Social Research*, Vol. 67, No. 2 (2002) 519.

MAYER, ANN ELIZABETH, 'The Islam and Human Rights Nexus: Shifting Dimensions', *Muslim World Journal of Human Rights*, Vol. 4, Issue 1, Article 4 (2007).

Mayer, Ann Elizabeth, 'Reform of Personal Status Laws in North Africa: A Problem of Islamic or Mediterranean Laws? WLUML Occasional Paper No.8, (1996), Middle East Journal, Vol.49, No.3, (1995) 432–446.

MEZGHANI, ALI, 'Le juge français et les institutions du droit musulman', *J.D.I.* 3 (2003) 721–764.

MILLER, JUDITH, 'The Challenge of Radical Islam' 72 *Foreign Affairs* 2 (1993).

MIR-HOSSEINI, ZIBA, 'The Conservative Reformist Conflict over women's rights in Iran', *International Journal of Politics, Culture and Society,* Vol. 16, No. 1 (Fall 2002) 37–53.

MODIRZADEH, N.K., 'Taking Islamic Law Seriously: NGOs and the Battle for Muslim Hearts and Minds' 19 *Harvard Human Rights Journal* (2006) 191–233.

MOHAMMED, KHALEEL, 'A Muslim Perspective on Human Rights', *Social Science and Modern Society,* Vol. 41, No.2 (January/February 2004) 29–35.

MTANGO, SIFA, 'A State of Oppression? Women's Rights in Saudi Arabia', *Asia-Pacific Journal on Human Rights and the Law* Vol. 5, No. 1 (2004) 49–67.

NEUMAYER, ERIC, 'Qualified Ratifications: Explaining Reservations to International Human Rights Treaties', *Journal of Legal Studies*, 36 (2) (2007) 397–430.

MURRAY, J. AND EL-MOLLA, MOHAMED, 'Islamic Sharia and Constitutional Interpretation in Egypt' in Cotran, E., and Sherif, A., (eds) *Democracy, the Rule of Law, and Islam* (Kluwer Law International, 1999) 435.

O'DONNELL, D., 'The reservation generation', *International Children's Rights Monitor* 9 (1992) 8–14.

PEIFFER, ELIZABETH, 'The Death Penalty in Tradtional Islamic Law and as Interpreted in Saudi Arabia and Nigeria'. 11 *William & Mary Journal of Women and the Law* (2005) 507–539.

PETERS, R., 'The Islamization of Criminal Law: A Comparative Analysis' *Die Welt des Islams,* Vol. 34, Issue 2 (November 1994) 246–274.

PETERS, RUUD, 'Islamic Law and Human Rights: a contribution to an ongoing debate', *Islam and Christian-Muslim Relations,* Vol. 10, No. 1 (1999) 5–14.

PIPER, C. L., 'Reservations to Multilateral Treaties: the Goal of Universality', 71 *Iowa Law Review* (October 1985) 295–322.

POSTAWKO, ROBERT, 'Towards an Islamic Critique of Capital Punishment', 1 *UCLA J. Islamic & Near E. L.* (2002) 269–295.

POWELL, E.J., and MITCHELL, S.M., 'The International Court of Justice and the World's Three Legal Systems', *The Journal of Politics* 69, No.2 (2007) 397.

PRICE, DANIEL, 'Islam and Human Rights: A Case of Deceptive First Appearances', *Journal for the Scientific Study of Religion* 21.2 (2002) 213–225.

QUOC-BENJAMIN, NGUYEN T.L.H., 'Women, Democracy and Islam, A Nobel Laureate's Views on Human Rights', *UN Chronicle* No.4 (2004).

QUOC-BENJAMIN, NGUYEN T.L.H., 'The Secretary-General's Lecture Series: 'who is afraid of human rights?', *UN Chronicle (*September–November 2004).

REHMAN, J., 'The Sharia, Islamic Family Laws and International Human Rights Law: Examining the Theory and Practice of Polygamy and Talaq', 21.1 *International Journal of Law, Policy and the Family* (April 2007): 108–127.

REZA, SADIQ, 'Endless Emergency: The Case of Egypt' *New Criminal Law Review*, Vol. 10, No. 4 (2007) 532–553

REZA, SADIQ, 'Torture and Islamic Law' *Chicago Journal of International Law*, Vol. 8, No.1 (2007) 21–41

ROTH, KENNETH, 'The Charade of US Ratification of International Human

Rights Treaties' *Chicago Journal of International* Law 1 (2000) 347–354.

RUDA, J.M., 'Reservations to Treaties' 146 *Recueil des Cours III* (1975) : 95–218.

SAADAWI, NAWAL EL, 'Woman and Islam', *Womens Studies Int. Forum,* Vol. 5, No. 2, (1982) : 193–206.

SAÏDI, K., 'La Réforme du droite algérien de la famille : Pérennité et rénovation', *R.I.D.C.* (1–2006): 120–152.

SAREHANE, FATNA, 'Le noveau Code marocain de la famille', *Gazette du Palais, Recueil* (Septembre – Octobre 2004).

SCHABAS, WILLIAM A., 'Reservations to the Convention on the Rights of the Child', *Human Rights Quarterly* 18 (1996): 472–491.

SCHABAS, WILLIAM A., 'Invalid Reservations to the International Covenant on Civil and Political Rights: is the United States Still a Party?', 21 *Brook. J. International of Law* (1995): 277 –325.

SENIAWSKI, BARBARA, 'Riba Today: Social Equity, the Economy, and Doing Business Under Islamic Law' 39.3 *Columbia Journal of Transnational Law* (2001): 701–728.

SHAH, NIAZ A., 'The Constitution of Afghanistan and Women's Rights', *Feminist Legal Studies* 13 (2005): 239–258.

SHIELD, ZABRINA, 'Constitutional Court strikes down Adultery and Succession laws', *Bulletin of International Legal Developments* 8, 92 (2007).

SHIELD, ZABRINA, 'Resignation of Attorney General Saeed Sheikh following the controversial suspension of Chief Justice Chaudhry', *Bulletin of International Legal Developments,* 6, 64 (2007).

SHIELD, ZABRINA, 'The right to peaceful expression in Indonesia', *Bulletin of International Legal Developments,* 5 (2007).

SHIELD, ZABRINA, 'Constitutional Court strikes down Adultery and Succession laws', *Bulletin of International Legal Developments,* 8, 92 (2007).

SMITH, JANE I., 'Women in Islam: Equity, Equality, and the Search for the Natural Order', *Journal of the American Academy of Religion*, Vol. 47, No. 4 (December 1979): 517–537.

SMITH, JANE I., 'Clothes and convictions: Women in Islam', *Christian Century,* (January 30–February 6, 2002).

STAHNKE, TAD, and BLITT, ROBERT C., 'The Religion–State Relationship and the Right to Freedom of Religion or Belief: A Comparative Textual Analysis of the Constitutions of Predominantly Muslim Countries' 36, *Georgetown Journal of International Law*, 947 (Summer, 2005).

STEWART, DAVID P., 'U.S. Ratification of the Covenant on Civil and Political Rights: the significance of the Reservations, Understandings and Declarations', 14 *Human Rights L. J.* 3–4, 77 (1993).

THOMAS, KATHERINE R., 'The Changing Status of International Law in English Domestic Law' *Netherlands International Law F* LIII (2006): 371–398.

THIRLWAY, H., 'The Law and Procedure of International Court of Justice', 60 BYIL, (1989).

VENKATRAMAN, BHARATI, 'Islamic States and the United Nations Convention of the Elimination of all Forms of Discrimination Against Women: Are the Shari'a and the Convention Compatible?' 44 *American University Law Review* (1995): 1949–2027.

WEINGARTNER, LAURA, 'Family Law and Reform in Morocco—the *Mudawana*: Modernist Islam and Women's Rights in the Code of Personal Status' 82 *University of Mercy University Law Review*, (2004): 687–713.

WITTE, JOHN JR., 'Law, Religion, and Human Rights' 28 *Columbia Human Rights Law Review*, 2 (1996): 1–31.

WYMAN, J.H., 'Vengeance is Whose? The Death Penalty and Cultural Relativism in International Law' 6 *Journal of Transnational Law and Policy* (1997): 543.

YAMANI, A. Z., 'The Eternal Shari'a' 12 *New York University Journal of International Law and Politics*, (1979): 205–212.

NEWSPAPERS/PRESS:

AFEDRARU, LOMINDA, 'Adultery No Longer a Crime, Says Court', *The Monitor* [Kampala], 6 April 2007. Available at : http://allafrica.com/stories/printable/200704050974.html

AL-JIFFRI, AHAIKHA YOUSSEF, 'Une femme élue pour la première fois au suffrage universel direct au Qatar', *L'Orient*, April 3, 2007.

BAUDRILLARD, JEAN, 'Interview with Nathan Gardels', *News Perspective Quarterly*, Spring 2002.

BEYER, LISA, 'The Women of Islam', *Time Magazine*, December 3, 2001.

BHOYRUL, ANIL, 'Business leader: Prince Alwaleed', *The Business,* May 19, 2007.

BROWNE, ANTHONY, 'Emboldened churches join forces to scupper new law on gay rights', *The Times*, 2 December 2006.

FOON FONG, LOH, 'Successful law reform', *The Star* [Malaysia], March 27, 2006. Available at: http://www.learningpartnership.org/news/press/032706morocco.

HERLINGER, C., 'Taliban revives in power vacuum', *National Catholic Reporter*, January 13 2006.

QUISTI, RAID, 'Saudi Constitution Guarantees Human Rights', *Arab news*, Wednesday 22 October 2003 (25 Sha`ban 1424)

RAMADAN, TARIQ, 'A Case for Reform', *New Statesman,* 10 April, 2006.

SADIQI, FATIMA, 'Morocco's Veiled Feminists', *Project Syndicate*, 2006 (last accessed 25/11/07). Available at: http://www.project-syndicate.org/print_commentary/sadiqi1/English.

TOUAHRI, SARAH, 'Morocco: Morocco's Nationality Code Amended', *Magharebia*, January 24, 2007 (last accessed 25/11/07). Available at: http://www.magharebia.com/cocoon/awi/xhtml1/en_GB/features/awi/features/2007/01/24/feature-01

ZAKARIYA, FUAD, 'Islam is what Muslim make of it', *Middle East Report*, July/August 1993.

'Ugandan adultery law too sexist', *BBC News*, April 5 2007. Available at: http://news.bbc.co.uk/go/pr/fr/-/1/hi/1world/africa/6528869.stm

'70 percent of Saudi Mobile Messages Pornographic', *Agence France Presse*, April 26 2007.

'Egypt Appoints First Women Judges', *Middle East Times*, March 14, 2007 (last accessed 25/11/07). Available at: http://www.metimes.com/storyview.php?StoryID=20070314-035749-4290r.

'Kuwaiti Panel Passes Landmark Women's Rights Bill', *Agence France Presse*, February 5, 2007. Available at: http://www.gulfinthemedia.com/index.php?id=282842&news_type=Top&lang=en.

'Une ministre koweïtienne prête serment sans le hijab, exigé par des islamistes', *L'Orient*, April 3, 2007.

'Pakistan Votes to Amend Rape Laws', *BBC News*, November 15, 2006 (last accessed 25/11/07). Available at: http://news.bbc.co.uk/2/hi/south_asia/6148590.stm.

ABBAS, ZAFFAR, 'Pakistani women to marry Freely', *BBC Online*. Available at: http://newsvote.bbc.co.uk/mpapps/pagetools/print/news.bbc.co.uk/2/hi/south_asia/333597.

ALBIN-LACKEY, CHRIS, AND RAWLENCE, BEN, 'What's next for Nigeria? The whole concept of African democracy is at risk', *Guardian unlimited*, 8 May 2007 (last accessed 25/11/07). Available at: http:// commentisfree.guardian.co.uk/chris_albinlackey_and_ben_rawlence/2007/05/whats_next_for_nigeria.html

'Women, nationality and citizenship', *Women 2000 and beyond*, June 2003.

ONLINE SOURCES

AKGUNDUZ, AHMET, 'Norms and values in Islam'. <http://www.uga.edu/islam/norms_values/html>

ALDEEB, SAMI, 'Conflicts entre droit religieux et droit étatique chez les musulmans dans les Pays musulmans et en Europe', 1997 <www.sami-aldeeb.com>

ALDEEB, SAMI, 'Sanctions pénales dans le pays musulmans – passé, présent et futur', 2006 <www.sami-aldeeb.com>

BINGÖLLÜ, MEHVES and TANRIKULU, SEZGIN, 'Legal Analysis of National and European Anti-discrimination Legislation: A Comparison of the EU Racial Equality Directive and Protocol 12 with Anti-discrimination Legislation in Turkey', *European Roma Rights, Migration Policy Group, and Interrights*, Brussels, 2002. Available at: http://www.migpolgroup.com/multiattachments/2414/DocumentName/Turkeyelectronic.pdf.

CARROLL, JILL, 'Secular Tunisia may Face a New, Younger Islamist Challenge' The Christian Science Monitor, 10 October 2007 (last accessed 15/05/2008) available at: http://www.csmonitor.com/2007/1010/p12s01-wome.html?page=2

DIAMOND, LARRY, 'Can the Whole World Become Democratic? Democracy, Development, and International Policies', Center for the Study of Democracy Paper 03-05, April 17, 2003 (last accessed 25/11/07). Available at: http://repositories.cdlib.org/csd/03-05.

INGLEHART, RONALD, KLINGEMANN, HANS-DIETER and WELZEL, CHRISTIAN, 'The Theory of Human Development: A Cross-Cultural Analysis', *Center for the Study of Democracy* Paper 02-01, February 1, 2002. Available at: http://repositories.cdlib.org/csd/02-01.

HIJAB, NADIA, 'Les femmes sont aussi des citoyennes: les lois de l'Etat, la Vie des femmes', report of an expert meeting organised by UNDP which was held in Casablanca in July 2002, UNDP RBAS (last accessed 14 August 2007). Available at: www.pogar.org/publications/gender/nadia/summaryf.pdf

HOFFSTROM, CHARLOTTE, 'States and Womens Rights: The Making of Postcolonial Tunisia, Algeria and Morocco' (last accessed 15/05/2008) available at: http://www.associatedcontent.com/article/442751/states_and_womens_rights_the_making.html

IBRAHIM, DINA, interview with MAYER, ANN ELIZABETH, 'Human Rights and Islamic Law – Are They Compatible?' (last accessed 21/01/08). Available at: http://www.geocities.com/CapitolHill/Parliament/3251/spring99/mayer.html

MCCARTHY, CAITRIONA, 'The Use of Reservations as a Hypocritical Escape Hatch?', *Cork Online Law Review*, VII, (2002).

MAYER, ANN ELIZABETH, 'The Convention on the Elimination of All Forms of Discrimination Against Women. The Political Nature of "Religious" Reservations' March 3, 2005. Available at: http://lgst.wharton.upenn.edu/mayera/Documents/frankfurtmay03edit.pdf

MESSARRA, ANTOINE, *Gérer le pluralisme religieux – Le champ du droit et les limites politiques de son effectivité. Le Liban en perspective compare* (last accessed 10/08/07). Available at: http://cedronma.usj.edu.lb/pdf/drreli/Messarra.prd

MILLER, JUDITH, *The Challenge of Radical Islam* (last accessed 25/11/07). Available at: http://www.foreignaffairs.org/19930301faessay5173/judith-miller/the-challenge-of-radical-islam.html.

MIR-HOSSEINI, ZIBA, *Is time on Iranian women protesters' side?*, Middle East Report, 16 June 2006 (last accessed 25/11/07). Available at: http://www.merip.org/mero/mero061606.html

MOHAMMADI, NAHID, *Cherchant une issue pour l'égalité en droit et en fait de la femme dans le monde Islamique,* Centrum voor Islam in Europa (last accessed 25/11/07). Available at: http://www.flwi.ugent.be/cie/CIE2/mohammadi1.htm

MOUSSA, JASMINE, *The Reform of Shari'a-derived Divorce Legislation in Egypt: International Standards and the Cultural Debate* (last accessed 25/11/07). Available at: http://www.nottingham.ac.uk/shared/shared_hrlcpub/HRLC_Commentary_2005/MOUSSA.pdf

MURAD, ABDAL-HAKIM, *Understanding the four Madhhabs – the problem with anti-madhhabism*. Available at http://www.masud.co.uk/ISLAM/ahm/newmadhh.htm

PAUL, JOEL R., *Cultural Resistance to Global Governance*, 5th November 2000 (last accessed 25/11/07). Available at SSRN: http://ssrn.com/abstract=272637

SAAD, GEORGES, 'Droits de l'homme, droit public musulman, droit administratif libanais', 2001 Conference, Beyrouth (last accessed 20/11/07). Available at: http://www.cedroma.usj.edu.lb/pdf/conf1/Pdf/Saad.pdf

STRAWSON, JOHN, *Encountering Islamic Law,* essay originally presented at the Critical Legal Conference held in New College, Oxford, September 9–12 1993 (last accessed 25/11/07). Available at: htttp://www.iiu.edu.my/deed/lawbase/jsrps/html

STAHNKE, T., BLITT, R. C., *The Religious–State Relationship and the Right to Freedom of Religion or Belief : A comparative textual analysis of the constitutions of the predominately Muslim countries*, USCRIF 2005, (last accessed 18/01/08). Available at: http://www.uscirf.gov/ countries/global/comparative_constitutions/03082005/Study0305.pdf

SUNDER, MADHAVI, 'Piercing the Veil', *UC Davis Legal Studies Research Paper Series*, Research Paper No.112 (last accessed 20/11/07). Available at: http://ssrn.com/abstract=413982

TABET, GIHANE, *Women in Personal Status laws: Iraq, Jordan, Lebanon, Palestine, Syria*, in SHS Paper in women's studies, Gender research, No 4, Unesco, July 2005 (last accessed 14/07/07). Available at http://portal.unesco.org/shs/en/file_download.php/273076fe9922d6d33343dba2c06a3edeWomen_in_Personal_Status_Laws.pdf

TIEFENBRUN, SUSAN, 'The Semiotics of Women's Human Rights in Iran', *Thomas Jefferson School of Law Legal Studies, Research Paper* No. 975512 (last accessed 21/11/07). Available at SSRN: http://ssrn.com/abstract=975512

WEICHMAN, D. J., KENDALL, J. D., and AZARIAN, M. K., *Islamic Law–Myths and Realities* (last accessed 25/11/07). Available at: http://muslim-canada.org/Islam_myths.htm

WRIGHT, WENDY, 'CEDAW: A Global Tool That Would Harm Women', *Concerned Women for America* (last accessed 21/01/08). Available at: http://www.beverlylahayeinstitute.org/articledisplay.asp?id=13101&department=BLI&categoryid=nation&subcategory&bliun

'Human Rights Brief', *American University Washington College of Law*, Vol. 10, Issue 2, (last accessed 21/01/08). Available at: http://www.wcl.american.edu/hrbrief/10/2women.cfm

'Opposing Ratification of CEDAW', letter from the *National Right to Life Committee*, 01/02/2007. Available at: http://www.nrlc.org/Federal/ForeignAid/ SenateCEDAWletter020107.html

'Review of the UK's Reservations to International Human Rights Treaty Obligations', JUSTICE (last accessed 08/01/08). Available at: www.justice.org.uk/images/pdfs/reservations.pdf

'Reparation for Torture: A Survey of Law and Practice in 30 Selected Countries (Lebanon Country Report)', *Redress*, May 2003 (last accessed 25/11/07). Available at: http://www.redress.org/www.redress.org/www.redress.org/studies/Lebanon.pdf

International Law in Domestic Courts, (last accessed 11/13/2007). Available at: http://ildc.oxfordlawreports.com/uid=5512/subscriber/?authstatuscode=202

'Country Reports on Human Rights Practices – 2006 (Senegal, Malaysia, Afghanistan, Kuwait, Tunisia, Morocco, Saudi Arabia, Iran, Egypt, Bahrain)', *Bureau of Democracy, Human Rights and Labor*, March 2006 (last accessed 15/11/07). Available at: http://www.state.gov/g/drl/rls/hrrpt/2006/78715.htm

'Egypt: New anti-terror law must not entrench systematic human rights abuses', *Amnesty International*, Press Release, 11 April 2007 (last accessed 25/11/07).<http://web.amnesty.org/library/print/ENGMDE120132007>

'Shadow report to the UN Committee Against Torture', *Bahrain Center for Human Rights and the National Committee for Martyrs and Victims of Torture* (last accessed 25/11/07). Available at: http://www.bahrainrights.org/node/35

'Gender and Law', *Answers.com*, (last accessed 25/11/07). <http://www.answers.com/topic/gender-and-law>

'Lebanon: Human Rights Developments and Violations', *Amnesty International*, Report, October 1997 (last accessed 25/11/07). <http://clhrf.com/reports/amnesty97.htm>

'Qatar: Country Reports on Human Rights Practices- 2001', *Bureau of Democracy, Human Rights, and Labor*, U.S. Department of State,

March 4, 2002 (last accessed 25/11/07). < http://www.state.gov/g/drl/rls/hrrpt/2001/nea/8292.htm>

'Death Penalty: Morocco to Abolish Capital Punishment', *AKI*, 1st February 2007 (last accessed 25/11/07). <http//www.adnki.com/index_2Level_ English.php?cat=Politics&loid=8.0.382342252>

'Egypt: Increasing Use of the Death Penalty', *Amnesty International*, June 13, 2002 (last accessed 25/11/07) <http://web.amnesty.org/library/Index/ENGMDE120172002>

'Iran: End Executions After Unfair Trials', *Human Rights Watch*, Report, 15th February 2007 (last accessed 25/11/07) <http://hrw.org/english/docs/2007/02/15/iran15339.htm>

'Report about press freedom in Egypt – Journalism in Egypt: Caught Between Laws and the Government', *Egyptian Organization for Human Rights,* EOHR report (last accessed 12/11/07). Available at: http://www.eohr.org/report/2006/re0821/shtml

'Islamic Family Law: Possibilities of Reform Through Internal Initiatives', *Emory University Law and Religion Program* <http://www.law.emory.edu/ifl/iflmain.html>

'Arab Political Systems: Baseline Information and Reforms – (Saudia Arabia, Egypt, Lebanon, Tunisia, Bahrain, Kuwait, Jordan), Carnegie Endowment for International Peace, and FundaciÓn para las Relaciones Internacionales y el DiÁlogo Exterior. Available at: www.carnegieendowment.org/arabpoliticalsystems www.fride.org/eng/Publications/Publication.aspx?Item=787

International Women's Rights Action Watch to CEDAW Country Report: Tunisia, 4th February 2008 (last accessed 14/04/08). Available at: http://iwraw.igc.org/publications/countries/tunisia.htm

'Morocco: Prosecution of Independent Newsweeklies', *Human Rights Watch,* background briefing, (last accessed 25/11/07). Available at: http://hrw.org/backgrounder/mena/morocco0506/1.htm.

'Nigeria: Under Islamic law, rights still unprotected', *Human Rights Watch*, report, 21 September 2004 (last accessed 25/11/07) Available at: http://hrw.org/english/docs/2004/09/21/nigeri9364.htm

'Political Sharia?' Human rights and Islamic law in northern Nigeria', *Human Rights Watch,* report, Vol. 16, No.9(A) September 2004. Available at: http://www.hrw.org/reports/2004/nigeria0904/index.htm

'Islam and Justice: Debating the Future of Human Rights in the Middle East and North Africa', *Human Rights First*, Human Rights First Publications, Executive Summary, (last accessed 25/11/07). Available at: http://www.humanrightsfirst.org/pubs/descriptions/islam.htm

'Democracy in the Arab World: Challenges, Achievements and Prospects', *International Institute for Democracy and Electoral Assistance* (last accessed 25/11/07). Available at: http://www.idea.int/publications/country/arabworld.cfm

'Arab Political Systems: Basline Information and Reforms: Tunisia', Carnegie Endowment for International Peace (last accessed 15/05/2008) available at: http://www.carnegieendowment.org/files/Tunisia_APS.doc

LECTURES, REPORTS AND SCHOLARLY ARTICLES

AKANDE, DAPO, 'The application of international law by English Courts: Doctrines of restraint and non-justiciability', *International Law in Domestic Courts*, BIICL Lectures, London, 2006.

AN-NA'IM, ABDULLAHI A., 'Islam and International Law: Toward a Positive Mutual Engagement to Realize Shared Ideals', *American Society of International Law Proceedings*, 89th Annual Meeting, 31 March–3 April 2004.

BARNES, HUGH AND BIGHAM, ALEX, 'Understanding Iran: People, Politics and Power' Report by The foreign Policy Centre (2006)

BADERIN, MASHOOD A., 'Identifying possible mechanisms within Islamic law for the promotion and protection of human rights in Muslim states', *a revised version of the paper delivered at the 3rd International Annual Conference of the Centre for the Study of Islam and Democracy*, Washington, April 2002.

BEN ACHOUR, S., 'L'ordre juridique Tunisien face a la repudiation islamique', in *Polygamie et repudiations dans les relations internationals, Tunis, Faculte des Sciences juridiques, politiques et socials*, Colloque du 16 Avril 2004.

BINGÖLLÜ, MEHVES, and TANRIKULU, SEZGIN, 'Turkey – A comparison of the EU Directive & Protocol 12 with anti-discrimination legislation', *European Roma Rights Migration Policy Group*, (Brussels, 2002).

'Concluding comments: Lebanon', *Committee on the Elimination of All Forms of Discrimination Against Women*, 33rd session, 5–22 July 2005, CEDAW/C/LBN/CO/2.

COLLECTIF95 MAGHREB ÉGALITÉ, 'One Hundred Steps, One Hundred Provisions', (London, Women Living Under Muslim Laws, 1995).

DIMITRIJEVIC, VOJIN 'United Nations Complaints Procedures after the Establishment of the Human Rights Council', *Human Rights and the International Arena: Means of Protection and Prevention*, BIICL Lectures, London, 7–8 February 2008.

EGYPTIAN ORGANIZATION FOR HUMAN RIGHTS, 'Your Excellency, Mr. President Mohamed Hosni Mubarak President of the Republic' (Letter to the president on 12/4/2006). Available at: http://www.eohr.org/report/2006/re0412/shtml

FADEL, MOHAMMAD, Public Reason as a strategy for principled reconciliation: the case of Islamic law and international human rights, University of Toronto Legal studies series, Research paper No. 981777, April 2007

GONTOWSKA, LUIZA M., 'Human Rights Violations Under Sharia'a: A comparative Study of the Kingdom of Saudi Arabia and the Islamic Republic of Iran' *Pforzheimer Honors College, Honors College Theses, Pace University*, (2005).

GREENWOOD, CHRISTOPHER, 'International Law and National Law', *Lecture Notes*, Magdalene College, Cambridge, Lent Term 2007.

HAMMARBERG, THOMAS, 'Protection and Promotion of Human Rights by International Structures – dilemmas and lessons learned' *Human Rights and the International Arena: Means of Protection and Prevention*, BIICL Lectures, London, 7–8 February 2008.

HIJAB, NADIA, 'Les Femmes Sont Aussi Des Cityoyennes: Les Lois de l'Etat, la Vie des Femmes', *Bureau Regional pour les Etats Arabes Programme de Dévelopment des Nations Unies.*

LEVINET, MICHEL, 'L'existence d'une conception des droits de l'homme propre aux états musulmans', DEA de droit international Faculté de droit de Montpellier I (last accessed on 04/02/08). Available at: http://memoireonline.free.fr/memoirepeggy.htmlo0

MOULAVI, M.H., BABU SAHIB, 'Justice and the Shariah' in Administration of the Shariah Court system, papers and proceedings of the conference Administration of the Shariah Court system, 7–13 August 1983, Manila Philippines, (University of the Philippines, Quezon City, 1985)

MURRAY, MARGARET, 'Le pacte international relatif aux droits civils et politiques, un atout méconnu et mal utilisé en vue de la promotion des droits des femmes et de leur droit à l'égalité', *De La Maîtrisse en droit international des droits de la personne, Université du Québec à Montréal,* 2001.

NAJAR, IBRAHIM, 'LES PRINCIPES GÉNÉRAUX DU DROIT SUCCESSORAL COMPARE', Les dénominateurs communs entre les principes généraux du droit, Colloque des 4, 5, et 6 Octobre 2001, Cedroma, Université du Saint-Joseph, Beyrouth

NOLLKAEMPER, ANDRE, 'The role of domestic courts in the implementation of international responsibility', *International Law in Domestic Courts*, BIICL Lectures, London, 2006.

SARDAR ALI, SHAHEEN, '(Re) claiming our Histories: A reflection on Women, Islam and Human Rights in Contemporary Muslim Communities', *Paper for Human Rights Day*, Organised by INGAD, Islamabad, 10 December 2003.

SMOCK, DAVID, 'Applying Islamic Principles in the Twenty-first Century – Nigeria, Iran, and Indonesia', *United States Institute of Peace Special Report* 150, (September 2005).

TABET, GIHANE, 'Women in Personal Status Laws: Iraq, Jordan, Lebanon, Palestine, Syria', *SHS Papers in Women's Studies/Gender Research*, No. 4, (July 2005).

VILJOEN, F., and MADLINGOZI, T., 'Taking stock of the debates on complementary international standards to strengthen and update international legal instruments against racism, racial discrimination, xenophobia and related intolerance', *Commission on Human Rights, 62nd Session, Intergovernmental working group on the effective implementation of the Durban declaration and programme of action, 4th session, High level seminar,* E/CN.4/2006/WG/21/BP.2, 9 January 2006.

WILDHABER, LUZIUS, Keynote Speech, *International Law in Domestic Courts*, BIICL Lectures, London, 2006.

ZARROKH, EHSAN, 'Islamic Law and Law of the Muslim World: Iranian Judicial System (Court's Structure)', *New York Law School,* Research Paper Series 07-02.

'Islam and Muslims in the World Today', International Conference, Hosted by the University of Cambridge, London, June 4 – June 5, 2007.

'Islam, International and Comparative Law: Current Issues', BIICL Conference, London, December 3, 2007.

Annual Report on Human Rights Situation in Syria 2006, Syrian Human Rights Committee, June 2006.

'Concluding Observations', *Committee on the Rights of the Child*: United Kingdom Report, CRC/C/15/Add.34 15th February 1995

'CEDAW: The Women's Rights Treaty', *Human Rights Watch*, Report 12 March 2007.

'Statement to commemorate the twenty-fifth anniversary of the adoption of the Convention on the Elimination of All Forms of Discrimination against Women', *Committee on the Elimination of Discrimination against Women*, October 13, 2004.

'Consideration of reports submitted by States parties under article 18 of the Convention on the Elimination of All Forms of Discrimination against Women', *Committee on the Elimination of Discrimination against Women*, CEDAW/C/TUR/4-5 (8 August 2003).

WOMEN FOR WOMEN'S HUMAN RIGHTS, 'Turkish civil and penal code reforms from a gender perspective: the success of two nationwide campaigns', (Women for Women's Human Rights, 2005)

The Relationship between International and Domestic Law: *Proceedings of the UniDem Seminar Organised in Warsaw on 19 to 21 May 1993 in Co-operation with the University of Wroclaw and the Pozna? Human Rights Centre and Supported by the Phare programme of the European Communities.* (Strasbourg: Council of Europe, 1994).

'The Talibanization of Nigeria: Radical Islam, Extremist Sharia Law and Religious Freedom', *Freedom House, Center for Religious Freedom*, New York (2002)

BOOK REVIEWS

MADELUNG, W., *Journal of Near Eastern Studies*, Vol. 47, No. 4. (Oct., 1988), 313–314, book review of: POWERS, DAVID S., *Studies in Qur'an and Hadith: The Formation of the Islamic Law of Inheritance* (Berkley: University of California Press, 1986).

LOWE, A.V., *International and Comparative Law Quarterly*, 36 (1987), 411–413, book review of: MANN, F.A., *Foreign Affairs in English Courts* (Oxford: Clarendon Press, 1986).

FAZAELI, R., & CASTELLINO, J., *Religion and Human Rights, (*Leiden: Koninklijke Brill NV, 2006), 1:197–199, book review of: MARTIN, LAU, *The Role of Islam in the Legal System of Pakistan* (Leiden: Martinus Nijhoff, 2006).

RIVERS, J., *Religion and Human Rights,* (Leiden: Koninklijke Brill NV, 2006), 1:201–203, book review of: GHANEA, NAZILA (ED.), *The Challenge of Religious Discrimination at the Dawn of the New Millennium* (Leiden: Martinus Nijhoff, 2003).

VOYIAKIS, E., *Religion and Human Rights*, (Leiden: Koninklijke Brill NV, 2006), 1:205–207, book review of: JANIS, M.W., & EVANS, C. (eds) *Religion and International Law* (Leiden: Martinus Nijhoff, 2003).

CONSTITUTIONS

Basic Law of Saudi Arabia (last accessed 22/01/08). Available at: http://www.mideastinfo.com/documents/Saudi_Arabia_Basic_Law.htm

Constitution of Algeria (last accessed 08/01/08). Available at: http://www.algeria-un.org/default.asp?doc=-const

Constitution of Egypt (last accessed 08/01/08). Available at: http://www.misr.gov.eg/english/laws/constitution/index.asp

Constitution of Jordon (last accessed 08/01/08). Available at: http://www.kinghussein.gov.jo/constitution_jo.html

Saudi Arabia Index (last accessed 22/01/08). Available at: http://servat.unibe.ch/icl/sa__indx.html

Constitution of the Islamic Republic of Iran (last accessed 27/03/08), available at: http://www.iranchamber.com/government/laws/constitution.php

Constitution of the Islamic Republic of Pakistan, (last accessed 27/03/08), available at: http://www.pakistani.org/pakistan/constitution/

Constitution of the Kingdom of Bahrain, (last accessed 27/03/08), available at: https://www.e.gov.bh/wps/wcm/connect/b220f880451bac569820f98d0e8f4425/constitutioneEN.pdf?MOD=AJPERES&CACHEID=b220f880451bac569820f98d0e8f4425&CACHEID=

b220f880451bac569820f98d0e8f4425&CACHEID=b220f880451bac5 69820f98d0e8f4425&CACHEID=b220f880451bac569820f9

Constitution of the Kingdom of Morocco (last accessed 27/03/08), available at: http://confinder.richmond.edu/admin/docs/Morocco.PDF

Constitution of the Kingdom of Saudi Arabia (last accessed 27/03/08), available at: http://www.the-saudi.net/saudi-arabia/saudi-constitution.htm

Constitution of Lebanon (last accessed 16/06/08), available at: http://www.servat.unibe.ch/icl/le00000_.html

Constitution of the Libyan Arab Republic, (last accessed 27/03/08), available at: http://www.servat.unibe.ch/law/icl/ly00000_.html

Constitution of Malaysia (last accessed 27/03/08), available at: http://www.malaysia-today.net/malaysia_constitution.pdf

Constitution of Tunisia (last accessed 16/06/08), available at: http://www.servat.unibe.ch/icl/ts00000_.html

Constitution of the Republic of Turkey (last accessed 27/03/08), available at: http://www.anayasa.gov.tr/images/loaded/pdf_dosyalari/THE_CONSTITUTION_OF_THE_REPUBLIC_OF_TURKEY.pdf

Constitution of Yemen (last accessed 08/01/08). Available at: http://www.al-bab.com/yemen/gov/gov.htm

INTERNATIONAL LEGAL INSTRUMENTS AND TREATIES

African Commission on Human and Peoples' Rights, African Charter on Human and Peoples' Rights, Nairobi, 1981, (last accessed 27/03/08), available at: http://www.achpr.org/english/_info/charter_en.html

Council of Europe, Convention for the Protection of Human Rights and Fundamental Freedoms, Rome, 1950, (last accessed 27/03/08), available at: http://www.echr.coe.int/NR/rdonlyres/D5CC24A7-DC13-4318-B457-5C9014916D7A/0/EnglishAnglais.pdf

Inter-American Specialized Conference on Human Rights, American Convention on Human Rights, San Josi, Costa Rica, 1969 (last accessed 27/03/08), available at: http://www.hrcr.org/docs/American_Convention/oashr.html

United Nations, General Assembly, Declaration of Human Rights, New York: United Nations, 1948 (last accessed 27/03/08), available at: http://www.udhr.org/UDHR/default.htm

United Nations, General Assembly, Convention on the Elimination of All Forms of Discrimination Against Women, New York: United Nations, 1979 (last accessed 27/03/08), available at:

United Nations, General Assembly, International Covenant on Civil and Political Rights, New York: United Nations, 1966 (last accessed

27/03/08), available at: http://untreaty.un.org/ENGLISH/bible/englishinternetbible/partI/chapterIV/treaty6.asp

United Nations, General Assembly, International Convention on the Elimination of All Forms of Racial Discrimination, New York: United Nations, 1966, (last accessed 27/03/08), available at: http://untreaty.un.org/ENGLISH/bible/englishinternetbible/partI/chapterIV/treaty2.asp

United Nations, General Assembly, Convention Against Torture and Other Cruel, Inhuman or Degrading Treatment or Punishment, New York: United Nations, 1984 (last accessed 27/03/08), available at: http://untreaty.un.org/ENGLISH/bible/englishinternetbible/partI/chapterIV/treaty14.asp

United Nations, General Assembly, Convention on the Rights of the Child, New York: United Nations, 1989 (Last Accessed 27/03/08), available at: http://untreaty.un.org/ENGLISH/bible/englishinternetbible/partI/chapterIV/treaty19.asp

United Nations, General Assembly, Vienna Convention on the Law of Treaties between States and International Organisations or between International Organisations, New York: United Nations, 1986 (last accessed 27/03/08), available at:
http://untreaty.un.org/ENGLISH/bible/englishinternetbible/partI/chapterXXIII/treaty3.asp

WEBSITES

Current Trial Library: http://www.antenna-tr.org/ctl/index.asp?lgg=en

Emory Law – Legal Profiles: http://www.law.emory.edu/ifl/legal/

Hauser Global Law School Program, GlobaLex: http://www.nyulawglobal.org/globalex/#

Middle East Research and Information Project: http://www.merip.org

Society for the Advancement of Community, Health, Education and Training (SACHET), '(Re)claiming our histories: A reflection of Women, Islam, and Human Rights in Contemporary Muslim Communities' by Shaheen Sardar Ali: http://sachet.org.pk/home/gender_columns/webcolumn_26.asp

Supreme Court of Pakistan: http://www.supremecourt.gov.pk

Turkish Constitutional Law Materials by Kemal Gozler: http://www.anayasa.gen.tr/english.htm

UN Convention on the Elimination of all forms of Discrimination Against Women, Country Reports: http://www.un.org/womenwatch/daw/cedaw/reports.htm

UNDP Programme on Governance in the Arab Region: http://www.pogar.org

UN News Centre: http://www.un.org/News/
UN Office of the High Commissioner for Human Rights: http://www.ohchr.org
Université Saint-Joseph de Beyrouth, Centre d'études des droits du monde arabe: http://www.cedroma.usj.edu.lb/files/documents.htm
U.S. Department of State, Bureau of Democracy, Human Rights and Labor: http://www.state.gov/g/drl/rls/hrrpt/2001/nea/8292.htm

CASES

As a consequence of some of the cases being drawn from secondary sources some primary case information may be missing in the citations.

EGYPT

Egyptian Supreme Constitutional Court, Appeal no 5257/43 of the 28th December 1997 (Egypt)
Supreme Constitutional Court of Egypt, 26 March 1994, Mahkama (1996, 6:23-60). (Egypt)
Egyptian State Security Tribunal judgment of April 1987, cited by CH Heyns, F Viljoen, *The Impact of the United Nations Human Rights Treaties on Domestic level* (The Hague: Kluwer, 2002) 234. (Egypt)

EUROPEAN UNION

Carlos Garcia Avello v Etat Belge, Case No. 148/02 of 2 October 2003 ECR I-II613 (European Union)

ICJ

Reservations Case I.C.J Reports, (1951) 15 ILR
Nuclear Test cases, I.C.J Reports, (1974) 57 ILR
The border and Transborder Armed Actions case (Nicaragua v. Honduras), I.C.J Reports, (1988) 84 ILR
Advisory Opinion on Reservations to the Convention on the Prevention and Punishment of the Crime of Genocide (1951) I.C.J. 15

IRAN

Case 23/h84-495, Esfahan

LEBANON

Criminal Court of Beirut, *judgment number 1119/2003*, 12 June 2003 (Lebanon)

High Sunni Court of Beirut decision of the 16th February 2000, cited in Ali Nadim Homsani, *Majmouaat al mabadi' wal kawai'd al chari'ya wal kanouniyya, Manchourat el Halabi el houkoukiyya*, 2003, 21–23. (Lebanon)

Highest Assembly of the Islamic Sunni courts decision of the 4th February 1987, cited in Ali Nadim Homsani, *Majmouaat al mabadi' wal kawai'd al chari'ya wal kanouniyya, Manchourat el Halabi el houkoukiyya*, 2003, 21–23. (Lebanon)

MALAYSIA

Government of the State of Kelantan v. Government of the Federation of Malaya and Tunku Abdul Rahman Putra Al-Haj. (1963) MLJ 355 (Malaysia)

Public Prosecutor v Orhan Olmez, [1987] Part 1 case 12 [SCM] (Malaysia)

Regional Centre of Arbitration v. Ooi Beng Choo & Anor (No. 2). [1998] 2 MLJ 383 (Malaysia)

MBF Capital Bhd v Dato' Param Cumaraswamy, [1997] 3 MLJ 824 (Malaysia)

MOROCCO

Moroccan Supreme Court decisions No. 49 of 1 October 1976, No. 5 of 3 November 1972 and No. 162 of 3 August 1979 (Morocco)

NIGERIA

Garba v Lagos State A-G Suit ID/599M/91 (31 October 1991), (Nigeria)

PAKISTAN

Pakistan v Public at Large (1986)PLD SC 304 (Pakistan)

Iftikharuddin v Federal Government (1992) PLD FSC 188 (Pakistan)

Hazoor Bakhash v Federation of Pakistan (1980) PLD FSC 145 (Pakistan)

Mst. Balqis Fatima v Najm-ul-Ikram Qureshi, (1959) PLD (Lahore) 566 (Pakistan)

Khurshid Bibi v Muhammad Amin (1967) PLD SC 97 (Pakistan)

Humaira Mehmood v State (PLD 1999 Lahore 494) (Pakistan)

Aurangzeb v Mst. Gulnaz PLD 2006 Kar 568

Subhan v Mst. Sabreen PLD 2007 Kar
Rukhsana Malik v Abdul Aziz PLD 2004 Lah 801

TUNISIA

Tribunal of first instance of La Manoba, *case number 34179* of 27 June 2000 (Tunisia)
Tribunal of first instance of La Manoba, *case number 53/16189* of 2 December 2003 (Tunisia)
Tunisia Administrative Tribunal, *case number 2193* of 1 June 1994 (Tunisia)
Tunis Appeal Court, case No. 120 of 6 January 2004 (Tunisia)
Tunis Administrative Tribunal, case No. 3,643 of 21 May 1996 (Tunisia)

TURKEY

Danistay 5. Chamber, No. 1991/933, cited in Mehves Bingöllü and Sezgin Tanrikulu *Turkey –son of the EU Directive & Protocol 12 with anti-discrimination legislation*, European Roma Rights Migration Policy Group, Brussels (2002)
Istanbul Second Criminal Court of First Instance, *case number 2006/140*, 4 June 2006 (Turkey)